ANTHROPOLOGICAL PAPERS

MUSEUM OF ANTHROPOLOGY, UNIVERSITY OF MICHIGAN
NO. 63

ECONOMIC AND SOCIAL ORGANIZATION OF A COMPLEX CHIEFDOM:

THE HALELEA DISTRICT, KAUA'I, HAWAII

BY
TIMOTHY EARLE

Illustrations by
Eliza H. Earle

ANN ARBOR, MICHIGAN
1978

© 1978 Regents of The University of Michigan
The Museum of Anthropology
All rights reserved

ISBN 978-1-949098-00-6 (paper)
ISBN 978-1-951519-08-7 (ebook)

To Eliza, for her hours of labor.

CONTENTS

I. EVOLUTIONARY SIGNIFICANCE OF CHIEFDOMS 1
    Chiefdoms 2
    Ecological Theories of Cultural Evolution 4
    Archaeology of Chiefdoms 6
II. SOCIAL ORGANIZATION IN POLYNESIA AND HAWAII 9
    The Polynesian Model 9
    Hawaiian Social Organization 11
        Hawaiian Society 12
        Local Management 16
        The Regional Hierarchy 18
    Summary 19
III. THE HALELEA DISTRICT 21
    Environment of the Hawaiian Islands 23
    Halelea 25
        Rainfall 25
        Soils 25
        Vegetation 29
    Halelea Ahupua'a 30
        Ha'ena 31
        Wainiha 32
        Lumahai 32
        Waikoko 33
        Waipa 33
        Waioli 34
        Hanalei 34
        Kalihikai 35
        Kalihiwai 35
    Summary 36
IV. THE EVOLUTIONARY SIGNIFICANCE OF IRRIGATION 37
    The Hydraulic Theories 38
        Construction of Irrigation Systems 39
        Maintenance of Irrigation Systems 41
        Reconstruction Following Natural Disasters 42
        Defense and Reconstruction Following Warfare 44
        Allocation of Water and Settlement of Disputes 45
        Nonmanagerial Hypotheses 47
        Summary of Hydraulic Theory 48
    Test of the Hydraulic Theory 49

V. MODERN TARO AGRICULTURE	51
Taro Cultivation	52
Taro (*Colocasia esculenta*)	52
Preparation	54
Planting	54
Crop Nurture	55
Harvest	55
Production Schedule	56
The Family Farm	56
Halelea's Modern Taro Irrigation	57
System 14	58
System 15	63
System 17	66
System 18	67
System 22	67
System 23	69
System 26	70
System 29	70
The Operational Requirements of Modern Irrigation	70
Construction of Irrigation Systems	71
Maintenance of Irrigation Systems	71
Reconstruction Following Natural Disasters	73
Warfare	75
Water Allocation and Settlement of Disputes	75
Summary	76
VI. ARCHAEOLOGICAL RESEARCH ON IRRIGATION	77
Site Descriptions of Irrigation Complexes	78
Ka-D5-4	79
Ka-D5-5	88
Ka-D5-6	90
Ka-D5-7	92
Ka-D5-8	93
Ka-D6-11	96
Ka-D10-9	100
Ka-D10-10	100
Types of Halelean Irrigation	101
Type A: Alluvial Terrace	103
Type B: Alluvial Coastal Plain	103
Type C: Alluvial Island	104
Type D: Alluvial Bottom	104
Archaeological Evidence for the Managerial Requirements of Halelean Irrigation	105
Construction of Irrigation Systems	105
Maintenance of Irrigation Systems	107
Reconstruction Following Natural Disasters and Warfare	107
Water Allocation	108
Summary	108

VII. HISTORICAL RESEARCH ON IRRIGATION	109
Explorer Accounts of Irrigation	110
Taro Cultivation	113
Construction of the Irrigation System	114
Soil Preparation	115
Planting	116
Harvest Procedures and Scheduling of Crops	118
Discussion of Traditional Taro Cultivation	118
Land Records of 1850	120
Sources	123
Length of Ditch	126
Net and Gross Area of an Irrigation System	127
Net and Gross Number of Farmers on an Irrigation System	127
Number of Communities	127
Cross-cultural Comparisons	128
Irrigation Systems	129
Social Organization	132
The Significance of Irrigation in Hawaii	135
Construction and Maintenance of Irrigation Systems	136
Allocation of Water and Settlement of Disputes	137
Reconstruction of Irrigation Systems Following Natural and Cultural Disasters	138
Conclusions	141
VIII. THE HAWAIIAN COMMUNITY	143
Social and Economic Organization of the Halelean Communities	143
The Household	146
The Interhousehold Cluster	153
The Community	155
Summary	158
A Consideration of the Theory of Redistribution	158
Evaluation of Service's Hypothesis: Halelea	159
Population Circumscription and Warfare	162
Conclusion	165
IX. A RECONSIDERATION OF CHIEFDOM ORGANIZATION	167
Polynesia: Structure and Process	168
The Evolutionary Transformation	168
Competition Among Polynesian Chiefs	171
The Hawaiian Chiefdom: The Evolution of Regional Centralization	173
Competition Among the Hawaiian Chiefs	174
The Role of Capital Investment in Status Rivalry	180
The Ahupua'a: The Local Community in a Regional Context	185
Land Tenure and Mobilization in the Ahupua'a	186
Community Isolation	190
Summary	191
X. SUMMARY AND CONCLUSIONS	193

FIGURES

1.1	Causal sequence for three ecological theories leading to sociopolitical centralization	4
3.1	The island of Kaua'i	22
3.2	Annual rainfall, Kaua'i	24
3.3	Halelea district, Kaua'i	26
3.4	Annual rainfall, Halelea district, Kaua'i	27
3.5	Soils map, Halelea district, Kaua'i	28
5.1	Taro	53
5.2	Wainiha, Kaua'i	59
5.3	Cross section of irrigation ditches	61
5.4	Farm 1, System 14, Wainiha, Kaua'i	62
5.5	System 15, Wainiha, Kaua'i	64
5.6	System 17, Wainiha, Kaua'i	66
5.7	System 22, Waioli, Kaua'i	68
6.1	Ha'ena, Kaua'i	80
6.2	Site Ka-D5-4, Ha'ena, Kaua'i, extensive irrigation complex	81
6.3	Site Ka-D5-4, Ha'ena, Kaua'i, sections a - j	82
6.4	Section g, Site Ka-D5-4, Ha'ena, Kaua'i	83
6.5	Site Ka-D5-5 and Ka-D5-6, section b, Ha'ena, Kaua'i	89
6.6	Site Ka-D5-8, Manoa Valley, Ha'ena, Kaua'i	Fold Out
6.7	Site Ka-D6-11, Wainiha, Kaua'i	97
6.8	Site Ka-D10-9, Hanalei, Kaua'i	99
6.9	Site Ka-D10-10, Anini, Hanalei, Kaua'i	101
6.10	Typology of Halelean irrigation systems	102
8.1	Historical (1850) land use pattern, Waioli, Kaua'i	152
9.1	Genealogy of Kaua'i chiefs	176

MAPS

1. Base map from USGS maps of the western, coastal portion of the Halelea district — Fold Out
2. Base map from USGS maps of the eastern, coastal portion of the Halelea district — Fold Out

TABLES

6.1	Characteristics of taro pondfields for archaeological sites in Ha'ena and Wainiha	85
7.1	Quantitative data on taro pondfields as described in early explorer/traveler accounts	111
7.2	List of Land Court Award numbers for the apana associated with the historical irrigation systems in the Halelea district	123, 124
7.3	Summary of data for the historical irrigations systems in the Halelea district	125
8.1	Mean distances from houselots to specified locations	150
8.2	Distribution of historical populations and resources for the Halelean ahupua'a	161
9.1	Approximate chronology for ahupua'a chiefs of Halelea and for paramount chiefs of Kaua'i	177

PLATES

1. Planting taro cuttings in Hanalei, Kaua'i
2. Harvesting in Hanelei, Kaua'i
3. System 29, Hanelei, Kaua'i
4. Site KA-D5-8, Ha'ena, Kaua'i. Looking up pondfield terraces. Photograph by Tom Dye
5. Site Ka-D5-8, Ha'ena, Kaua'i. Detail of construction of retaining wall. Photograph by Tom Dye
6. Site Ka-D5-8, Ha'ena, Kaua'i. Terrace walls of ceremonial complex. Photograph by Tom Dye

PREFACE

During 1971 and 1972, I was fortunate to be a member of Marshall Sahlins' research project investigating the protohistoric and early historic periods of Hawaiian society (Sahlins 1971). This project combined ethnohistorical, archaeological, and limited ethnographic research to gain an understanding of the economic and social organization of Hawaiian chiefdoms and the early Hawaiian state. My work concentrated on a single political unit, the Halelea district, Kaua'i, and my dissertation under the direction of Richard Ford contains the primary analysis of these data (Earle 1973).This monograph is a follow-up of that research and it incorporates a reanalysis of the original data with additional data on community organization collected during the summer of 1974. Since completing my dissertation, I have presented the Hawaiian material to students and colleagues at UCLA and benefited from their many constructive comments. Because my ideas concerning Hawaii have changed considerably since 1973, this monograph is not a restatement of my dissertation but represents a new manuscript which hopefully complements and expands upon the earlier work.

My dissertation research was assisted by numerous individuals whom I acknowledged then (Earle 1973:iii-iv) and wish to thank again. I am especially grateful for the continued assistance of Dorothy Barrère, Sophie Cluff, Molly and the late Howard Moore, and Mabel Wilcox during the 1974 field season.

I wish to express again my thanks to the National Science Foundation (Grant GS-28718X1) which supported the primary research for the Sahlins project and to the Wenner-Gren Foundation for Anthropological Research, which supported an initial reconnaissance survey to determine an area suitable for combined archaeological and ethnohistorical investigations. A grant from the Academic Senate of the University of California, Los Angeles (Grant 3040) permitted continued analysis and the field research during summer, 1974. The publication of this present manuscript is made possible by a generous gift from John Gregg

Allerton, underwriting in part the publication cost. For all this assistance, I am particularly grateful.

Finally, as with the original dissertation, this volume has been enriched greatly by the efforts of Eliza Howe Earle. She prepared the illustrations included here and provided extensive editorial assistance. In so many ways, this is as much her manuscript as it is mine.

CHAPTER I

EVOLUTIONARY SIGNIFICANCE OF CHIEFDOMS

Fundamental to modern anthropological thought is the concept of culture as a system of interrelated parts. Culture may be studied within a synchronic, functionalist framework for which the primary goal is to determine how cultural systems operate; or, as in this present volume, culture may be viewed from a dynamic, evolutionary perspective whereby explanations of cultural change become the main interest. After a long period of disfavor, renewed research on cultural evolution is now an important emphasis within American cultural anthropology. Initially, various anthropologists attempted to deal with this subject by delineating stages of general evolution (cf. Steward 1955 a; Fried 1967; Service 1962). Although heuristically useful, this typological approach has shown itself to be largely incapable of explicating the general processes of cultural change. The research in this present volume diverges from this typological approach by analyzing in detail the organizational transformations of a single society, Hawaii. The context of analysis is not a world-wide series of evolutionary stages but instead is the variability in chiefly organization within Polynesia. As pioneered by Eggan (1950) and Sahlins (1958), controlled comparison will be used to investigate various theories which have been proposed as explanations for evolutionary change.

Polynesia holds particular importance for anthropological research on the evolution of social organization. The Polynesian culture area is characterized by a wide range in sociopolitical complexity within a background of cultural uniformity. During the last two thousand years, a single biological and cultural population expanded to occupy the islands of the central Pacific. This greatly simplifies the anthropologist's task for the following reasons. Since evolution itself is not a creative process but can only select among existing biological and cultural materials, the observed structure and content of an organic or cultural system is determined largely by its history. For controlled comparisons within Polynesia, it is possible to analyze variability as an outcome of the evolutionary process because history is shared between the diverse cultures.

In this present study, the central concern is the social organization of chiefdoms. As Service (1975) has recently stressed, chiefdoms are especially significant for evolutionary research. Structurally, they are intermediate between the elemental kin-based organization of segmental (egalitarian) societies and the complex, specialized organization of states. Since archaeological evidence now suggests that chiefdoms temporally preceed states in many areas, a good argument may be made for the evolutionary development from chiefdom to state. The term "chiefdom" is widely and loosely used in anthropological literature to refer to hierarchically organized societies which lack the strong governmental apparatus diagnostic of state societies. In the precolonial era, chiefdoms were widely distributed through Oceania, the Americas, Asia, and Africa, but an expanding Western society has caused their rapid alteration or extinguishment. Since new ethnographic fieldwork on the traditional patterns of chiefly organization is virtually impossible, the anthropologist interested in chiefdoms must shift his research interests to archaeological and ethnohistoric data sources. Archaeology and ethnohistory are now responsible for the primary research on precolonial, traditional societies and, with this in mind, a major aim of the present volume is to demonstrate the feasibility of using an integrated archaeological and ethnohistorical strategy for research on chiefdoms.

CHIEFDOMS

Chiefdoms are based on two organizational principles: (1) the ranking of individual statuses within the local community; and (2) the regionally centralized organization of local communities. Social relationships within the local community are organized on the basis of kinship in such a way that an individual's status is determined by his genealogical distance from the senior line. The highest ranking individual, the local chief, represents the group's senior line and thus acts as the group's focal member to which all trace relationship. The status of chief is dual — he is, at the same time, local aristocrat and local leader. As local aristocrat, his position is religiously sanctioned and symbolically marked. He holds titular ownership of group property, such as land and capital equipment, and he holds broad rights of request for food, goods, and services. Conversely, as leader, he allocates use rights in group property and he is generally responsible for the group's welfare. This involves him in the recruitment of public labor for beneficial projects such as religious ceremonies and construction of irrigation systems. This responsibility also includes the mediation of internal disputes and the defense against external threat. As Service (1975) recognized, the dual status of aristocrat and leader is inseparable in chiefdoms, and these two facets may be viewed respectively as the rights and obligations of the chiefly office.

On the regional level, the central integration of local communities is a striking evolutionary development from segmental societies. A segmental society is characteristically composed of independent local groups. Each local group should be structurally identical to the next and largely self-sufficient. The relationships amongst groups are based on reciprocity, which emphasizes the equality or symmetry of the relationship. As denoted by the term segmental, the relationship between the parts is not governed by a centralized organization, and, although it is common to speak of an ethnic or dialectical tribe, the relationships within such regional units are diffuse and the boundaries vague. For all intents and purposes, the local community is the dominant social unit of a segmental society.

The chiefdom is, in contrast, a regionally organized society composed of a number of local communities tied by their placement in the chiefly hierarchy. This hierarchy is based on a nested series of social and territorial groups (e.g., the village community, the district, and the chiefdom) and the highest ranking member of each unit functions as the group's focal member. In such a way, the highest ranking member of the community is the local chief; the highest ranking local chief is the district chief; and the highest ranking district chief is the paramount chief. At each level, the focal individual serves both as leader for his respective social unit and as conduit for decisions made at higher levels in the hierarchy. The specific way in which this operates will be described for the redistributive hierarchy in Hawaii (Chapters 8 and 9). The chiefly hierarchy serves very general social, political, economic, and religious functions within the society. The general rights and obligations of chiefs at each level of the hierarchy are similar, expanding in scope relative to the scale of the social unit involved. At any level, the representative chief is both aristocrat and leader. He is the elite member of the social unit (district or chiefdom) for which he directs activities involving the social unit as a whole. Specific activities vary greatly from one chiefdom to another but they characteristically include religious ceremonies, warfare, diplomacy, and large-scale public works.

A key to understanding chiefdoms is the recognition of a trend towards the differentiation and centralization of leadership. By distinguishing an elite set of chiefs apart from the groups they represent, leadership has become *externally specialized* as distinct from other social roles. The ranking of chiefs on a regional basis then establishes a centralization of leadership on the basis of *precedential decision making* by which decisions made at one level on the chiefly hierarchy supersede lower level decisions. The present investigation of causes for the development of chiefdoms will focus on factors which might affect differentiation and centralization of leadership. Interestingly, these developments may be viewed as an evolutionary progression toward state organization for it is just these trends, with the addition of *internal specialization* of leadership, which characterize state bureaucracies (Wright 1977). An explanation of chiefdoms should, therefore, also be a preliminary explanation for the evolution of the state.

ECOLOGICAL THEORIES OF CULTURAL EVOLUTION

As discussed in the previous section, the evolution of chiefdoms involves centralization and specialization of the social system. The present research project was designed to test three popular theories of cultural evolution based respectively on the cultural factors of irrigation, redistribution, and warfare. As seen in Figure 1.1, these theories are logically similar. Initially, population density determines various conditions; these conditions, in conjunction with particular environmental circumstances, select for specific cultural adaptations which, in

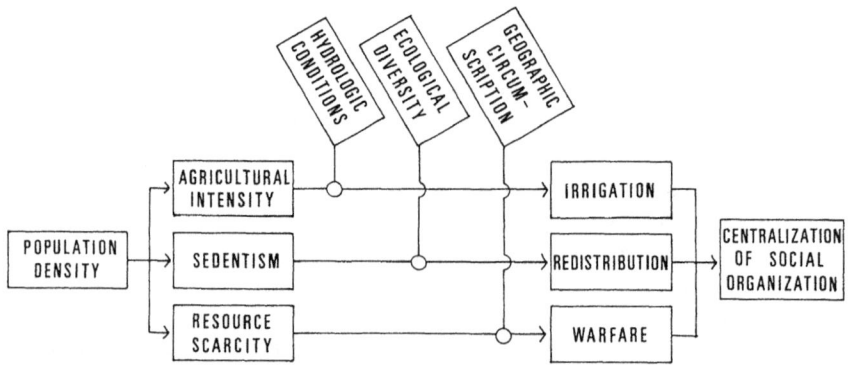

Fig. 1.1 Causal sequence for three ecological theories leading to sociopolitical centralization.

turn, require the centralization of decision making for adequate control. I will briefly summarize the logic behind these theories although each will be discussed in more detail later (Chapters 4 and 8).

The theory emphasizing the central role of irrigation was developed in greatest detail by Wittfogel (1957). His main proposal was that centralized authority evolves as a response to the managerial requirements of complex irrigation technologies — "the bulkiness of all except the smallest source of water supply creates a technological task which is solved either by mass labor or not at all" (1957:15). Wittfogel's own formulation was "volunteeristic" in that the farmers seeing the advantages of irrigation would select freely this strategy and its concomitant central organization. This specific aspect of the theory has been criticized by Carneiro (1970) and recent reinterpretations of the irrigation theory (cf. Price 1971) emphasize its ecological basis. In the reinterpretation, increasing population density requires an increased intensity of subsistence production (cf. Boserup 1965). One, but by no means the only, way to increase productivity is through irrigation. Therefore, where there is both an increasing population density and favorable hydraulic conditions, irrigation will be the solution to the problem of intensification and result, in part at least, in the rise of centralized sociopolitical organization.

An alternative but logically very similar theory has been proposed by Service (1962). He argued that in an ecologically diverse area with a sedentary settlement system, a centralized redistributional economy would evolve to distribute the specialized products produced in ecologically differentiated zones. In other words, given sedentism, ecological diversity causes economic specialization which in turn requires centralized coordination for proper distribution. Like the irrigation theory, the initial critical factor is a high population density which requires the sedentary agricultural economy.

The final theory considered here emphasizes the importance of warfare in the evolution of centralized social organization. As formulated by Carneiro (1970), population growth in a circumscribed area, for which emigration is restricted, results in warfare over scarce agricultural resources. The formation of chiefdoms, and later states, is the outcome of the political domination of several communities by a militarily successful group. This results in a centralized social system in which the conquerors extract tribute from the subjugated communities. In a situation of frequent warfare, central organization would also be necessary for military success. The initial importance of population density and the secondary significance of management in this third theory are logically parallel to the first two theories.

Hawaii is ideal for testing these three evolutionary theories for two reasons. First, prehistoric Hawaiian society showed definite evolutionary trends towards specialization and centralization of leadership. Second, all the necessary preconditions for the theories are present — hydrologic conditions suitable for irrigation, high environmental diversity, and geographic circumscription. When the research strategy for field work was initially worked out, the aim was to collect data to test these theories because it seemed highly likely that one or more of them would offer an adequate explanation for the observed evolutionary development. The striking results of the research reported here were, however, negative. Although initially attractive, each theory in turn proved inadequate. I will try to show that the inadequacies of these theories stem from their simple causal sequences, which do not sufficiently take into account feedback relationships between social organization, economy, and environment. After indicating the inappropriateness of each theory for explaining the Hawaiian case, I will direct attention to a reevaluation of chiefly organization in order to show that, given specific ecological conditions, the internal structuring of the organization could result in developmental change.

ARCHAEOLOGY OF CHIEFDOMS

The archaeology of intermediate (chiefly) societies will be a central focus of considerable research in the next few years. Although chiefdoms are critical for understanding evolutionary processes, chiefdoms are presently poorly defined and poorly understood. Descriptions of societies under the general term *chiefdom* have ranged from the village chiefdoms among the Yaruro of Venezuela (Leeds 1962) to the interisland chiefdoms of Hawaii (Sahlins 1958). The variability in scale and complexity within socieites described as chiefdoms is large, but the factors affecting this variability are poorly understood. Our lack of knowledge on intermediate societies is a reflection of their rapid extinction during the last few centuries. If anthropologists are to understand the evolution of chiefdoms it must be through archaeological and ethnohistorical research and not another ethnographic project.

The archaeological work on chiefdoms is already well under way. Excellent work analyzing the neolithic Wessex monuments from England (Renfrew 1973), the megaliths of Malta (Renfrew 1974) and the Mississippian complex from the Eastern United States (Brown 1971; Peebles 1971, 1974) all indicate the tremendous potential for archaeological research on chiefdoms.

Since the key organizational feature of chiefdoms is their centralized hierarchy, it is this aspect which must be analyzed in the archaeological data. There are three basic data sources useful for this research. First, the social, political hierarchy is an organizational structure involved in a full range of cooperative productive activities. Research on those activities involving labor outside the extended family (lineage) is therefore critical. Evidence for such activities is represented in the archaeological record as field monuments, like the British megaliths, the Easter Island statues, and the Hawaiian *heiau*. The techniques of their manufacture and the amount of labor required (Renfrew 1973) reflect the organization of construction activities. In a similar vein, capital improvements, such as irrigation systems, fishponds, and weirs, may be further evidence for cooperative labor crews.

Second, the regional nature of a chiefly hierarchy is represented by a system of central places. As indicated by the monuments of the Wessex chiefdoms, the importance of these centers can be measured by the labor expended in their construction (Renfrew 1973). The number of levels in the site hierarchy and the intersite structure both within and between levels is direct evidence for the size and differentiation of the chiefly organization (cf. Earle 1976). Minimally, it is possible to delineate the approximate territory or support area for a given center and, thus, estimate the population size of the social unit.

Third, mortuary practices are a direct source of data on social status and wealth differentiations. Although there are many methodological problems (cf. Earle and D'Altroy n.d.), the distribution of primitive valuables in burials can be used to investigate social stratification of the burial population (Brown 1971; Rathje 1970; Peebles 1974; Earle and D'Altroy n.d.).

Archaeological evidence for chiefdom organization is both varied and extensive, and future archaeological research, in conjunction with ethnohistorical work, should offer opportunities to study the evolutionary processes involved in the formation of hierarchical societies. For example, the monumental features of the Chavin and the Olmec have presented an enigma to the archaeologists, although it seems evident that these ancient societies were stratified, hierarchical societies comparable to the complex chiefdoms of Polynesia (e.g., Hawaii, Tahiti, and Tonga). Attempts to classify arbitrarily societies into either state or nonstate categories have created an artificial break in the developmental sequence. It is my belief that evolutionary process can be profitably investigated in these intermediate societies where a dynamic interplay between social organization and environmental conditions is vividly displayed.

CHAPTER II

SOCIAL ORGANIZATION IN POLYNESIA AND HAWAII

The complexity and scale of Polynesian societies vary greatly from the small social groups on the coral atolls of Tokelau and Pukapuka to the extensive regional chiefdoms on the island groups of Tonga and Hawaii. Polynesian social organizations are characteristically chiefdoms and the variability within these organizations represents many transformations of chiefly hierarchical structure. In this chapter, I will first describe a model of Polynesian social organization, summarizing the general principles common to Polynesian societies, and then outline a historical description of Hawaiian society at the time of first western contact. In both the general model and the specific Hawaiian case, the focus will be on the hierarchical structure and its operation in economic, political, and religious activities. This contrast between the general model and specific Hawaiian examples will be used to highlight the marked increase in both centrality and differentiation in Hawaiian chiefdoms. The explanation of this evolutionary development is the stated goal of this volume.

THE POLYNESIAN MODEL

The Polynesian environment typically is pictured as small clusters of tropical islands isolated in the central Pacific. There is, however, considerable environmental variability both between and within island groups. The macroclimatic variability in rainfall, temperature, and soils is determined by global patterns of solar radiation and winds. For example, the pattern of trade winds largely determines an expected range in sea level rainfall of 1000-1500 mm, for Easter Island and northern New Zealand, to 3500-4000 mm for Samoa (Thomas 1965:34). Microclimatic variability is equally great. The specific geography of an island group is largely determined by its geological history. Starting as massive volcanic cones which rise sometimes to a height of more than 3000 m, these high islands gradually erode to jagged mountains and finally disappear, marked only by the coral caps of atolls. As will be described specifically for the Hawaiian islands, the size and relative position of an island greatly influence its pattern of rainfall. Even within a single island, environmental diversity resulting from orographic rainfall and temperature patterns is pronounced.

Because of the historical relationship between Polynesian societies, it seems reasonable to construct a generalized model for a prototypical social system from which the specific island societies evolved. This prototypical society would have been adapted to the typical high volcanic island, rich in diverse resources, but severely limited in total land area. The basis for Polynesian social organization is the localized lineage imbedded in a conical clan structure. Kirchoff (1955:6-8) defines the conical clan as ambilateral, nonexogamous, and ranked. The basic hierarchical organization is formed by the principle of measured distance from the senior line of the clan. In the ambipatrilateral case, characteristic of Polynesia, the highest ranked individual is the eldest son in the direct line of eldest sons. Theoretically, each person has a unique rank "precisely in proportion to his distance from the senior line of descent" (Sahlins 1958:141).

By population growth of the original founding group, assumed to represent one lineage unit, the clan expands to become the single, all-inclusive organization for the newly colonized island. As local groups continue to grow in size, they occasionally fission while retaining a defined kinship relationship between themselves. This process may be referred to as the *ramification* or branching of the original lineage and the resulting conical clan is composed of related lineages ranked both internally and externally. Internally, lineage mates are ranked by their genealogical distance from the senior member who should be the lineage chief. Externally, the lineage chiefs are ranked by their genealogical distance from the senior line of the conical clan. The ranking of the chiefs determines the regional hierarchical structure and, by extension, a hierarchy of social groups as represented by the chiefs.

The conical clan structure is closely related to the system of land tenure. Typically, an island is divided into pie-shaped segments each of which contains the necessary subsistence resources. By occupying a land segment, the localized lineage has a generalized subsistence economy which is largely self-sufficient. The lineage chief is titular owner of the land division with rights to allocate unused lands. The chief is also responsible for group activities like the construction of canoes, the building of irrigation systems, and the performance of rituals. The local land divisions of several closely related lineages together form a district, which has various political and administrative functions. The district chief is the highest ranking lineage chief and is responsible for all district-wide activities which are generally either ceremonial or political in nature. He has the right to mobilize from the district resources such as food, raw materials, and labor, but he must request these through the lineage chiefs. The island is ideally the realm of the whole conical clan with the paramount chief at its head. The paramount should be the highest ranking of all chiefs. Although he is titular owner of the island as a whole, he must channel his requests through district-level chiefs. In general, the political-economic system is hierarchical, while retaining some autonomy at each level. The degree of autonomy at each level varies greatly through Polynesia and this variability is an excellent measure of the centrality of the chiefly organization.

In sum, chiefs hold dual statuses: the first is determined by their focal position in their local group; and the second is determined by their relative position in the regional hierarchy. The typical Polynesian chief is closely tied, by kinship bonds, to his local group. He is not a member of an elite class; rather, he is the elite member of his group. As such, he performs a wide range of leadership roles. Key to understanding the leadership roles of the chiefly hierarchy is their *generalized* nature. Chiefs are distinguished as general leaders in all group affairs — economic, political, and religious — but there is no specialization of leadership roles except as to level in the hierarchy. In other words, the differentiation of group leaders forms an incipient governmental structure but this structure is *not* marked by the internal specialization characteristic of state bureaucracies.

HAWAIIAN SOCIAL ORGANIZATION

When the Hawaiian Islands were first contacted by European expeditionary and mercantile vessels during the last quarter of the eighteenth century, the traditional social organization was recognized by the European visitors as politically sophisticated. These early explorers were impressed by the extreme deference paid to the islands' aristocracy and by the despotic power of the paramount chief. In recent anthropological reviews of the culture area (Sahlins 1958; Goldman 1970), Hawaii is unequivocally placed at the apex of Polynesian development.

> Polynesian social evolution reached its greatest development in the Hawaiian Islands, where all changes in direction or further elaborations of traditional forms under way elsewhere finally came to fruition.... The Hawaiian chiefs had finally succeeded in replacing substantially the traditional lineages with a tightly controlled administrative organization. All other Stratified societies had brought out fully all the political capacities of the Traditional order. Hawaii had begun to introduce a new order and to move in a new direction. [Goldman 1970:200]

It is generally accepted that Hawaiian social organization evolved to a complexity beyond the simple chiefdom and approached the state. The specific features which marked this development most clearly are the following: (1) discontinuity in rank between chiefs and commoners; (2) specialization in leadership roles; and (3) increased centrality in the regional hierarchy. The sections that follow will first describe the traditional social organization of Hawaiian chiefdoms and then describe the operation of leadership in productive activities.

Hawaiian Society

The following reconstruction of aboriginal Hawaiian society relies heavily on the traditional description written by four Hawaiians in their native language: David Malo (1951 [1898]),born 1795; John Papa Ii (1959), born 1800; Samuel M. Kamakau (1961; 1964), born 1815; and Kepelino Keauokalani (Beckwith 1932), born 1830. These ethnohistorical descriptions were compiled from personal observation (Malo and Ii) and informants (Kamakau and Kepelino); they all suffer from similar problems. Since they were written after considerable social and economic contact with western nations, many changes from the aboriginal situation had taken place but these changes are often difficult to recognize. In addition, the accounts are presented, for the most part, as idealized reconstructions which do not discuss important regional and social differences. Supplementary work on traditional Hawaii has been done by the anthropologist, E. S. Craighill Handy (Handy 1940; Handy and Pukui 1972 [1958]; Handy and Handy 1972). Working with native informants in the 1930s, Handy was able to obtain a wealth of data; however, the question of its applicability to the precontact period must be carefully considered. Since Malo (1951 [1898]) provides the oldest and most comprehensive of the traditional descriptions, his work is the main source for the following analysis.

A striking departure from the Polynesian model is the marked stratification in the social organization of the Hawaiian islands. Unlike the typical Polynesian chiefs, who were closely linked to local lineages as most senior members, the Hawaiian chiefs were a genealogically separate group, more closely related to each other than to the members of the local commoner populations. The chiefs (*ali'i*) were both structurally and economically distant from the commoners (*maka'ainana*). Structurally, chiefs and commoners followed different rules of kin relationship. Economically, the class distinction was defined by differential access to strategic resources. The distinction is made particularly clear by Malo:

> It was the *ma-ka-aina-na* also who did all the work on the land; yet all they produced from the soil belonged to the chiefs; and the power to expel a man from the land and rob him of his possessions lay with the chief. [1951 (1898):61]

The chiefs were organized internally on principles of rank similar to those described for the conical clan. Distance to the senior line was still critical, but this distance was traceable through both males and females. The traditional histories (e.g., Kamakau 1961) record the dominance of patrilineal inheritance of rank in the early (mythological) period, but by time of western contact, male and female links were of equal importance. In other words, the early period resembled closely the prototypical Polynesian inheritance system; however, this original pattern had shifted to a more cognatic one.

As a result of this shift, marriage became an important political tool to maintain or to build the rank of offspring.

> Special care was taken in regard to chiefs of high rank to secure from them noble offspring by not allowing them to form a first union with a woman of lower rank than themselves . . . .
>
> It was for this reason that the genealogies of the kings were always preserved by their descendants, that the ancestral lines of the great chiefs might not be forgotten; so that all the people might see clearly that the ancestors on the mother's side were all great chiefs, with no small names among them; also that the father's line was pure and direct. [Malo 1951 (1898):54-55]

Within the senior line, the most suitable mating was a marriage between full siblings of the paramount's "first union," because these came with the highest guaranteed pedigree. Royal incest acted to concentrate high status within the senior line and to minimize competing claims to the paramountship.

In addition, marriages between members of the ruling lines of two islands were prevalent. Such marriages were strongly political, as they were used to form political alliances and to increase political position. For example, Ka'eo, a high ranking chief in the Maui line, married the paramount chiefess of Kaua'i. By this marriage, an alliance was formed between these islands and Ka'eo, who had no immediate claim to the Maui paramountship, became paramount of Kaua'i (see Chapter 9). Multiple unions were a common practice for chiefs, who could solidify their political position by marrying women representing different social and regional groups.

The combination of both bilateral inheritance of status and multiple marriages created a very complex kinship web, contrasting sharply with the neat pattern of a conical clan. Most chiefs could trace multiple relationships to the paramount and these relationships could be used to political advantage. Malo (1951 [1898]:191-92) described an institutionalized means for establishing the legitimacy of status claims. Upon the succession of a new paramount chief, the *hale nauwa* was established to review claims. Each chief would present himself before a group of genealogical specialists to whom was recited his genealogy and especially how he was related to the paramount. If the genealogists considered the relationship to be legitimate, the chief was allowed entrance to the hale nauwa and become eligible for political appointment. "In this way they learned who were closely related to the king, who also were in his direct line, as well as the relative rank of the *ali'i* to each other and to the king" (Malo 1951 [1898]:192).

Consequently, a pseudo-conical clan structure, with its carefully defined individual ranking, was redefined with each new paramount. The use of genealogies and genealogists was critical to the Hawaii chiefs, for this largely determined their political position and, as will be shown, their access to resources.

In direct contrast, commoners had no conical clan organization and recognized no rank distinctions. As Kamakau makes clear, the commoners were an undifferentiated stratum ranked below, and cut off from, the chiefly elite:

> To the commoners [genealogies] were of no value, for their parents were of equal status, and they produced "back country" children (*keiki kua'aina*) who could not become chiefs (*'a'ole pi'i aku na lii*). Therefore, the children of the commoners did not learn any genealogy except for the names of their fathers and mothers and grandparents. [ms.:172]
> ... it used to be kapu for the *maka'aina,* the people in general, to know these things [genealogies]. [ms.:173]

The commoners were organized in nuclear families or bilateral extended families which, apparently, were largely independent of each other economically. Marriage took place, typically, within the local community (*ahupua'a*). Migration was uncommon and a family was closely identified with the local community.

The social organization, both in terms of the chiefly hierarchy and the stratification between chiefs and commoners, was manifest in the system of land tenure. Land tenure was based on a system of overlapping ownership/stewardship whereby an individual's rights were determined by his sociopolitical status. After the genealogical review at the hale nauwa, Malo reports that "A plan was then made as to what office the king should give one another chief and commoner related to him" (1951 [1898]:192). An individual was assigned stewardship of a given land division from which he had: (1) the right to obtain goods and services for his support; and (2) the obligation to manage the social, religious, and economic affairs to provide adequately for the needs of both the higher levels of the chiefly hierarchy and the local commoner population.

There were apparently four significant, overlapping levels of land tenure—the chiefdom or island (*moku*); the district (*'okana*); the local community division (*ahupua'a*); and the family farm (*kihapai*). The paramount chief, as focal member of the reconstructed conical clan, was residual owner of all lands and held the title *ali'i 'ai moku* (chief who rules the island). The Hawaiian word *'ai* has as its standard meanings "agricultural produce" or "to eat." As such, the chiefly title clearly denotes the paramount's right to live off the produce of his chiefdom. According to the closeness of the established relationship, the paramount distributed stewardships at the next two levels to individuals who then received the titles *ali'i 'ai okana* and *ali'i 'ai ahupua'a*, respectively. Similar to the paramount, these chiefs enjoyed rights to personal support from their land division. These chiefs were, however, only rarely involved directly in productive activities. They held rights to food produced by the commoners, whether on the commoners' subsistence plots or *ko'ele* land, which was set aside specifically for the support of the chiefs. Finally, the commoner received use rights in a small piece of land used for his own subsistence; however, this right was theoretically revocable at any time. The commoner's holding was contingent on his labor on the *ko'ele* land and on his periodic gifts to the chiefs. In general, the system of land tenure was based on the principle that rights to a land unit were contingent on the fulfillment of obligations to higher levels in the hierarchy. This principle applied equally to commoner and to chief. An *ali'i 'ai ahupua'a* whose land division did not meet the expectations of the higher level chiefs was subject to removal from his stewardship.

In sum, the traditional Hawaiian social organization was stratified into two classes — chiefs and commoners. Removed from direct productive activities, the chiefs were supported by the goods and services produced on the land division they controlled. The commoners were the laborers of the land — producing both for themselves and their chiefs. The chiefs were not without responsibilities both to the higher levels in the hierarchy and to the commoners whom they controlled. The next section will describe the important managerial role of the chiefs in the local productive activities.

Local Management

Although the social classes in Hawaii were structurally detached from each other, economically they were interdependent. The elites depended on the commoners for all necessary manual labor and commodities; in return, the commoners were dependent on the elites for leadership and support. In the land tenure system, associated with the chiefly office are specific rights and obligations. On the one hand, a chief held the right to a percentage of the yield from his land division; on the other hand, the chief held the obligations to guarantee the smooth functioning of the subsistence economy for the commoners and to supply higher levels in the hierarchy with their requirements. As was typical of the simple Polynesian chiefdom, these two aspects of land tenure were often associated with a single individual, the local chief. In Hawaii, however, the managerial obligations were usually delegated to a specialist, the *konohiki*.

It was this delegation of managerial responsibility to the konohiki which most gives Hawaii the appearance of having an incipient state bureaucracy.

> ... the *konohiki* and their aides were government-supported fulltime functionaries. The organizational and acquisitive network that they spread over the countryside probably contributed more than any other political institution to making the government of ancient Hawaii a crude, agrobureaucratic hydraulic state. [Wittfogel 1957:241]

As described below, the konohiki were the generalized managerial specialists responsible for a wide range in productive activities.

The traditional subsistence economy of Hawaii was composed of three major sectors — wetland agriculture, dryland agriculture, and fishing. A konohiki was appointed to each local land division with express managerial responsibilities in each sector. It was his role to organize productive activities which required more labor than was available to the nuclear or extended family.

As described in later chapters, the dominant subsistence strategy was wetland taro. Taro (*Colocasia esculenta*) is a tropical root crop belonging to the Araceae or Aroid Family, a tropical family adapted to hydromorphic soils and annual rainfall in excess of 1250 mm distributed evenly throughout the year (E. Earle 1971:5). Wherever possible in Hawaii taro was grown by irrigated methods. As is well documented both historically and archaeologically, traditional Hawaiian irrigation systems consisted of a short irrigation ditch which fed water from a permanent water source into a series of pondfields. The konohiki was important in both the construction and the regulation of these irrigation systems. He was responsible for the construction of the ditch, the monitoring of the system for defects, and the allocation of water and land within the system (Nakuina 1894; various water cases before the Hawaiian Supreme Court). The construction of large pondfields and fishponds also involved large labor crews managed by the konohiki (cf. Kamakau 1976).

Dryland (non-irrigated) agriculture was an alternative strategy practiced primarily in areas where the lack of permanent streams made irrigation impossible. The dominant crops were taro and sweet potato (*Ipomoea batatas*). Although secondary to taro in both nutritional and ritual importance, sweet potato was an extremely important crop to the Hawaiians because it could be grown in areas of restricted rainfall where taro was not a viable staple crop. Sweet potato is suited to "light, well drained soils" (Massal and Barrau 1956:25) and in Kona, Hawaii it was grown in the zone of 760-1800 mm of annual rainfall (Newman 1970:128). Therefore, taro and sweet potato in combination allowed for a dryland agricultural strategy broadly adapted to Hawaii's wide range in rainfall.

The traditional techniques of dryland planting were labor intensive, requiring the initial clearing of all vegetation and the mounding of soil. In some situations, these tasks were done by communal work parties of "ten, twenty, or more men" who were bedecked in their ceremonial finery (Kamakau 1976). It seems likely that this group labor was used to plant fields quickly after rain and the recruitment of the group on short notice was probably handled by the konohiki.

Since taro and sweet potato are both poor in protein, it was necessary to combine the tuber diet with a good protein source, most often fish. Fishing and simple aquaculture were an important part of the traditional subsistence economy. Some fish ponds were constructed in conjunction with the irrigation systems, but particularly it was the larger fishponds and fish traps which involved cooperative labor crews for construction. In Summers' (1971) excellent summary description of the ponds and traps on the island of Molokai, there is good documentation for the recruitment and management of labor crews, including people from several ahupua'a for such activities. On a smaller scale, the canoes used in offshore fishing were probably constructed under the direction of the konohiki who then would have retained the use rights in them.

In sum, there is ample evidence for the many ways in which the konohiki acted as manager in local subsistence activities. This management was involved both in the construction of capital equipment and in the allocation of its use. It is, however, important to emphasize that the role of the konohiki was still very generalized and included many social and religious duties as well as the economic ones summarized here. The separation in status between chief and konohiki is, however, still a significant organizational development.

The Regional Hierarchy

The regional organization of the Hawaiian chiefdoms had important military, religious, and economic activities which required the mobilization of extensive surpluses from the subsistence economy. The Hawaiian chiefdoms were based on a redistributional economy. There were several large-scale collections each year at which raw materials, manufactured goods, and food were collected and stored in central places for use by the paramount chief. A primary purpose of the collection was political — support of the existing chiefly hierarchy. Food was distributed to the chiefs and their dependents for their personal support. Additionally, raw materials like bird feathers and whale ivory were converted by specialists attached to the chiefs into fine valuables like feather cloaks, feather helmets, and ivory pendants which were symbols of political office.

The mobilized goods were also used to support a small retinue of administrative and military specialists attached to the court of the paramount. The foremost administrative specialist was the *kalaimoku* who was the main advisor to the paramount. Malo (1951 [1898]:198) reports that an individual kalaimoku might hold office under several different paramounts. He was an advisor both in domestic affairs and in battle. Additionally, the paramount retained a number of military specialists who formed the core armed force of any warfare. Since warfare was endemic both within and between chiefdoms, the military specialists offered stability to the paramount and security to the local population against raiding.

Religious affairs were equally important and the paramount was responsible for the support of ritual specialists (*kahuna*). During the yearly cycle, the paramount supported various ceremonial occasions, the most important of which was the *makahiki* ceremonies lasting several months. These ceremonies were considered absolutely necessary for the productivity of the land and the sea. The ceremonies were also a ritual sanctification of the paramount's leadership.

There were further, strictly economic functions for the regional hierarchy. Because local disasters including floods and tidal waves were regular but unpredictable occurrences, it was not unusual for the yearly subsistence crop of a whole local community to be virtually destroyed; and, in this situation, the paramount chief would be responsible for the support of the destitute population. This was critical in Hawaii where regional kinship ties were limited by a high rate of community endogamy for commoners.

SUMMARY

Hawaiian social organization, although similar in many ways to the general Polynesian model, shows several distinct modifications which indicate an evolutionary trend towards state organization. Most obvious was the stratification into economic classes. The commoners were without the extensive kinship organization of the Polynesian conical clan. While the commoners were the primary subsistence producers, their rights to land were derived from the chiefs. The chiefs were organized regionally into a sociopolitical hierarchy based on land tenure; however, a chief was only steward for a land division rather than the highest ranking local individual of the division. His rights derived from the paramount and were revocable for reasons of poor management. This social stratification and political centralization were striking characteristics of aboriginal Hawaiian social organization.

Additionally in Hawaii, the generalized leadership position of the Polynesian chiefs had developed into the elites' right to an income and with it the managerial responsibility for surplus production. The Hawaiian economy was carefully managed by the konohiki to produce a surplus which was used to support the elite stratum and to underwrite governmental activities like warfare, ceremonies, and disaster protection necessary for the local population.

The governmental apparatus in the Hawaiian islands was still elemental but the trends towards administrative specialization and regional centralization are clear. Possible causes of this evolutionary development will be examined in this volume; irrigation, warfare, and redistribution were all common aspects of traditional Hawaiian chiefdoms, but their effects on Hawaii's development must be carefully evaluated.

CHAPTER III

THE HALELEA DISTRICT

Located on the north coast of the island of Kaua'i (Fig. 3.1), Halelea is a district of unusual natural beauty. The luxuriant vegetation, coral sand beaches, and mountain ridges fulfill our image of the tropical Pacific. Before modern plantation agriculture and international tourism, Halelea was a traditional administrative district composed of nine ahupua'a communities. These ahupua'a were characteristic of a Hawaiian "wet" valley community subsisting on a mixed strategy of irrigated farming, fishing, and dryland farming.

Halelea was chosen (from all the appropriate research sites in Hawaii) because of the ample and diverse documentation available on traditional irrigation practices there. Since the research plan was to test Wittfogel's theories with field data, an area with extensive irrigation systems was needed to investigate the relationships between irrigation technology and social organization. Halelea seemed ideal because information — archaeological, historic, and contemporary — indicated the continued importance of irrigated taro in the local economy.

In selecting Halelea, the deciding factor was the presence of several well preserved archaeological sites which included large irrigation systems for farming the alluvial soils near the sea. Traditional Hawaiian irrigation systems ranged greatly in size, from small terrace complexes in the valley interiors to extensive systems on the coastal plains. Archaeological research previous to this project had concentrated on the smaller sites because the larger ones are seldom preserved; however, since historical sources indicate that the coastal sites were economically dominant, our understanding of the complexity of Hawaiian irrigation may have been seriously biased by the available archaeological sample. The coastal Halelean sites, therefore, offered an unusual opportunity to rectify this situation. In addition, these systems were well described in the historical records and several were still operating. The contemporary taro industry was seen as particularly important because some of the basic irrigation practices are little changed from earlier periods.

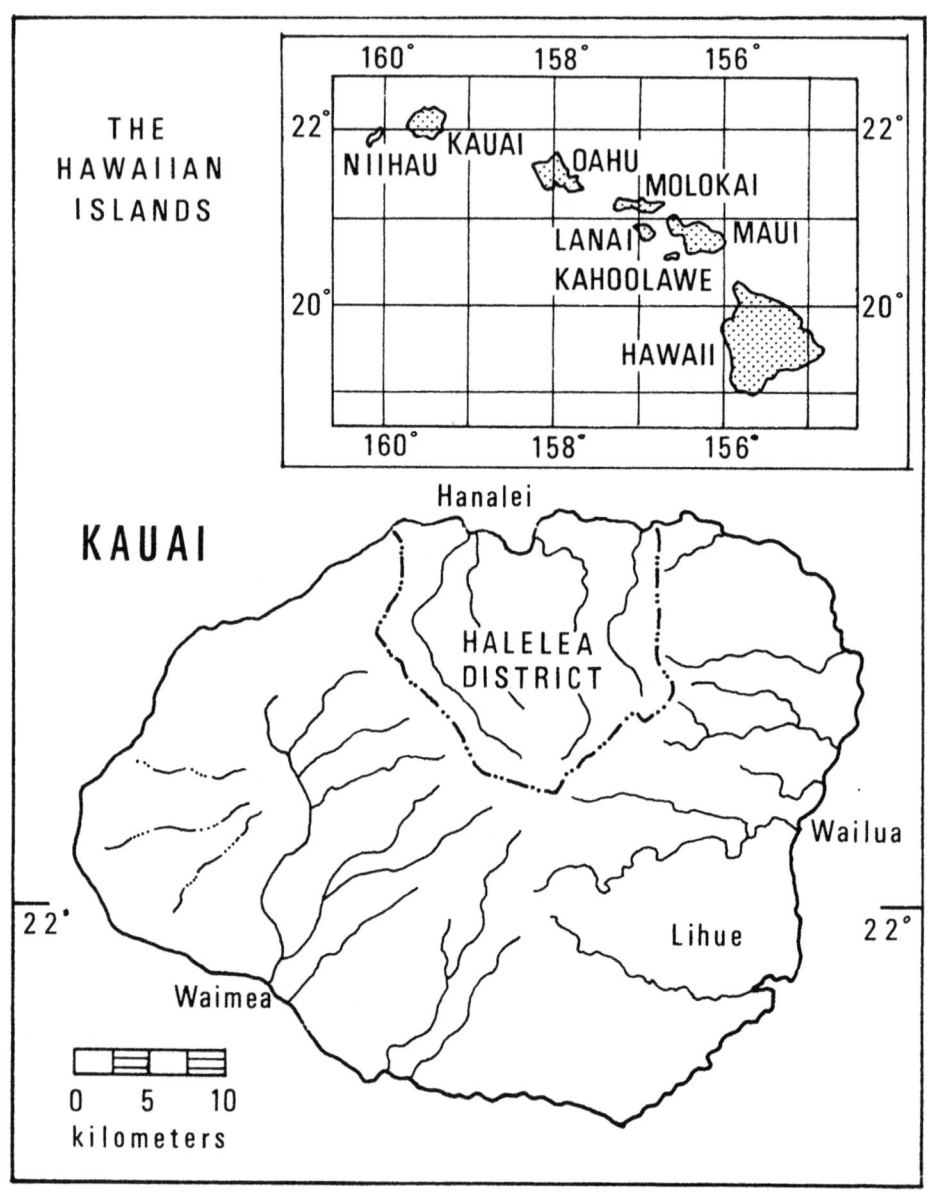

Fig. 3.1 The island of Kaua'i showing the location of the Halelea district.

ENVIRONMENT OF THE HAWAIIAN ISLANDS

The Hawaiian Islands are located in the central Pacific, just within the tropics at 20 degrees north latitude. Isolated from all other major land masses, this chain of eight major islands is composed of peaks of a volcanic mountain range, which protrude above the sea. As described by Carlquist (1970), the natural history of the Hawaiian Islands is determined by an interplay of climatic, geologic, and biogeographic processes.

The Hawaiian chain typifies the geological history of a Pacific volcanic island. After the building stage of primary and secondary volcanic activity, the island is sculptured by erosion. The extent of erosion is determined largely by the geological age of the island and its rainfall pattern. Kaua'i is among the oldest of the major Hawaiian islands and its dramatic topography testifies to this fact. The deep valleys and knife-edged ridges of the Halelea district illustrate particularly well the long established patterns of erosion in this zone of high rainfall.

Rainfall is the creative agent in erosion and the pattern is established by the interaction of tradewinds with the local geography. During the summer (May to October), the trade wind belt moves northward to dominate the Hawaiian climate. Because the trade winds are the result of air circulating from the cooler northern latitudes towards the warmer tropics, the capacity of the air to hold water increases continuously. As a consequence, these are drying winds, and the summer months have little precipitation except on the windward (northern) coasts and in the mountains. Orographic rainfall occurs where the ocean winds encounter the mountains and are forced upwards. As the air cools, the moisture held in the air condenses to rain. During the winter months (November to April), this pattern is broken as the band of trades move to the south and the Hawaiian climate becomes dominated by irregular warm/cold fronts and frequent storms. Several major winter storms produce general rainfall especially concentrated on the southern coasts and at lower elevations (Carlquist 1970:66). Winter is considered the rainy season but seasonality in rainfall is not marked on the north coasts.

The pronounced variability in rainfall within a single island is well documented for the island of Kaua'i (Fig. 3.2). At sea level, the expected yearly rainfall is 1500-2000 mm (Thomas 1965:34), but the observed rainfall for Kaua'i deviates markedly from this figure (Carlquist 1970:76-77). Kaua'i's climate may be described in terms of a windward-

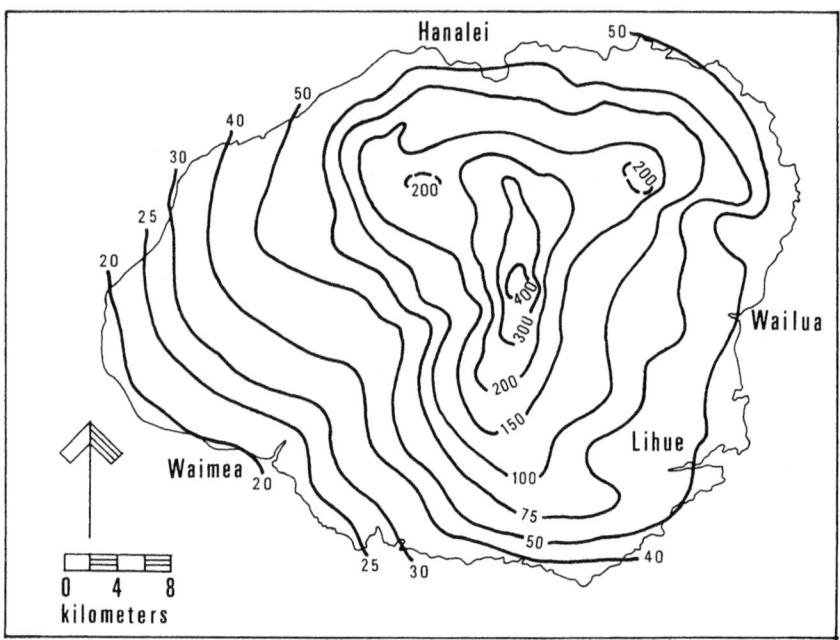

Fig. 3.2 Annual rainfall, Kaua'i. Isohyetals indicate inches of annual rainfall (after Murabayashi et al. 1967:1).

leeward, wet-dry dichotomy. On the windward, northern coast, the mean yearly rainfall is about 2500 mm. This contrasts to the more restricted rainfall on the southwestern, leeward coast which receives only about 600 mm per year. The mountains, which cause higher than expected rainfall in northern Halelea, result in a rain shadow effect on the south coast. In the mountains themselves, rainfall may reach 11,500 mm per year at the highest elevations (1548 m).

The effect of variability in rainfall on subsistence and settlement is mitigated by two factors — irrigation and mixed subsistence crops. First, taro is more dependent on a permanent water source for irrigation than on local rainfall patterns. Although there is a marked windward-leeward difference in rainfall, the heaviest rain is in the central mountains. For the leeward coast of Kaua'i, mountain runoff feeds several large streams, such as Waimea, Makaweli, and Hanapepe, which are excellent sources of irrigation water for taro. Second, the combination of the subsistence crops taro and sweet potato allows for considerable range in the amount of rainfall acceptable for dryland agriculture. The short growing season and reduced water requirements of sweet potato make it well suited to the restricted seasonal rainfall on the south coast. These points are important because it is often assumed that all districts could not be economically self-sufficient because of marked variabilities in rainfall. There is little evidence to reinforce this notion (cf. Chapter 8).

HALELEA

Since Halelea is located on the northern coast of the geologically old island of Kaua'i, the district is characterized by a heavily eroded land surface, well developed stream systems, ample rainfall, and luxuriant vegetation. Figure 3.3 indicates the distribution of streams within Halelea. There are four major streams and numerous smaller ones which drain the rainfall from the mountains to the sea. Halelea is divided into nine ahupua'a, the boundaries of which were determined by topographic features. The four largest ahupua'a — Wainiha, Lumahai, Hanalei, and Kalihiwai — are each based on the catchment basin of a single large stream. The catchment areas of these streams are separated from each other by the dramatic ridges which form the political boundaries between ahupua'a. As will be discussed in more detail in the descriptions of the ahupua'a these boundaries deviate from the dominant, natural divisions so as to divide sections of critical resources between ahupua'a. The five smaller ahupua'a — Ha'ena, Waikoko, Waipa, Waioli, and Kalihikai — are based on the catchment areas of one or more smaller, permanent streams.

Rainfall

Following the orographic pattern already described, rainfall in Halelea increases regularly as one moves inland (Fig. 3.4). On the coast, mean annual rainfall is about 1700 mm and this increases to more than 10,000 mm to the rear of the valleys near the summit of Mt. Wai'ale'ale. Traditionally, the major farming and habitation was concentrated near the coast where rainfall is between 1700 and 2600 mm.

Soils

The distribution of soils in Halelea is shown in Figure 3.5. The most important soils for traditional agriculture were the alluvial deposits located along the permanent streams but concentrated near the coast. The coastal plain was particularly critical for subsistence farming, for it

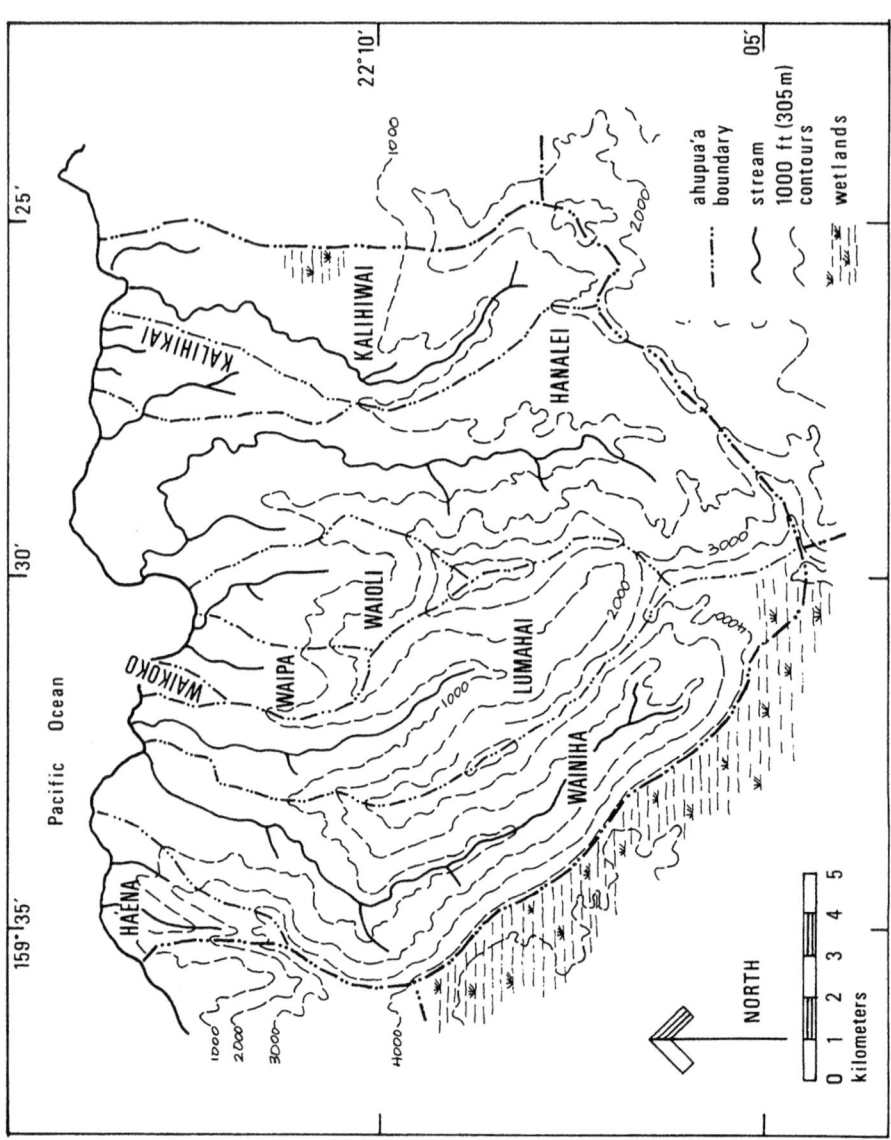

Fig. 3.3 Halelea district, Kaua'i. The territorial boundaries of the nine historical ahupua'a are shown in relationship to the topography.

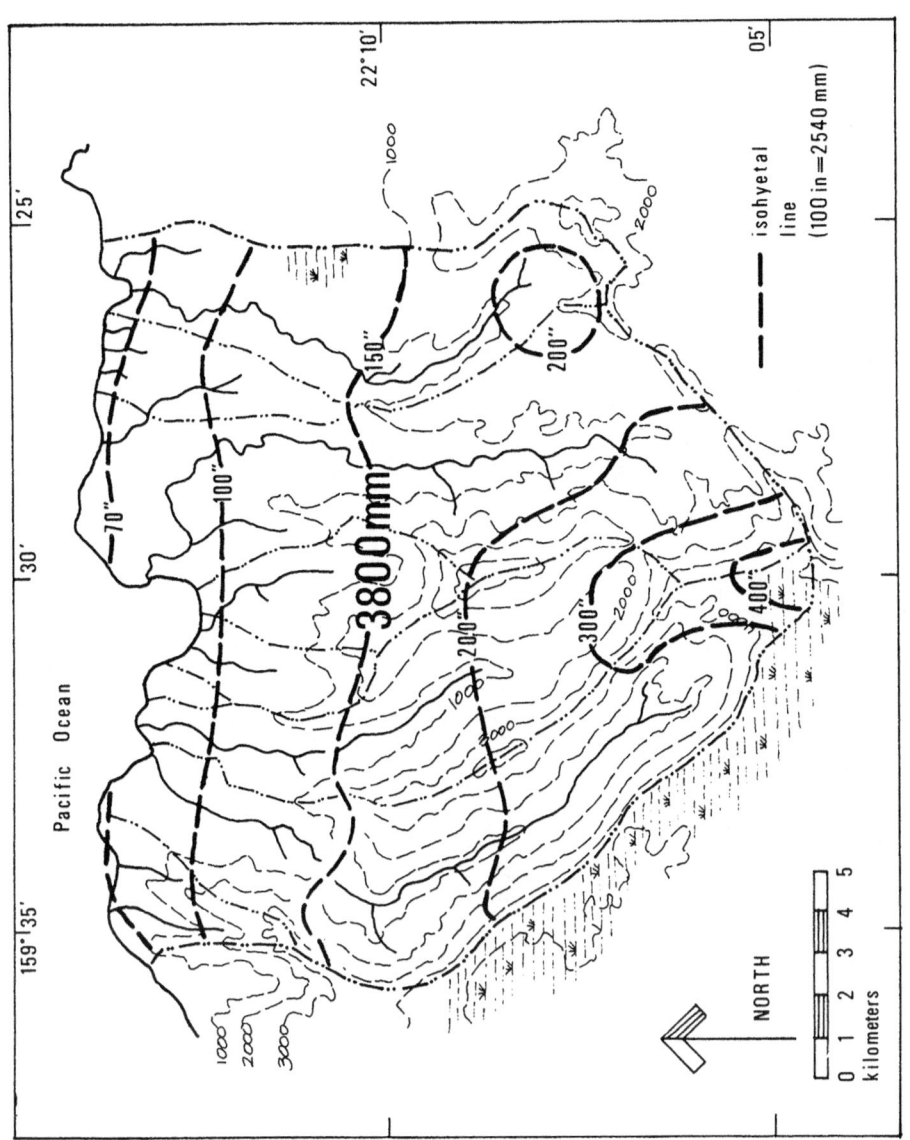

Fig. 3.4 Annual rainfall, Halelea district, Kaua'i. The isohyetal of 3800 mm is the approximate boundary between lowland vegetation (phase D₁) and upland vegetation (phase D₂).

28 ORGANIZATION OF A COMPLEX CHIEFDOM

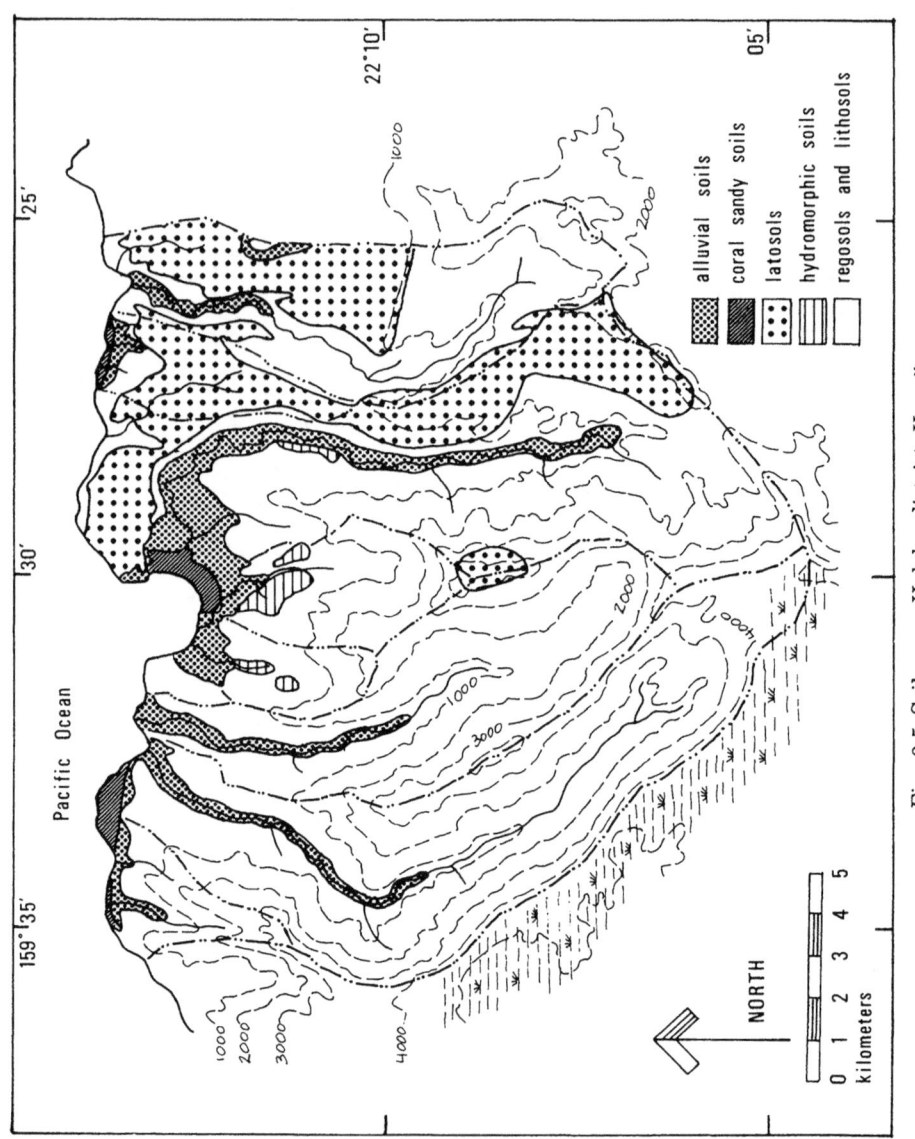

Fig. 3.5 Soils map, Halelea district, Kaua'i.

was in this zone that the large irrigation systems, with their taro pondfields and fishponds, were located. Of secondary importance were the areas of coral sandy soils found along the coast. These well drained soils were excellent for several crops and were the preferred area for house sites. The soils of greatest proportion in land area were regosols, lithosols, latosols, and hydromorphic soils; these soils were little used for traditional agriculture although they supported numerous wild and feral species used as auxiliary food and for other products.

Vegetation

For the Halelea district, Ripperton and Hosaka (1942) identify two phases of the major vegetation zone D, which requires at least 1500 mm of rainfall at sea level. The division into the two phases is based on elevation and, more specifically, rainfall. The "low phase" (D_1) is found at lower elevations with rainfall less than 3800 mm per year, the "middle phase" (D_2) is found at higher elevations with rainfall greater than 3800 mm (cf. Fig. 3.4). The modern phases of zone D contrast sharply with each other on the basis of the ratio of introduced to native species — D_1 is composed predominantly of introduced species; D_2 is dominated by natives.

During the field research for this present project, three plant communities associated with specific geographic situations were distinguished within phase D_1. These three communities were as follows: (1) the coastal community, restricted to the sandy soils near the sea; (2) the lowland community, found on alluvial soils along the valley bottoms; and (3) the upland community, located on the rolling, heavily eroded upland soils.

These communities are differentiated from each other by distinctive dominant species. The coastal community is characterized by the recently introduced species of ironwood *(Casuarina equisetifolia)* and false kamani *(Terminalia catappa)*. In the lowland community, the dominant species are the aboriginally introduced hau *(Hibiscus tiliaceus)* and kukui *(Aleurites moluccana)* and the recently introduced guava, Java plum *(Eugenia cuminii)*, and various grasses *(Gramineae)*. The upland community is more uniformly covered with guava and grasses, but the native *Pandanus* is locally dominant. Various nineteenth century accounts (e.g., Jarves 1844:162-63; Wilkes 1845:69) described an extensive *Pandanus* forest covering the latosolic uplands of Hanalei, Kalihikai, and Kalihiwai. More recently, this area has been converted to pasture land.

Many of the wild and feral species found in the D_1 phase vegetation zone were important economically to the ancient Hawaiians. In the coastal community, the chief economic species is the coconut palm *(Cocos nucifera)*. The economic species of the lowland and upland communities are more diverse and include four major supplemental food plants — banana *(Musa* sp.), breadfruit *(Artocarpus altilis)*, mountain apple *(Eugenia malaccensis)*, and ti *(Cordyline terminalis)*. The bananas are found in the wettest conditions, sometimes associated with rough pocket terraces. Breadfruit trees are rarer but they grow in the lower parts of Kalihiwai and Ha'ena. The mountain apple is feral in Ha'ena and Wainiha, and it is grown locally in the sandy soils near houses in Waioli. The ti is widespread. The important famine foods of these communities include *Pandanus, noni (Morinda citrifolia)*, wild taro *(Colocasia* sp.), and the tree fern *(Cibotium* sp). Other species, including *hau, kukui,* bamboo *(Bambusa* sp.), *ohia-lehua,* and *koa (Acacia koa),* were utilized for fibre, wood, dye, medicine, and other non-food purposes.

Phase D_2 of the vegetation zone is in areas receiving more than 3800 mm of rain a year. The geology of this zone comprises the steep talus slopes and pockets of alluvial soils found in the upper valleys. The dominant species are the native trees ohia-lehua and kukui. The vegetation also includes many important economic species, especially the wild and feral food plants such as banana, taro, and yam *(Dioscorea sp.)*. Bananas and taros grow profusely in the wetter alluvial soils on the valley floors. In an early account of the interior of Wainiha, Bingham (1969 [1849]) described "bananas of spontaneous growth"; in 1885, Stolz (1912) described this same area as a "banana jungle." Native tree ferns are common in this community, and *'awa (Piper methysticum),* a beverage source, is also present. In addition, important fibre sources include *olona (Touchardia latifolia)* and *'ie'ie (Freycinetia arborea)*.

HALELEA AHUPUA'A

To introduce this section, I will give a generalized description of a Halelean ahupua'a. The boundaries of the ahupua'a run along ridges from the mountains to the sea so as to include the full catchment area of at least one permanent stream. The hydrology of the central stream dominates the ahupua'a. In the interior, the steep-sided mountain valley of the stream's headwaters is engulfed in luxuriant vegetation which climbs the many side ravines. Nearer the sea, the valley widens, the stream begins to meander, and it is often braided. In the bends and central islands, pockets of alluvium are common, and aboriginally these were developed into small irrigation systems. The flanking hillsides are clothed with vegetation. Just before the sea, the stream emerges from the valley onto a narrow coastal plain which slopes gradually from the mountain ridges to the shore. Just in back of the low sand dunes, the water table reaches the surface where there is a narrow swamp. This coastal alluvium was the critical farming area for each community. Shallow bays have developed at the mouths of the stream and areas of fringing coral reef are scattered along the coast.

The variability in the ahupua'a is shown best by the individual descriptions of the nine Halelean land divisions. In the following subsections, the geography of these ahupua'a is described with regard to size of the land divisions, their geomorphic formations, and their land use. The particular geomorphic features noted include (1) the structure of the catchment areas for the streams, (2) the location of alluvial soils, (3) the length of coast, and (4) the presence or absence of reefs. (Additional quantitative information is presented in Chapter 8). The modern, historical (based on descriptions of land awarded to commoners in 1848-1852; see Chapter 7), and archaeological land uses are summarized briefly. To amplify the descriptions, the reader is referred to Maps 1 and 2 which reproduce the coastal strip of the United States Geological Survey topographic maps of Halelea.

Ha'ena

The ahupua'a of Ha'ena (Map 1) is relatively small (7.7 km^2) and has no major stream system. Although Ha'ena has a long coast (4.9 km) with several coral reefs, its boundaries do not extend far into the interior. The ahupua'a encompasses the catchment areas of two permanent streams. The dominant stream, Limahuli, flows through a narrow valley until 0.5 km from the sea where it enters a sloping alluvial plain between the coastal sand dunes and the steep, mountain slopes. An extensive marsh area is located behind the sand dunes just east of Limahuli stream. This marsh is fed by water from Limahuli and a series of separate springs along the base of of the ridge east of Limahuli. A second, smaller stream, Manoa, is in the eastern part of Ha'ena and runs through a narrow mountain valley, entering almost directly into the sea.

All irrigated taro production has now been abandoned in Ha'ena, but in 1850 eleven systems were in use. The major taro area was on the alluvial plain extending to both sides of Limahuli stream. In this area, there were extensive irrigation systems, and Handy's informants reported that the marsh was planted in taro and the sand dunes in sweet potato (Handy and Handy 1972:411). Several of the irrigation systems are well preserved and they were mapped in detail by this project. Other smaller systems, one of which was studied, are located on the narrow alluvial benches along the Limahuli and Manoa streams.

Wainiha

Wainiha (Map 1) is the second largest ahupua'a (43.5 km^2) in the Halelea district. It includes the catchment area of the Wainiha stream which runs about 20 km from Mt. Wai'ale'ale to the sea. The coast is 2.9 km long and includes a small bay and two coral reefs. The boundary separating Ha'ena and Wainiha is interesting because it appears to divide equitably two major coral reefs between the ahupua'a. The Wainiha stream itself begins in a narrow mountain valley with many small tributary streams. About 3 km from the sea, the valley widens somewhat and the stream becomes braided with numerous islands. There are alluvial areas along the stream and on the islands, but there is no alluvial plain at the valley's mouth. An alluvial plain has, however, developed to the west of the Wainiha stream in an area fed by several periodic streams.

Presently, there are three irrigation systems in the lower valley, and in 1850 this area was extensively developed in irrigation systems on the islands in the stream and along the stream banks. In the interior of Wainiha, many small irrigation systems utilized alluvial pockets along the central stream and its many tributaries, but most of these were apparently abandoned by 1850. Six small irrigated terrace sites were located between 4.5 and 10.0 km from the sea by Bennett (1931:136) and by this present project. Other terraced areas have been described by hunters farther inland. The separate alluvial plain to the west of the central valley was apparently not farmed aboriginally by irrigation due to the lack of a convenient water source.

Lumahai

Lumahai (Map 1) is a large ahupua'a (36.9 km^2) including the catchment area of the major stream, Lumahai. Like Wainiha, the Lumahai stream starts in a deep valley thrusted into the central mountains of Kaua'i. The upper part of the stream is joined by numerous tributaries which rush down the steep valley slopes. About 1.5 km from the sea, the stream enters a compact alluvial plain bounded on either side by the valley ridges and on the sea by low sand dunes. The coast is 1.2 km long with no significant reefs.

THE HALELEA DISTRICT

Very little is known about the land use of this ahupua'a. Around the turn of this century, there were extensive rice plantations in the alluvial area near the sea. For the earlier historic period (1850), only limited information is available because no land awards were granted to commoners in Lumahai. The reason for this absence is unclear but it was not for want of a community population (see Schmitt 1966, 1973 for nineteenth century census data). Perhaps the ahupua'a chief and/or konohiki were instrumental in discouraging awards. Extensive bulldozing for pasturage has destroyed all archaeological evidence of pondfields in the lower section of the valley, but various small terrace sites are to be found in the interior. One such site was identified 2.5 km from the sea, during a rapid reconnaissance survey, and others have been described by local hunters.

Waikoko

Waikoko (Map 1) is the smallest ahupua'a (1.8 km^2) in the district. The ahupua'a boundaries include the catchment area of a small permanent stream and an area of alluvial plain. The eastern boundary arbitrarily divides a large alluvial flat between Waikoko and Waipa. Along the coast (1.4 km long), Waikoko has access to a section of Hanalei Bay and to a coral reef.

The land division of Waikoko is unusually small and its status as an independent ahupua'a community should be questioned. The alluvial area presently supports a small taro farm irrigated with water from Waipa. Little is known about aboriginal land uses in this ahupua'a because there are no recorded archaeological sites and no land awards from 1850.

Waipa

The ahupua'a of Waipa (Map 1) is relatively small (6.8 km^2) but it includes several good areas for irrigated agriculture. Waipa has a coastal strip (1.1 km long) on Hanalei bay, but no coral reefs. The boundaries extend inland to include the catchment area of the Waipa stream. This stream travels through a narrow valley until, 0.8 km from the sea, it enters a flat alluvial plain about 1.2 km across. The westerly 0.2 km of this plain is divided off as part of the ahupua'a of Waikoko. In addition to the dominant stream, there is a small stream called Kiwa'a which empties into the same alluvial flat. Discharge from this second stream has made the central and eastern parts of the flatland quite marshy. At present, there is only one irrigation system in production; in 1850, four were present in the coastal plain. There are reports of the archaeological remains for several irrigation systems in the valley interior.

Waioli

The ahupua'a of Waioli (Maps 1 and 2) is of moderate size (14.2 km^2). It encompasses the whole drainage basin of the Waioli stream which originates about 8 km from the sea. The Waioli stream travels through a narrow valley until about 1.4 km inland where it enters a flat alluvial plain which is divided between Waioli and Hanalei. A band of the plain about 0.8 km wide belongs to Waioli. The northern edge of the ahupua'a is a sandy coastal strip (0.6 km long) bordering Hanalei Bay.

Presently, the alluvial plain on both sides of the Waioli stream is extensively farmed with two irrigation systems. In 1850, this area was dominated by several large systems; little archaeological evidence remains because rice cultivation, around the turn of the century, heavily altered the traditional systems. A local farmer mentioned several small terraced sites in the valley interior.

Hanalei

The ahupua'a of Hanalei (Map 2) is the largest (68.5 km^2) in the Halelea district. It includes the whole catchment basin for the Hanalei stream which runs about 21.5 km from Mt. Wai'ale'ale to the coast. Like Wainiha, the stream's headwaters flow through a narrow mountain valley with numerous tributaries. Perhaps 9 km inland, the valley widens somewhat and the stream begins to meander. Here there are considerable alluvial deposits in the bends of the stream. About 3 km from the sea, the Hanalei valley opens onto a large alluvial plain (2.7 km wide) which is divided arbitrarily between the ahupua'a of Hanalei and Waioli. The eastern section (about 1.9 km wide) belongs to Hanalei; much of this area is very low and marshy. The alluvial plain is bordered on the north by a broad sandy strip along Hanalei Bay with fringing reefs. The eastern boundary of the ahupua'a is interesting, as it deviates from the normal pattern of following the watershed ridge-line, to include the mouth of the Anini stream. This greatly increases the length of the coast (6.9 km) and incorporates a large area of coral reef into Hanalei ahupua'a.

The large alluvial flat on both sides of the Hanalei stream is still farmed extensively for taro. The area is irrigated by three ditches: two parallel ditches on either side of the Hanalei stream and a third ditch which taps the Waioli stream. In 1850, this same alluvial flat was farmed by a mixture of irrigation and swampland cultivation of taro. Western plantation agriculture had, however, already altered the traditional irrigation systems by 1850; and, since then, large-scale rice farming has obliterated all archaeological evidence. Anini stream was a secondary but important area for irrigation agriculture in 1850, but very little physical evidence of it is preserved today. Additional small irrigation systems were probably once common in the interior sections of Hanalei valley. Two of these are described by Bennett (1931:134) and a local resident mentioned seeing numerous terraced sites deep in the interior.

Kalihikai

Kalihikai (Map 2) is a moderate sized ahupua'a (9.9 km^2) composed of several catchment areas. The most important section for the traditional subsistence economy was the series of catchment areas of three small streams. These streams drain a section of low, rolling upland within 2 km of the shore. The streams originate in narrow gulches opening onto a continuous alluvial flat, which lies between the uplands and the sea beach. This alluvial area is only about 0.25 km from uplands to sea but is about 1.3 km from end to end. The coast extends 1.8 km along a straight sandy beach, and offshore there is a large coral reef. The interior part of Kalihikai extends 6.6 km from the sea into an area of latosolic uplands which form the partial catchment areas for the Anini stream and for two tributaries of the Kalihiwai stream.

There is no contemporary taro production in this ahupua'a and recent bulldozing for pasturage has apparently destroyed all archaeological remains. In 1850, a series of irrigation systems tapped the three small streams and farmed the flat alluvial soils near the sea. The uplands are now pasture but, during the nineteenth century, there were extensive *Pandanus* groves.

Kalihiwai

The ahupua'a of Kalihiwai (Map 2) is 22.3 km^2 in size. Its boundaries enclose the entire watershed of the Kalihiwai stream except for the headwaters of two small tributaries located in the ahupua'a of Kalihikai. The main stream originates in the central mountains and, for most of its length, flows through a narrow valley. Near the sea (1.9 km), the valley widens somewhat and there are extensive alluvial areas in the large bends of the main stream and at the confluence of the main stream and side streams. Additionally, a small unnamed stream and the lower sections of the Pu'ukumu stream are included within the ahupua'a. Along the coast (2.9 km) the Kalihiwai stream empties into the broad Kalihiwai Bay. There are coral reefs along the shore to both sides of the bay.

No modern taro farming is found in Kalihiwai and recent land uses have apparently destroyed all archaeological remains of traditional agricultural systems in the lower valley areas. In 1850, several irrigation systems were active in the lower valley and on both of the independent streams. A local resident described numerous small terraced sites along the narrow valley interior.

SUMMARY

Despite the obvious differences in extent, the nine ahupua'a of Halelea are similar in basic resource composition. Each land unit holds a permanent water source, sections of alluvial soils, a coastal segment with access to open sea, and reefs or shallow water areas. As discussed in Chapter 8, the ahupua'a boundaries were laid out to include, within a single territorial unit, all the resources necessary for a generalized subsistence economy. Within the Halelea district, the ahupua'a pattern is characterized by a strong similarity between land divisions.

CHAPTER IV

THE EVOLUTIONARY SIGNIFICANCE OF IRRIGATION

In the recent explanations of cultural evolution stressing material causes for change, researchers have formulated hypotheses which seek to isolate the ecological and economic conditions causing the evolution from tribes to chiefdoms and, finally, to states. Irrigation has been one of the most persistently discussed causes of cultural evolution; although no one totally discounts the importance of irrigation, the precise causal relationship between irrigation and social development remains clouded. For the last twenty-five years, investigation of the significance of irrigation has involved both archaeologists and cultural anthropologists studying a wide range of societies, from simple tribes to ancient civilizations. Excellent reviews of this extensive research are available in Price (1971), Lees (1973), Mitchell (1973), and Hunt and Hunt (1974).

Karl Wittfogel is usually identified as the central figure in the anthropological debate over the significance of irrigation. From his research on Chinese history, Wittfogel formulated an interrelated set of theories on "Oriental society" and applied these theories cross-culturally to explain the development of managerial ("despotic") societies. His intricate treatise, *Oriental Despotism* (Wittfogel 1957), was a monumental effort to explicate the web of interactions between many components of environment, technology, and culture.

As stated in *Oriental Despotism,* Wittfogel's main proposition was that centralized authority in society evolves as a response to the complexity in an irrigation economy. According to this argument, environmental factors essential to agricultural production may be divided into the three following categories: (1) factors unalterable by primitive technology, such as climate; (2) factors manipulable only by the individual farmer, such as soils; and (3) factors manipulable only by suprafamily work crews, such as water. It is the third category that

Wittfogel says is of particular evolutionary significance, because it requires the development of a suprafamily organization.

Wittfogel believed that, for all but the smallest irrigation systems, mass labor is required for construction and maintenance activities and that this mass labor requires coordination. Central managers, therefore, originate to coordinate mass labor activities and to allocate rights in the water; hence their economic power as managers becomes extended to general political power in society. To summarize Wittfogel's line of reasoning — large-scale irrigation results in managerial controls which lead to a centralized governmental apparatus.

The work of Wittfogel was introduced to a general anthropological audience in a symposium volume edited by Julian Steward (1955b). This symposium established a firm correlation between centers of ancient civilization (China, India, Mesopotamia, Egypt, Peru, and Mesoamerica) and irrigation, but Steward (1955b) himself questioned the exact nature of this relationship. The debate which has developed around irrigation has centered on the issue of causality. In ethnology, some detailed case studies have tended to support Wittfogel's ideas (cf. Gray 1963), but most have concluded with negative results (cf. Leach 1961; Millon, Hall, and Diaz 1961; Sahlins 1962; Lees 1973). Similarly, in archaeology, many researchers (cf. Wolf and Palerm 1955; Adams 1966; Lanning 1967) have argued that large-scale irrigation is more a result of, than a cause of, state formation; although a few (cf. Sanders and Price 1968; Price 1971) have cautiously supported the critical significance of irrigation.

As the debate has continued, emphasis has wandered erratically from one aspect of irrigation to another. Authors have not so much disagreed with each other as addressed themselves to different issues. To clarify this debate, it seems necessary to cease thinking of irrigation as a single phenomenon and to conceive of it, instead, as composed of various aspects potentially significant in the evolution of centralization. In sum, Wittfogel's hydraulic theory should not be tested as a single proposition; rather, its specific hypotheses should be carefully segregated and investigated separately.

THE HYDRAULIC THEORIES

In this section, a synthetic model of irrigation will be formulated based on the major issues identified in past anthropolgical research (cf. Wittfogel 1957; Steward 1955b; Millon 1962; Service 1962; Adams 1966; Fried 1967; Sanders and Price 1968; Price 1971; Lees 1973; Downing and Gibson 1974). This model attempts to systematize the various lines of reasoning concerning the relationship between irrigation technology and centralized authority, as presented in the literature. Five aspects of irrigation are identified as potentially significant: (1) construction; (2) maintenance; (3) response to natural disasters; (4) warfare; and (5) allocation of water and settlement of disputes. Under specific conditions, each of these may require local or regional management of productive activities. The specific type of management varies greatly — direction of labor crews, mediation of conflict, central storage of staples — but they all would promote centralization of authority.

In the discussions which follow, I will describe: (1) the specific hypothetical relationship between irrigation and centralized management; (2) the numerous factors complicating these relationships; and (3) possible archaeological tests of the hypotheses.

Construction of Irrigation Systems

In *Oriental Despotism*, Wittfogel (1957:23-29) discusses the significance of construction. Irrigation, like heavy industry, requires high initial capital investments, including dams, ditches, and protective dikes. Wittfogel believes that if the hydraulic technology were of large enough scale, construction would require amassing and central direction of sizable labor crews. As formulated by Wittfogel and later authors, this argument is a tautology, because scale is usually measured by the organization of production. Instead, measurements of physical size should be the basis of defining the scale of a system.

To rephrase this argument in a testable form: the scale of an irrigation system (I) determines the man-days of work required for construction (Wc); in turn, this work affects the size of the requisite labor crews (L). Furthermore, as the size of labor crews increases, the need for centralized management (M) should also increase. Simply put, management should be a function (f) of the size of an irrigation system.

$$I \rightarrow Wc \rightarrow L \rightarrow M$$
$$Wc = f(I)$$
$$L = f(Wc)$$
$$M = f(L)$$
$$M = f(I)$$

This simple chain of relationships is greatly complicated by various exogenous factors. The first relationship — scale of an irrigation system determines the man-days of work required — seems straightforward but, in fact, unrealistically assumes that the technology of construction is constant. As an example, the introduction of metal tools increases the efficiency of labor and thus decreases the total number of man-days required in a given task. The introduction of mechanized equipment, of course, dramatically alters the relationship.

The second relationship — work determines the size of the labor crew — is tenuous because it does not consider the factor of time. For any given amount of work, there is a trade off between the size of the construction crew and the time span of the task — one man working ten days is equivalent to ten men working one day (as long as size of labor force does not affect efficiency). This time factor results in the situation described by Woodbury (1961), whereby an irrigation system of large size may be built slowly over a long period of time with only small labor crews. The economic constraints operating on a society to select one alternative over another are, therefore, of critical importance. Some tasks, particularly the construction of dams, must be performed in a restricted time frame; while the size of labor crews on other tasks may greatly affect efficiency. Political requirements are equally important, as discussed in Chapter 9.

The third relationship — size of labor force determines the centralization of management — enters a nebulous domain where social factors become critical. Two of the most important factors appear to be: (1) the payoff to participating members and (2) the social organization among participants. First, the type of payoff to participants is critical for determining the control necessary for recruitment and direction of a labor crew. If the crews are organized on the basis of share-out, whereby each individual receives land and water corresponding to his labor commitment, self-interest is a powerful incentive for recruitment and efficient cooperation. On the other hand, if crews are corvée, supervision may be necessary to guarantee satisfactory work. Second, the established social relationships among crew members also determine the need for supervision. For example, if all members belong to a single local community, patterns of relationship including leadership roles are already established and so additional controls are unnecessary. As Lees (1973) notes, the organization of a labor crew is determined more by the society's social structure than the size of the labor crew itself. On Moala, now a part of the Fijian nation state, government headmen recruit and direct labor for irrigation despite the fact that this involves only a dozen or so individuals (Sahlins 1962:44, 46). In sum, although there is undoubtedly a relationship between crew size and management, this relationship is a complex one which cannot be analyzed outside of the broader social context.

Archaeologically, it is possible to test a simplified version of the construction-managerial hypothesis by examining the relationship between construction work per unit time and centralization of authority. If technology is held constant, work may be estimated by the volume of earth moved during construction. Since time is a critical factor, a reliable measure of the time span of construction is necessary.

Maintenance of Irrigation Systems

Irrigation systems require regular maintenance, such as the cleaning of ditches and the shoring up of dams, in order to operate effectively. Wittfogel (1957) notes the similarity of maintenance to construction activities because both, if large enough, require mass labor and management. More recently, authors (cf. Price 1971:40) have emphasized the role of maintenance rather than construction because of the major operational difference between the two; maintenance is required by all systems on a regular basis, and, unlike construction, maintenance cannot be distributed over long time spans. In other words, the labor required for maintenance is dependent on the *present* state of the system. Similar systems have similar maintenance requirements, regardless of whether they were initially constructed slowly by accretion, or quickly by planned mass labor.

To restate this argument, the scale of an irrigation system (I) determines the man-days of maintenance work (W_m). The magnitude of this work determines the size of the labor crews (L) and the size of the labor crews determines the centralization of management (M). Thus management should be a function (f) of irrigation scale.

$$I \rightarrow W_m \rightarrow L \rightarrow M$$
$$W_m = f(I)$$
$$L = f(W_m)$$
$$M = f(L)$$
$$M = f^1(I)$$

This simple set of relationships, however, is complicated by several factors.

First, in the relationship between the scale of an irrigation system and the maintenance required, only those parts of the system which require regular maintenance should be considered. While ditches and dams may involve maintenance by cooperative labor crews, field areas are maintained individually as part of cultivation activities. This means that the physical dimensions of the dam and ditch complex are critical, but the total acreage in production is of little importance. Many environmental and technological factors, including climate, vegetation, and system technology, greatly affect the specific amount of work required in regular maintenance.

Second, the relationship between the magnitude of maintenance and the size of labor crews is complicated by the ability to subdivide tasks into separate, repetitious subtasks handled independently by small social units within an irrigation system. An excellent example of this organizational pattern is found in the "Twelve Village Irrigation Cooperative" in Japan, where, although the main irrigation system is twenty miles long and there are more than 10,000 acres of irrigated paddy (Eyre 1955:200), most maintenance activities involve only small work teams, each maintaining separate segments of the system. A cooperative group, representing the whole system, is responsible for maintaining only the head dam and the main ditch *before* the first diversion. This subdividing of maintenance tasks greatly reduces the size of any given maintenance crew.

Third, as discussed in the section on construction, there is no simple relationship between size of crew and type of managerial control. The contrast between the segmental Ifugao and the hierarchical Moalans illustrates this point. The extensive irrigation systems of the Ifugao are maintained by informal cooperation between owners of a ditch complex (Barton 1919:60), while the very small Fijian systems are maintained by government directed labor crews (Sahlins 1962:44, 46).

Archaeologically, the maintenance-management hypothesis is difficult to test because of the additional factors which, in conjunction with physical size, determine the maintenance work. In certain instances, it may be possible to examine the work involved in a specific task. For example, the periodic cleaning of an irrigation ditch requires the removal of silt, and the volume of this silt may be estimated from the archaeologist's cross sectioning of the mounded banks bordering the ditch. For all intents and purposes, however, the best test of this hypothesis usually available to the archaeologist is to investigate the correlation between the size of dam and ditch complex and the centralization of authority.

Reconstruction Following Natural Disasters

Irrigation systems are subjected to natural disasters and environmental degradation including floods, drought, salinization, and waterlogging. According to the severity of the disaster, reconstruction may involve considerable work or capital expenditure. The possible significance of disaster reconstruction, as distinct from regular maintenance, has been discussed recently in the Downing and Gibson volume (cf. Spooner 1974; Lees 1974; Hunt and Hunt 1974). Basically, it can be argued that only centralized authority has access to the labor and capital that are necessary for reconstruction.

To formalize this reasoning, the scale of any irrigation system (I) in conjunction with the magnitude of the disaster (D) determines the man-days necessary for reconstruction (W_r).[1] This work determines the requisite labor force (L) which in turn determines the centralization of management (M). Thus management should be a function (f) of the scale of the irrigation system and the severity of disasters.

$$\begin{matrix} I \\ D \end{matrix} \searrow W_r \to L \to M$$
$$W_r = f(I,D)$$
$$L = f(W_r)$$
$$M = f^1(I,D)$$

The relationships involved in disaster reconstruction are very similar to those for construction and maintenance except for the initial part — tasks in disaster reconstruction are a function of the size of an irrigation system and the intensity of the disaster. An irrigation system represents a major capital investment for an area. Over a period of time, labor is invested in the construction of dams, ditches, and field terraces so as to increase the area's agricultural productivity. Although a system may have been constructed by accretion, its present value is represented by the total labor and materials necessary to rebuild the system. This point is dramatized in a disaster. Because irrigation systems are compact and highly organized, they are susceptible to extensive damage during a natural disaster. Any specific disaster, according to severity, will destroy a certain percentage of the capital improvements of the system. This is an abrupt loss which must be reconstructed in order to regain the previous productivity of the area.

Critical to the reconstruction program and the size of work crews required are the economic dependence of an area on irrigation and the possible alternative sources of subsistence. If a population is heavily dependent on irrigation and has no sufficient alternative food source, an irrigation system must be rebuilt quickly and large labor crews may be necessary; conversely, if irrigation agriculture is relatively unimportant, or there are alternative food sources, rebuilding may be spread over a longer period of time (cf. discussion on importance of time factor in initial construction).

Disasters are particularly interesting because of their potential role in the evolution of regional management (cf. Gall and Saxe 1977). With the diversified agriculture of most segmental societies, a disaster

---

[1] In a monetized economy, as described by Spooner (1974) or Lees (1974), the critical factor is the capital requirement of reconstruction. In such a situation, only a centralized agent may have access to the necessary capital to hire labor, technocrats, and/or machinery.

usually affects only a small portion of a local group's production. In contrast, a society based heavily on irrigation agriculture is highly susceptible to disasters because of the specialized nature of its production. A centralized regional organization could lessen this risk in two ways. First, the organization could recruit large labor crews from several communities to rebuild the system and restore the area's self-sufficiency. Second, the organization could maintain food stores to support disaster victims until they are able to rebuild their own systems more slowly. Although local communities often keep stores as a hedge against hard times, it is inefficient for them to hold individually sufficient stores to withstand an infrequent but extensive disaster. Assuming that such disasters are localized and random, the probability of a disaster occurring within a region is the sum of the probabilities for each community. Therefore, storage by a centralized regional agency could be used effectively to support *any* afflicted community under the agency's jurisdiction.

It is possible, albeit difficult, to study the effects of disasters archaeologically. By studying the depositional history of an irrigation system, one might be able to isolate the frequency, extent, and source of major damage to the complex, although reconstruction would tend to obscure such evidence. In most situations, it is only feasible to know the frequency and severity of disasters from modern data and to make educated guesses concerning the expected percentage of damage to irrigation complexes.

Defense and Reconstruction Following Warfare

Irrigation systems are susceptible to social "disasters" in warfare. The effects of warfare include both raiding and destruction. In raiding, the effective yield is reduced by predation and so must be compensated for by surplus production. In competitive warfare, irrigation systems are frequently destroyed to decrease an enemy's productive capacity. In this latter situation, the severity of warfare's impact is measurable as the percentage of a system's technological improvements that are destroyed. Since such destruction requires reconstruction, warfare has an effect similar to a natural disaster.

Defense is another aspect of warfare which may select for centralized management. Irrigation systems represent both considerable capital investments and high agricultural yields. There is an obvious need to protect these systems against both purposeful destruction, described above, and regular parasitic raiding. The significance of warfare to a society based on irrigation is made clear in several ethnographic cases. For the El Shabana of Southern Iraq, Fernea (Millon 1962) describes a centralized social organization focused on the *shaykh*, the individual who holds regional political power. Fernea argues that, historically, the shaykh was unimportant for management of irrigation, but was critical for defense of the area's production. Similarly, Hackenberg (1962) describes the centralization of authority among the Pima, of the Southwestern United States, as caused by the dual conditions of concentrated irrigation agriculture and predatory raiding by the Apache.

In chiefdoms like Hawaii (see Chapter 9), there was apparently a positive feedback loop involved in the relationships between warfare, irrigated agriculture, and regional political organization. Chiefdoms, with their intensive competition both internally and externally, depend on constant expansion by conquest warfare. This constant warfare, especially where there is irrigated agriculture, requires a strong defensive posture which further strengthens the importance of regional political organization. The regional organization becomes important in the recruitment of a defensive force from local communities and in the maintenance of military specialists (cf. Chapter 9).

Archaeologically, warfare is difficult to study quantitatively. For the purposes of this study, all data on warfare come from ethnohistoric sources.

Allocation of Water and Settlement of Disputes

As a corollary of the hydraulic theory, Wittfogel (1957:52-54) states that the distribution of water among irrigators may require centralized allocation. The inherent antagonism between irrigators is described in detail by Millon, Hall, and Diaz (1961) who show that the interests of fellow farmers are in direct conflict when water is scarce. Sanders and Price stated the evolutionary significance as follows:

> ... this conflict [over scarce water] stimulates the selective process in favor of centralized authority — the more severe the conflict, the greater the need for and probable evolution of centralized control. [1968:183]

This "severity of conflict" would be determined both by the relative scarcity of water and by the scale of the irrigation system. In this case, scale could be measured by the number of participating farmers.

To restate the above argument, the scale of an irrigation system (I) and the scarcity of water (S) results in a given probability of conflict (C). As conflict increases, the selection for a centralized managerial authority (M) also increases. Thus, the probability of centralized management should be a function (f) of the scale of irrigation and the scarcity of water.

$$\genfrac{}{}{0pt}{}{I}{S} \searrow C \to M$$
$$C = f(I,S)$$
$$M = f(C)$$
$$M = f^1(I,S)$$

In the first relationship, scarcity of water (measured as the ratio of water available to water required), is in a direct and logical relationship to potential conflict. The relationship between number of farmers and conflict is theoretically equally simple; as the number of households dependent on a single water source increases, the potential frequency of conflict increases with the number of dyadic relationships.

The structuring of these relationships must be considered according to (1) the physical structure of the irrigation system and (2) the social structure of the farmers. The physical design of an irrigation canal, with the associated pattern of water distribution, establishes a hierarchical set of relationships between farmers. These relationships are structured according to a pattern of conflict and cohesion similar to the fission – fusion model of segmentary lineages (cf. Evans-Pritchard 1940). Although farmers along a secondary ditch are in competition (potential conflict) for water in that ditch, they form a cohesive group in competition with other secondary-ditch groups for water in the primary ditch. At the next level, the farmers in the system, as a whole, form a cohesive group opposed to other irrigation systems on the same water source. As discussed by Eyre (1955:203,205) and Netting (1974:73), the major diversion points are usually the focus for disputes, because it is at these junctures that farmers, either isolated or in groups, stand in opposition to each other's interests.

In order to predict the likely outcome of opposed interests, one must examine the social relationships among the groups. As long as groups share membership in a traditional community, it is likely that disputes will be resolved through established channels. In contrast, disputes between members of separate communities are likely to result in conflict resolvable only by open hostilities or by regional mediation. Barton described this situation for the Kalinga of the Philippines:

> The first users of water from a stream have the right to prohibit any division of water upstream from them. Enforcement within the bounds of a single town is accomplished without trouble . . . [however] Flowage rights often cause great trouble and perpetual feuds between towns. [1949:104]

Competition between local communities would select for a regional organization to mediate disputes and keep the irrigation systems functioning efficiently (cf. Price 1971).

It should be noted that various ethnographic studies (cf. Leach 1961; Netting 1974) have emphasized that allocation may be handled by traditional patterns of water rights. This may often be the case, but such findings do not contradict the basic hypothesis. As noted by Netting (1974:73), Leach (1961:165) and Eyre (1955:203), such traditional systems are conservative and resist alteration. Although there is a certain flexibility, major changes required by such factors as changing demography would inevitably result in severe conflicts of interests requiring mediation. A centralized system of allocation may seldom be required for the day-to-day functioning of a system, but it would be necessary during periods of rapid change and transition.

Archaeologically, the major variables of this hypothesis may be studied relatively easily. For any given water source and irrigation system, it is usually possible to determine the number of participating communities and to estimate roughly the number of farmers. Water scarcity is more problematical, but it may be investigated by attempts to project modern hydraulic patterns back into past conditions.

Nonmanagerial Hypotheses

There are several nonmanagerial hydraulic hypotheses which should be mentioned, although they will not be dealt with in any detail here. One frequently mentioned and uncontroversial effect of irrigation is the increase in agricultural yields per unit area. As discussed by Price (1971:10), irrigation is first and foremost a means of increasing productivity to meet both the subsistence needs of a growing population and the social needs of a stratified society. Childe develops, at length, the notion that civilization is based on surplus production and dense population. In his formulation, irrigation by increasing productivity would play an important role in the evolution of civilization. Service (1975:273-76), however, is most correct to point out that surplus production and high population density may be necessary, but they are not sufficient cause for the evolution of the state.

Another line of argument postulates that irrigation may result in social stratification, although it does not directly cause state formation (Adams 1966; Flannery et al. 1967:467; Fried 1967:211). Lees develops this idea as follows:

> The potential difference in access and control inherent in the physical nature of the flowing resource may have important implications for differential political or economic control, since the actions of upstream irrigators will directly affect the productive capacity of downstream cultivators, but not the reverse. [1973:123]

Although she sees differences in access as inherent to all irrigation, she cautiously notes that a society's response to this condition may vary greatly (Lees 1973:128); as in Pul Eliya (Leach 1961), there may be specific mechanisms to insure that water is equally distributed to all community members regardless of their relative positions on the irrigation system.

Finally, several researchers (cf. Pasternak 1972) have argued that irrigation results in the weakening of the extended family as the primary production unit and an increased emphasis on the nuclear family. In societies dependent on rainfall agriculture, the extended family recruits the labor necessary to plant a field quickly following the first rains. In contrast, there is no such critical planting time for irrigated crops because water is controlled artificially. As a result, the economic significance of the extended family, for agriculture at least, is negligible and so the extended family breaks apart from internal conflicts. This is a most intriguing hypothesis for it predicts the breakup of the strong lineage organization, so typical of acephalous society. This would tend to create an organizational vacuum on the local level which could be filled, in part, by a state organization. Many researchers have noted the general deemphasis of kinship as an organizational principle after state formation.

Summary of the Hydraulic Theory

In brief, the basic hydraulic theory postulates a causal chain, whereby under specific conditions an irrigation system selects for centralized management. The scale of the physical irrigation system (dams, ditches, terraces) results in work requirements for tasks (construction, maintenance, reconstruction, defense) which require labor crews of varying sizes. According to a complex set of relationships, the size of labor crew then determines centralization and specialization of management. A corollary is that the scale and complexity of the physical system (number of farmers and major diversions) determines the possibility of conflict over water. Conflict, in turn, results in a need for mediation. There are, however, numerous mitigating factors which affect each of the postulated relationships. These factors may be loosely grouped into aspects of the adaptational system (population, mixture of subsistence strategy, frequency of disasters, scarcity of water, etc.) and aspects of the social system (social relationships between laborers and farmers, economic payoffs, demands of a social elite on production, etc.). Although the basic managerial hypothesis and its mediational corollary are very simple, these additional factors greatly complicate the theory.

TEST OF THE HYDRAULIC THEORY

In the following three chapters, I will present the ethnographic, archaeological, and historic data on irrigation agriculture in Halelea district, Kaua'i. In *Oriental Despotism,* Wittfogel (1957:241) characterized traditional Hawaii as a "crude, agrobureaucratic state." In Polynesia, irrigation agriculture is a widespread form of traditional subsistence production where hydrologic conditions are favorable (cf. Barrau 1961; Sahlins 1958); but nowhere in Polynesia is irrigation so extensive or so well developed as on the Hawaiian islands. Because Hawaiian social organization was also the most highly evolved of the Polynesian societies, the probable evolutionary significance of irrigation seems plausible. The following chapters will examine whether the technological scale and complexity of Hawaiian irrigation was sufficient to require management, which would have, in turn, selected for a centralized organization.

In the synthetic hydraulic theory described in the previous sections, the specific aspects of the physical irrigation system that might require the centralization and specialization of managerial control were isolated. The theory generally states that, as scale and complexity of these critical aspects increase, so too must the centralized management. To test this theory for Hawaii, it is essential to know if the irrigation technology described for Halelea was both necessary and sufficient for strong centralized management. This can be accomplished by comparing the scale and complexity of the Halelean irrigation system, with irrigation practiced by four relatively well documented societies — (1) Sonjo, Tanganyika (Gray 1963 and 1972: personal communication); (2) Ifugao, Philippines (Barton 1919, 1922; Conklin 1967, 1972, 1974); (3) Moala, Fijian Islands (Sahlins 1962); and (4) Pul Eliya, Sri Lanka (Leach 1959, 1961). As this comparison shows (Chapter 7), despite a basic similarity in irrigation technology, these five societies are distinct from each other in level of management and in centralization of sociopolitical organization. In short, at the scale of the Halelean systems, irrigation does not necessitate management and it is an insufficient cause for the political evolution of complex chiefdoms.

CHAPTER V
MODERN TARO AGRICULTURE

In Halelea district, taro is a major agricultural crop cultivated, as it has been since precontact times, in basinlike pondfields irrigated from the local streams. Presently, there are about thirty-two farms concentrated on the low alluvial soils bordering Hanalei Bay and in Wainiha valley. Most local farmers are only part-time and their farms are usually less than a hectare in area. The taro is produced almost exclusively for market, and the farmers sell their taro to the commercial mills which manufacture *po'i* for the Honolulu market. Only small amounts of the taro is grown for home consumption and ceremonial occasions, such as wedding and baby luaus. This is very different from the prehistoric and early historic periods, when the numerous irrigation systems, distributed throughout the district, produced large quantities of taro as the primary staple in the diet of the local Hawaiian population. Taro was a way of life for the Hawaiian farmers of Halelea.

During the nineteenth century, however, three factors — the growth of large-scale plantation agriculture, a marked decrease in the Hawaiian population, and the importation of Oriental laborers — radically altered the whole Halelean society and its subsistence base. Oriental and Western entrepreneurs leased the taro lands and converted them into massive areas of rice, produced for export sales. The local agricultural economy was irreparably transformed from subsistence to market oriented production. After the rice industry collapsed, the fields were reconverted to taro, but the goal remained cash cropping. Many of the Orientals simply retooled for taro production and the district's largest farms are now run by Japanese (about forty percent of the local taro farmers).

Although much has changed, many aspects have remained similar to traditional patterns. The purpose of the present chapter is to describe modern taro agriculture in Halelea and, in particular, to describe the present practices of hydraulic engineering. As I will discuss later, the irrigation technologies are very similar to their traditional prototypes and their operation should greatly help us understand the archaeological and historic data on the earlier systems. This chapter will also focus on ethnographic description of the relationship between irrigation agriculture and the organization of production. Because the changes in the local social and economic milieu have been so great, this description does not represent traditional Hawaiian agriculture or organization, but, since the irrigation technology itself is little changed, the present control of these systems helps to illuminate the organizational requirements of traditional Hawaiian irrigation.

TARO CULTIVATION

Modern practices of taro cultivation are very different from the traditional methods, as described by Handy (1940), Kamakau (1976), and Malo (1951[1898]), because they are heavily dependent on mechanization, artificial fertilization, and an urban market. The most striking feature of taro production, however, remains unchanged — taro cultivation is largely nonseasonal. For every taro patch, there is a cycle of production activities, including soil preparation, planting, crop nurture, and harvest, but the individual cycles can be staggered so that a group of patches produce continuously throughout the year. This means that there is neither a planting nor a harvest season; rather there is continuous production lacking the peaks and troughs in labor needs, so familiar to the western farmer.

In this section, I describe the modern practices of taro cultivation and show that some are dependent on the horticultural requirements of the plant while others are linked to modern technological innovations and marketing (cf. Peterson 1972). The purpose of this description is to demonstrate that the modern schedule of labor inputs for taro cultivation can be fulfilled by an independent nuclear family organization.

Taro *(Colocasia esculenta)*

Taro is an economic species of the family Araceae. It is naturally adapted to a tropical climate and hydromorphic soils, and cultivation aims to duplicate these conditions wherever possible. *Colocasia esculenta* can be easily identified by its peltate leaves (see Massal and Barrau 1956:11). The Hawaiian planter distinguishes four significant parts of the taro plant: corm *(kalo)*; cutting *(huli)*; leaf *(lau)*; and flower

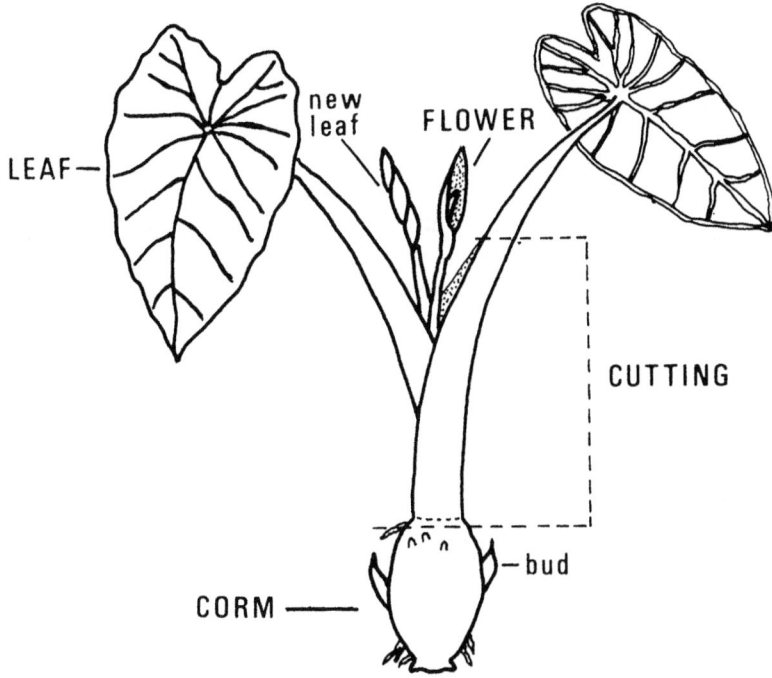

Fig. 5.1 Taro *(Colocasia esculenta)*. (Illustration redrawn from Handy 1940:78).

(pua) (Fig. 5.1). The corm is a thickening of the underground stem in which the plant accumulates reserve materials for future growth. The flesh of the corm is protected by a thick cortex. Both roots and buds come from the corm. The buds develop into either aerial shoots or rhizomes, which are the specialized adaptation for vegetative reproduction in the wild (Handy 1940:8). Domesticated plants send up shoots closely encircling the parents. The cutting, the planting material for the Hawaiian agriculturalist, consists of a new aerial shoot, which is a terminal meristem enclosed by a sheath of young leaf bases, all in the axil of an older leaf that is cut off at the petiole just above the level of the sheath. The corm is cut off about 6 mm below the junction with the petiole base and so a small piece of corm is left on the cutting. Leaves are peltate and have prominent ribs and veins. The new, unfurled leaves appear from the sheath of the next older petiole, and young leaves are important greens in the Hawaiian diet. The flower consists of a bisexual spadix enclosed in a modified yellow leaf form, the spathe. The spathe is

considered a delicacy. On Kaua'i, flowering was observed from May to August. During this period several fields were seen with about 10-30% of their plants in blossom.

Throughout the corm, petiole, and leaves are found microscopic capsules holding needlelike crystals of calcium oxalate. "These crystals ... are set free explosively by mastication or maceration. They set up irritation of the buccal and pharyngeal mucous membranes ..." (Massal and Barrau 1956:10). In comparison with closely related aroids, *Colocasia* is fairly low in these oxalate crystals but cooking is still necessary to make it edible.

Preparation

Taro patches are kept almost constantly in production, and a field will be replanted normally within a week to several months after harvest. During the very short fallow period, the patch is kept flooded to prevent weed growth. The farmer tills under any weeds which sprout, along with the leaves and petioles of the harvested taro. This tillage both controls weeds by eliminating viable seeds and incorporates organic matter into the soil. Before planting, the soil horizon is usually prepared by a Japanese hand tractor so as to create a 10 to 15 cm "puddled" zone in which the cutting is planted and the corm will mature. This puddling restricts loss of water to seepage.

Planting

Following the final preparation of the soil, the field is planted with cuttings collected during the previous harvest. Some farmers dry their fields for planting, while others plant in flooded fields. The cuttings are planted about 50 cm apart by implanting the individual cutting about 10 cm into the puddled soil(Pl. 1). Various techniques, including stretching strings across the field, pacing, and simple "eye-balling," are used to standardize spacing. After the first leaf appears (about one to three weeks), unsuccessful cuttings are removed and replanted with fresh stock. This is not a major task and requires less than two man-hours per hectare.

A hectare of taro field uses approximately 45,500 cuttings and requires about 75 man-hours for planting. As only one field is planted at once and an average field is about .06 ha (cf. System 15, next section), this would require 2730 cuttings and 4.5 man-hours per planting session.

Crop Nurture

Between planting and final harvest, the taro is nurtured by irrigation, weeding, and fertilization. Irrigation is central to this type of taro cultivation and farmers recommend continuous flooding through the period of growth and maturation. The taro field is an artificial pond surrounded by an earth embankment (the bund). Water, about 8 to 10 cm in depth, is kept constantly flowing through the patch by at least one intake and one exhaust channel cut through the upper and lower bunds respectively. This irrigated pondfield is an entirely artificial environment created to benefit the taro. The water serves many functions — it creates the favorable hydromorphic soil, it introduces fresh sediments which help maintain fertility, and, perhaps most important, it acts as a mulch to inhibit weed growth. Within a farmer's fields, water flows from field to field and both the rate of flow and its depth are easily controlled by adjusting the size of the intake and exhaust points of the individual patches. Some care is required for fields removed from a secondary ditch because the flow in such a field is determined in part by flow in the intermediary fields between it and the ditch.

Weed control is handled by careful flooding and periodic weeding by hand. Although weeding may require many man-hours of labor, there is no tight schedule for weeding and this task is broken into short segments which are fitted into times when labor is not required elsewhere. Weeding the fields entails little physical effort, so both children and grandparents are often involved. The weeds grow thickest near the bunds, which act as dispersal points for the seeds, and so herbicides are sometimes used on the banks.

Fertilizer is now used on most fields and farmers emphasize its importance for sustained yields. It is applied several times during the growth cycle and requires about 0.5 man-hours per field (.06 ha in area) to apply. No study of the economics of fertilizer was attempted during this research project.

Harvest

About fourteen to eighteen months after planting, the taro crop is harvested. Still done entirely by hand, harvesting is the most arduous part in taro cultivation and it involves several tasks with a definite division of labor. Initially, the root system of the taro clone is broken up with a long metal pole (Pl. 2). This task requires a fair degree of skill and it is usually done by the father or the oldest son working in the fields.

While he works, the major job of "pulling" the taro is begun by the other helpers. The corms are separated, quickly washed, and roots removed. If no planting material is needed, the corm is snapped from the leaf stalk and thrown into a bucket. When planting material is collected, healthy plants are selected and placed to the side. From this pile, an experienced worker (perhaps the mother or an older child) will select a plant and cut all but 1 cm of the corm off into the bucket. After trimming off the leaves, the planting material is ready and is set aside for replanting. The filled buckets are carried to the field bank where they are loaded into bags which are calibrated to weigh either 80 or 100 pounds when filled. Finally, the bags are lugged from the fields and transported, by truck, to the taro agent in Hanalei town.

Although no accurate measurements were made, farmers report yields to be about 350 bags (100 lb) per acre or about 39,000 kg per hectare. An average field (.06 ha) yields 52 bags or about 2,360 kg of taro.

Production Schedule

The market demand for taro is year around and production to meet this demand is continuous. Each farmer enters into an agreement with a local buyer to deliver a specified number of bags on a given day each week. This affects the production in two ways. First, for any given farmer it designates one day each week as harvest day when he must pull his quota. Second, it requires the farmer to stagger his yields for year-round production. Individual fields are treated as production units for planning purposes. The farmer is careful to adjust planting schedules so that a patch is always available for harvest. In order to handle this effectively, a farmer must maintain a minimum number of patches, and even small farms are elaborately subdivided (Peterson 1972:41-42).

The Family Farm

Halelea's seven modern irrigation systems are divided into farms which vary in size from about 0.2 to 8.9 ha of active taro fields. Although small, these farms are an important source of income for many local households. Taro farming is a "family" level industry with field labor contributed largely by the household head (father) and his sons but with other family members (wife, daughters, grandparents, etc.) helping as they are available and needed. The farmer is responsible for production decisions and management. As he is usually the hardest worker, he leads by example. In a Hawaiian household, usually only the males are responsible for farm labor. The division of labor is informal and based on age: father, eldest son, second son, etc. The oldest male in any production crew is responsible for coordination and for the skilled or arduous tasks, such as loosening the taro clones or carrying taro bags.

The basic production unit is the resident nuclear or minimally extended family; more specifically, the males of the household unit. Most tasks can easily be performed with this labor pool because of the nature of irrigated taro agriculture. Although the labor needed for a given pondfield is cyclical (preparation, planting, crop nurture, and harvest), the staggering of individual patch cycles through the year equalizes labor requirements. (As will be discussed in Chapter 7, this lack of seasonality also applies to traditional systems of production.) Because of this nonseasonal pattern, labor from outside the household is recruited usually only for harvest days which are designated by the marketing structure. Additional harvest laborers are compensated for their work by wages or by housing privileges on the farmer's land.

In sum, modern taro cultivation is organized at the level of the household; both the labor and management are based on this residential unit. Only the harvesting for market now requires additional labor.

HALELEA'S MODERN TARO IRRIGATION

The modern taro irrigation system in Halelea is structurally similar to an aboriginal prototype, consisting of dam, ditch complex, and pondfields. A low, loose stone dam is typically constructed at a natural shallow or river bend to divert a portion of the waterflow into the main irrigation ditch. Presently, these stone dams are being replaced by permanent cement head dams, but some of the traditional ones still remain. The main ditch is a plain earth channel about 80 cm deep and 100 cm wide. Secondary or feeder ditches branch off from the central ditch, but the main ditch continues the length of the system. The pondfields themselves are flat terraces surrounded by an earthen bund about 1 m across. Water for the pondfields is fed alternatively from the main ditch, from a side ditch, or from exhaust of a higher patch. In order to maintain adequate aeration, the water is kept constantly flowing through the pondfields by means of active intake and exhaust channels cut in the surrounding bund. After water is led from one patch to the next, much of it returns to the central ditch to be used by lower patches. In some flat, low areas, a system of drainage ditches is used to prevent waterlogging in the lower fields.

Although structurally similar to the historic systems described in Chapters 6 and 7, many changes have also taken place. Perhaps most noticeable has been an increase in patch size related to mechanization. First, earth moving equipment reduces the labor required in patch construction and eliminates the advantage to smaller patches (cf. Chapter 6). Second, it is a general rule that the efficiency of tractors increases with larger field sizes and so, as tractors become increasingly important, fields will be enlarged. Third, mechanization has increased the potential size of family farms by decreasing labor requirements. Since number of fields is related to a constant production schedule, field sizes tend to increase with increased farm size. For example, one small farm (.24 ha) in Wainiha has ten patches (mean 241 m^2) while a large farm (8.9 ha) in Hanalei has only about twenty-three patches (mean 3870 m^2) (cf. Systems 14 and 26).

Other changes include the extension of irrigation systems by the use of extensive drainage ditches and flumes and the gradual introduction of modern hydraulic technology, like cement weirs and restricted orifice devices.

In the subsections to follow, I describe the three functioning irrigation systems (Systems 14, 15, and 17; see Fig. 5.2)[1] which were mapped with transit and alidade. In addition, brief notes on the other modern systems (18, 22, 23, 26, 30) in Halelea are given to extend the coverage. These descriptions will be used in following sections to examine the relationship between irrigation technology and the organization of irrigation tasks.

System 14

The modern segments of the ditch of System 14 irrigate two clusters of pondfields on the westerly side of the Wainiha stream (Fig. 5.2). The system's source is a side stream created by the effluent from the Wainiha hydroelectric generating station. At the intake (2.3 km from the sea), a stone percolation dam diverts water into the central ditch. This head dam is constructed of irregular stream cobbles piled roughly between several, larger in situ boulders. The dam measures roughly 13 m across the stream, 1.2 m wide, and 0.5 m high. It is positioned at a natural bend in the stream so that the ditch line continues the direction of stream flow above the dam.

---

[1] As shown in Maps 1 and 2, both modern and historic taro irrigation systems are numbered consecutively from west to east.

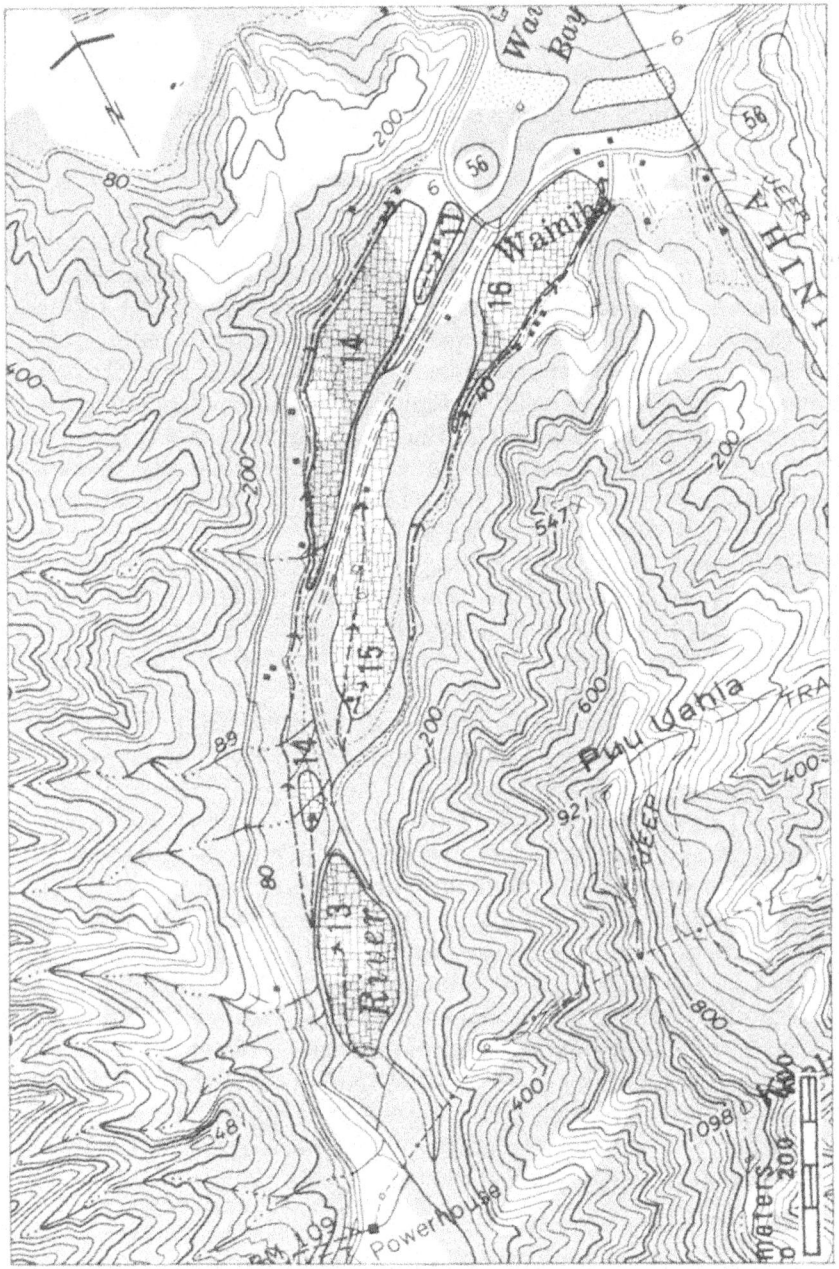

Fig. 5.2 Wainiha, Kaua'i. Enlargement of United States Geological Survey map for the lower section of the Wainiha valley. Systems 15 and 17 are fully functional. System 14 is only partially in use; with the exception of Farm 1, the lower part of this system is now abandoned. System 13 is abandoned and has been mapped as Ka-D6-11 (cf. Chapter 6). System 16 is abandoned.

About 10 m below the intake, the main ditch divides in two. The left or westerly fork (Ditch 1) continues straight on down the valley to a small farm (Farm 1); and the right or easterly fork (Ditch 2) branches out onto an alluvial island where a second farm (Farm 2) is located. For the first 350 m, Ditch 1 follows what appears to be a natural flood channel with slope of .013.[2] Where this natural channel bends sharply back to the main Wainiha stream, a stone and earth dam diverts the flow straight into the segment of the ditch which is clearly artificial. This dam controls excess water which tops the dam and is returned to the central stream. The cross section of Ditch 1, just below this point, is shown in Fig. 5.3. The ditch is unlined and approximately 1.9 m wide and 0.7 m deep at natural ground level. From here, the artificial ditch line maintains a gentle slope (.005) as it channels water 540 m along the base of the valley ridge to Farm 1. Because the ditch slope is more gradual than the Wainiha stream, the ditch water gradually gains a height advantage over the stream and, at the top of Farm 1, the ditch is elevated about four meters above the stream.

Farm 1 is small, with only .24 ha of field area and ten pondfields (Fig. 5.4). The pondfields are the smallest (mean 241 m^2; Standard Deviation 143) recorded for functioning systems. They have been constructed with earthen bunds on land sloping moderately (.052) towards the central Wainiha stream.

Just before reaching the pondfields of Farm 1, Ditch 1 divides, watering separately two series of pondfields with five patches each. Only the top patch in each series receives water directly from the main ditch, while all others receive water through higher patches. As discussed in Chapter 4, the number of fields through which water must flow in order to irrigate any specific field is a measure of the difficulty in controlling the water in that field. This measure is called "the number of distributary patches" and the mean number of distributary patches for this farm is 1.5 (S.D. 1.08). The circulation of water between patches is controlled by channels cut in the separating bunds, but water also seeps through the bunds. The bunds are earth mounds averaging 2.6 m in width (range 1.3 to 4.5 m). Scattered stones indicate that the bunds may have been reinforced by stone retaining walls at an earlier period.

The farmer, whose mother's family has farmed these pondfields for generations, has a house just above the fields where he lives on

---

[2]In this volume, slope is calculated as the difference in elevation between two points divided by the distance between these points.

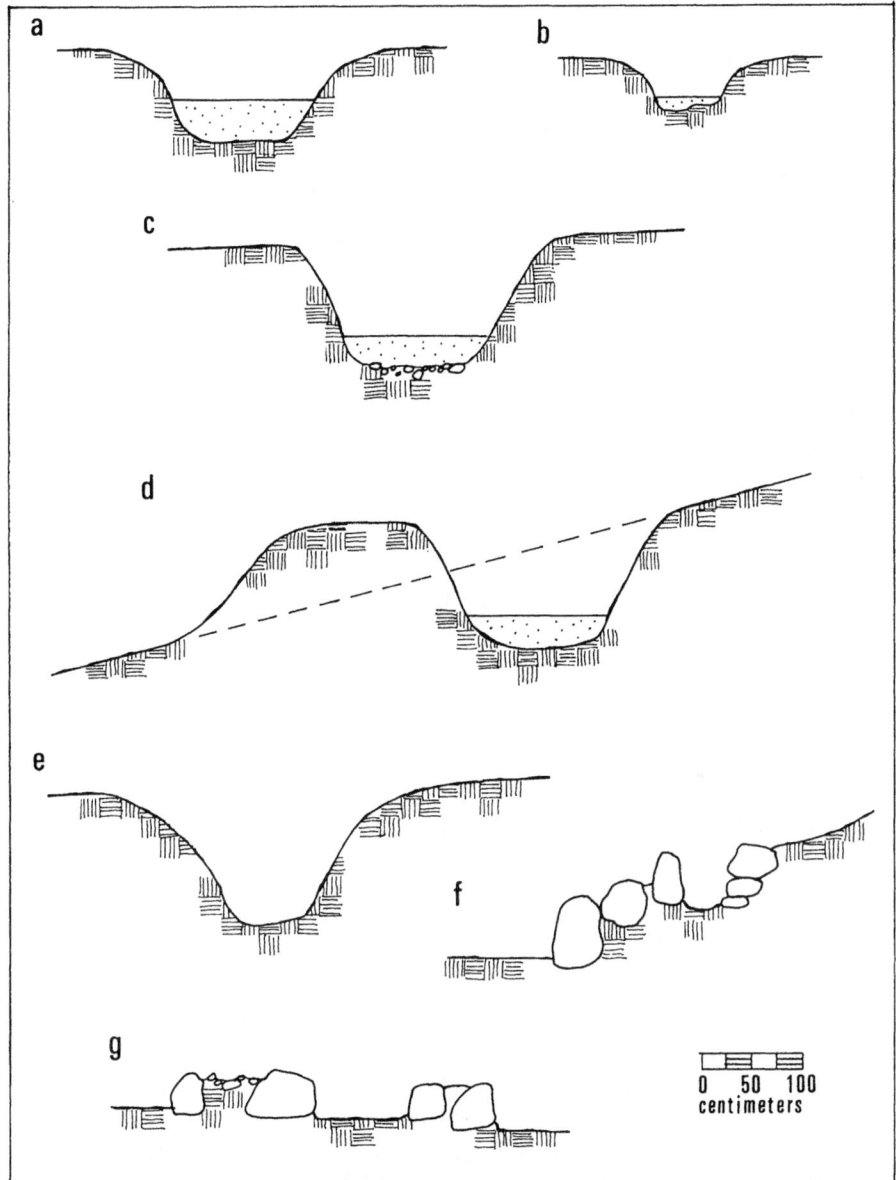

Fig. 5.3 Cross section of irrigation ditches: (a) System 14, Ditch 1; (b) System 14, Ditch 2; (c) System 15, near intake; (d) System 22, schematic representation of contour ditch; (e) Site Ka-D6-11, near intake; (f) Site Ka-D10-10, contour ditch; (g) Site Ka-D6-11, among patches.

62 ORGANIZATION OF A COMPLEX CHIEFDOM

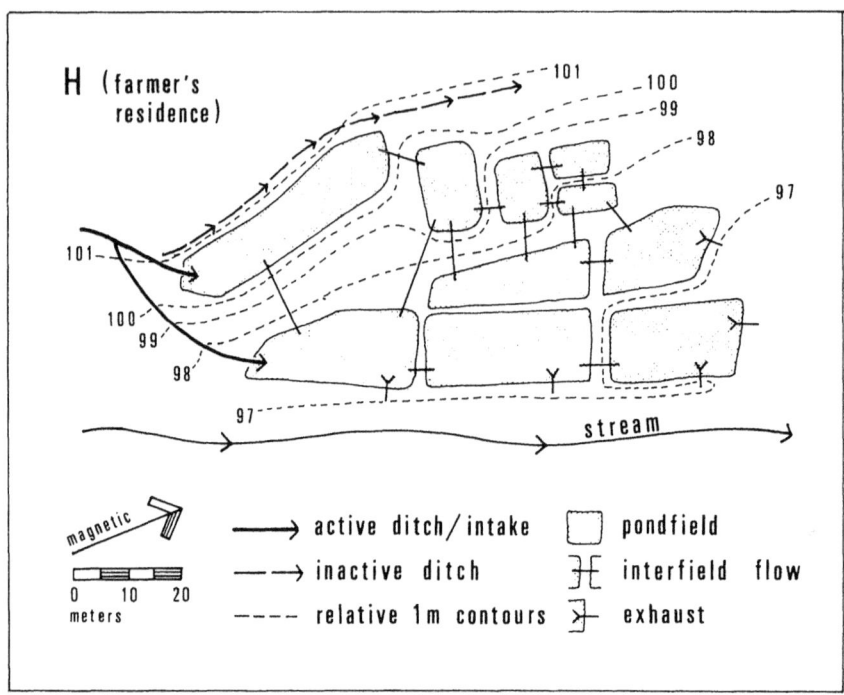

Fig. 5.4 Farm 1, System 14, Wainiha. The pondfield complex comprises the single farm on Ditch 1.

weekends. During these weekend stays, he is able to do most of the work on the taro himself; however, in the summer of 1974, he was having difficulties salvaging the fields from damage done during severe winter flooding.

To return to the intake of System 14, Ditch 2 branches off the main ditch 10 m below the head dam. At the division, the main ditch is partially dammed by a line of stream cobbles which divert water into the side ditch; the stones are necessary because Ditch 2 has a more gradual slope (.004) than the main ditch (.013). A few meters below the start of Ditch 2, a spillway leads excess water back into the stream. This spillway is a simple control device; as the water level of the ditch rises, excess water automatically spills into the lateral ditch and is removed from the system. Ditch 2, itself, runs down the central ridge of an island which lies between Ditch 1 and the Wainiha stream. A cross section of Ditch 2 is illustrated in Figure 5.3. It is unlined and roughly 1.2 m wide and 0.34

m deep at natural ground level. After 521 m, the ditch enters the top of Farm 2.

Farm 2 consists of fourteen pondfields with a combined area in taro cultivation of .57 ha. The mean size of these pondfields is 408 m^2 (S.D. 266.5), but the farmer reported that he recently altered the structure of the pondfields by removing several bunds and thus creating the fourteen larger patches from what had been twenty-five small patches. The pondfields are defined by earthen bunds on gently sloping (.016) land. The topography of the farm is typical for pondfield areas on islands. An island is high along a central ridge and slopes down towards the streams on either side; thus by running along the ridge, an irrigation ditch maintains a maximum height advantage and can irrigate pondfields to either side. Nine of the fourteen pondfields are irrigated directly from this ditch by means of narrow channels cut in the ditch bank. The control of water flow to the pondfield is a simple procedure — (1) to increase flow, place a few stream cobbles in the ditch, or (2) to decrease flow, place a stone or two in the channel cut into the bank. Because the number of distributary patches is low (mean 0.64; S.D. 0.93), controlling flow for each patch is uncomplicated. Circulation of water between patches is made possible by narrow channels cut in the earthen bund. These bunds average 1.8 m wide (range 1.1 to 3.3 m) and are occasionally reinforced with stone retaining walls. No drainage ditches are necessary, as excess water is simply returned to the stream by various short spillways.

The farmer directs the operation of this farm but most of the work is done by his sons who still live at home. Their house is down-valley about 1.0 km, though they have built a field shack on an abandoned field to store equipment.

System 15

System 15 (Fig. 5.5) is located on an island between two major channels of the Wainiha stream (cf. Fig. 5.2). The island itself is about 1 km long and 0.2 km wide. It is topographically quite simple with a dominant slope (.010) paralleling the stream flow. The main ditch of System 15 taps the Wainiha stream as it forks to either side of the island (1.6 km from the sea). Until a cement dam was constructed in the summer of 1972, the head dam was a loose stone mound stretching 50 m across the smaller of the two stream forks. The main ditch is a continuation of the direction of water flow in the stream above the fork. A cross section of the ditch near the intake is shown in Figure 5.3. It is

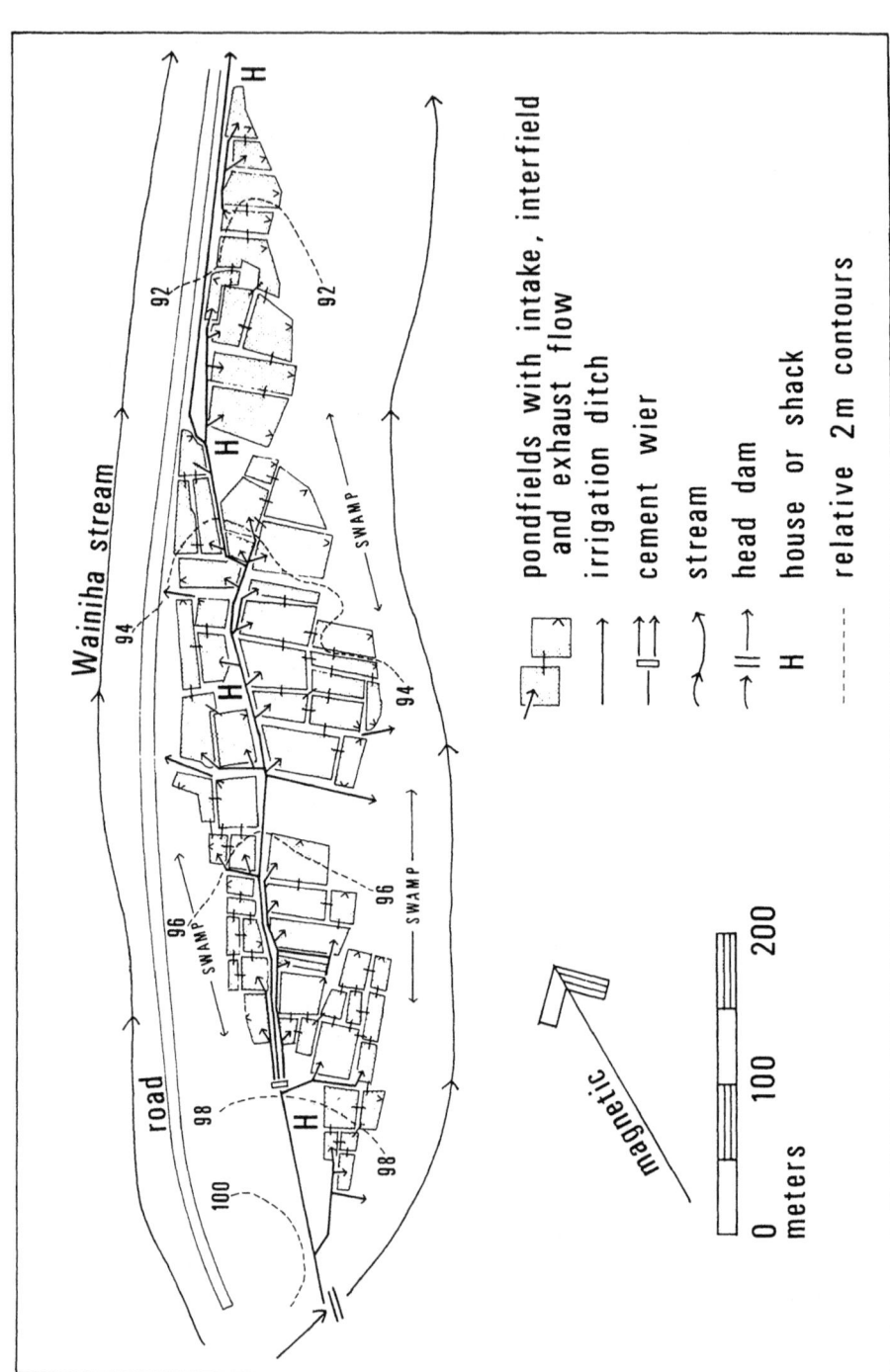

Fig. 5.5 System 15, Wainiha, Kaua'i. Typical island irrigation system.

unlined and roughly 2.2 m wide and 1.0 m deep at natural ground level. From the intake, the ditch runs down the central, low ridge of the island and secondary ditches branch off to water patches on either side. The first secondary ditch starts off only 6 m from the intake, but the main ditch continues for about 120 m before entering the main area of pondfields where its cross section is much reduced (perhaps 1 m across and 0.6 m deep). For the whole system, the total length of ditch is 680 m of primary ditch and 440 m of secondary ditch.

At present, there are sixty-six pondfields in taro cultivation with a total area of 4.07 ha. In addition there are six abandoned pondfields comprising 0.25 ha. The mean patch size is 607 m^2 (S.D. 378) but this apparently represents the recent combining of smaller patches. The pondfields have been constructed by building up earth terraces on gently sloping (.015) land. The surrounding bunds are usually simple earthen mounds, 2.2 m wide on the average, but they are occasionally reinforced by stone retaining walls.

The most interesting aspect of System 15 is the technology of water distribution. The main ditch is diverted at seventeen points either directly into a small cluster of pondfields or into a secondary ditch which feeds five to ten pondfields. In all but one case[3], the technology used for the diversion is simple and traditional. When the secondary ditch has a slope steeper than the main channel, flow is controlled by the opening which is altered by adding or subtracting stones in the entrance to the side ditch. When the secondary ditch is less steep than the main channel, the flow is determined by the number of stones used as a diversion dam in the main channel. The secondary ditch and its associated patches are cultivated by a single farmer, so that only the initial diversion is a matter of public concern. The circulation of water between patches is handled in a manner similar to System 14. The problem of controlling flow is simplified by direct feed from the secondary ditches in many cases, and the mean number of distributary patches is low (0.75; S.D. 0.98). Numerous spillways channel excess water into the uncultivated swampy area between the fields and the stream. Also, the main ditch receives exhaust water from patches and continues past the lowest patches to return excess water to the Wainiha stream.

The three or four farmers who cultivate taro in System 15 do not live on the island. There are, however, four shacks scattered among the fields used both for equipment storage and to house individuals who

---

[3]As shown in Figure 5.5, a modern cement weir is used to divide water between the main ditch and the two parallel secondary ditches which water large pondfield clusters.

help in the harvest. Some dry crops, especially bananas, are cultivated in nonirrigated sections.

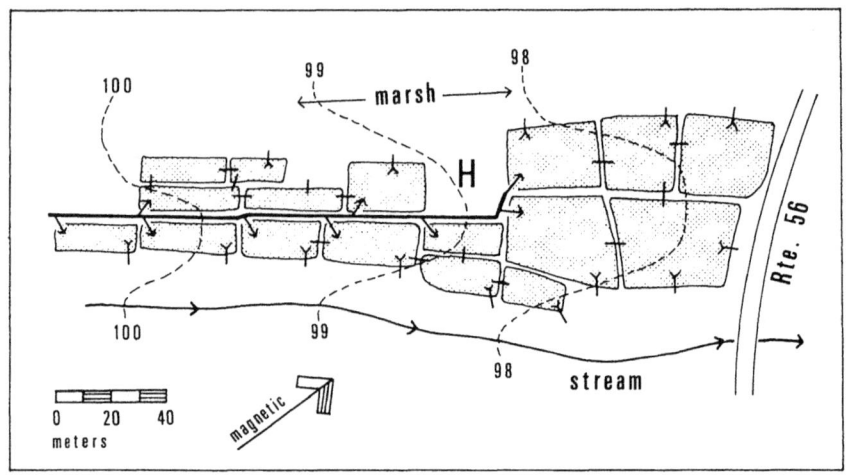

Fig. 5.6 System 17, Wainiha, Kaua'i. Example of a single farm irrigation system.

System 17

System 17 (Fig. 5.6) is located on flat alluvial soils west of the Wainiha stream and close to the sea (Fig. 5.2). This area lies between the stream and the lowest, now abandoned, section of System 14 but separated from that system by a low, marshy area. In 1850, the land records noted that this land was used for dryland cultivation, but it is now a taro farm.

The primary ditch of System 17 taps the Wainiha stream and leads water about 0.4 km to the top of the system's farm. There are seventeen pondfields in this one-farm irrigation system, a combined cultivation area of 0.85 ha. The pondfields themselves are constructed on low terraces with surrounding earthen bunds which average 1.6 m in width. Average patch size is 500 m^2.

The topography of the farm is similar to an island system, with a central low ridge sloping gently (.008) west to the marshy area and east to the stream. The primary ditch follows along this ridge and waters pondfields to either side. There are no secondary ditches; the primary ditch feeds directly into the bordering patches. The water then flows from patch to patch through narrow channels cut in the bunds or, in one case, through a pipe under a wide bund used as a path. In sum, the island topography makes it possible for the ditch to run down the center of the pondfields, making irrigation a very simple matter. The mean number of distributary patches is only 0.53 (S.D. 0.62).

System 17 is operated entirely by the farmer and his oldest sons. The farmer lives in a house above the farm, but his father occupies a small house in the midst of the patches. There is also a taro shack used to store equipment.

System 18

In 1850, System 18 irrigated a major section of the ahupua'a of Waipa but now it is used only to irrigate one taro farm in the neighboring ahupua'a of Waikoko. The primary ditch of System 18 taps the Waipa stream in the narrow valley just before the stream enters the broad alluvial plain. The intake is placed at a natural bend in the stream so that the main ditch line continues the direction of stream flow above the dam. The head dam, itself, is a standard stone mound percolation dam using in situ boulders. River cobbles (15-30 cm) are heaped between the boulders to create a mound wall 8 m long, 1 m wide, and 0.6 m high. The primary ditch, then, channels the water around a small hill and through the alluvial plain. This ditch is a simple earth channel about 1.1 m wide by 0.5 m deep at natural ground level. Along much of the ditch's length, roots of the hau, which grows exuberantly, clog the ditch and present a major maintenance problem. Excess water is handled simply by a spillway to the Waikoko stream.

The primary ditch is now about 1.32 km long. The ditch follows the line of an old ditch for the first 0.84 km and then it turns at right angles to the west where it is flumed across the Waikoko stream to water a farm with twelve pondfields. This westerly extension of the system is apparently recent, dating after the introduction of rice. The system is presently operated by a single oriental farmer.

System 22

System 22 (Fig. 5.7) irrigates the extensive alluvial plain east of the Waioli stream. This area is a broad zone of nearly flat, naturally swampy, alluvial soils which extend from the base of the mountain ridges to the sandy soils bordering Hanalei Bay.

The intake for the primary ditch of System 22 is located in the narrow valley of the Waioli stream before it enters the broad alluvial flatlands of Hanalei Bay. At the intake, the Waioli stream is braided into three channels at a shallow rapids. The modern cement head dam

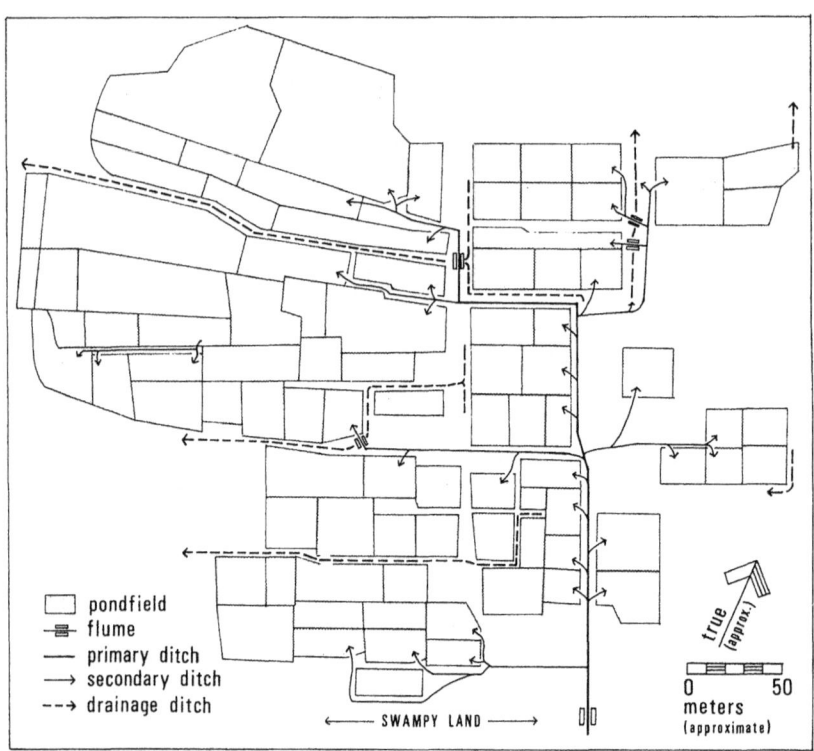

Fig. 5.7 System 22, Waioli, Kaua'i. Schematic representation showing the pattern of feeder and drainage ditches in an operational irrigation system.

(7 m long, 1.5 m high), which replaced a stone percolation dam in 1972, completely blocks the eastern channel. The ditch leads water away from the stream bed and along the lower slopes of the ridge which forms the eastern edge of the Waioli valley. This ditch is a good example of a contour ditch which maintains an approximate contour line along the slope of a ridge by keeping a gradual grade (less than .008). The ditch itself is dug into the natural slope and the fill is used to construct a down-slope bank which in places is up to 2 m high (cf. Fig. 5.3). Archaeologically, stone retaining walls were often used to reinforce the bank of a contour ditch.

The ditch finally rounds the northern face of the ridge and lies above the broad alluvial plain. Here, it divides into three segments. The highest fork of the ditch continues along the ridge to the Ma'ahana section in the ahupua'a of Hanalei. The middle fork of the ditch continues straight to a section of pondfields in the western section of Hanalei. The lowest fork turns north and cuts down into the main alluvial flatland of Waioli. This Waioli alluvium is relatively flat with an overall slope less than .005 but the topography gently undulates with alternating ridges and sloughs. The primary ditch cuts directly across the sloughs and so it is either built up or flumed across low areas. Secondary ditches branch off from the main ditch at right angles and run down the crests of the higher land. Drainage ditches are dug in the sloughs to lead excess water back to the Wainiha stream. The extensive use of both flumes and drainage ditches has permitted the expansion of System 22 into the flattest areas near the sea. Historically, the pondfields were concentrated closer to the ridge line. The present length of the main ditch is 1.40 km (.63 km below the main diversion).

The highest (Ma'ahana) branch of System 22 continues along underneath the rear ridge of Waioli and, after entering the ahupua'a of Hanalei, it descends to the broad alluvial plain. Topographically, the area is nearly flat (.003 slope), but it is criss-crossed by several sluggish streams. The main Ma'ahana ditch runs through the center of a pondfield series, which is fed either directly or by secondary ditches. The modern ditch runs 1.26 km beyond the main fork with the Waioli ditch, but this represents a considerable extension over the traditional system, made possible by the extensive use of flumes and drainage ditches.

The central branch of System 22 irrigates an area of pondfields between the other two sections of the system. There is no evidence that this area was in production before the major expansion of irrigation during the period of rice cultivation.

System 22 is now one of the major taro producing areas in the Hanalei district. It represents a nearly continuous area of pondfields including a gross area of 53.8 ha. Although no study was made, I estimate that there are about ten to twelve farmers on this system. The development of drainage systems and the use of flumes has permitted considerable expansion of the total area under cultivation from the traditional system.

System 23

System 23 is located on the alluvial plain west of the Waioli stream. The source for this system is the Waikunono stream, a tributary of the Waioli stream. At present, the Waikunono is diverted completely by a stone, earth, and plastic sheeting dam located where the stream emerges from a narrow canyon onto the plain. A contour ditch then leads the water along the base of the ridge which forms the western edge of the Waioli valley. The area of modern cultivation has only eight pondfields and these are located well downstream from the historic pondfield area. The modern fields are all cultivated by a farmer whose main fields are in System 22.

System 26

System 26 is the longest taro irrigation system in Halelea district. The primary ditch taps the Hanalei stream 6 km inland in the narrow section of the valley. This contour ditch then channels water 3.4 km along the base of the ridge which forms the western edge of the Hanalei valley. Secondary ditches branch off to irrigate three or four small farms located below the ditch. Just before the ditch enters the alluvial plain west of the Hanalei stream, there is a major spillway returning excess water to the stream. This spillway is controlled by a restricted orifice device in the ditch which allows only an established rate of flow. As flow rate increases beyond this amount, water backs up in the ditch, overflows the spillway dam, and is returned to the stream.

The primary ditch finally enters the alluvial plain where it irrigates the largest taro farm in the district. This farmer, who cultivates taro full-time, has about twenty-three pondfields with 8.9 ha in cultivation. He is presently the only farmer in the alluvial plain area. In total, the primary ditch for System 26 runs about 4.5 km. As will be discussed later, much of this is maintained by the bottom farmer.

System 29

Directly across the Hanalei stream from System 26, System 29 consists of an extensive area of about fifty pondfields on the alluvial flats east of the Hanalei stream (Pl. 3). The primary ditch taps the stream in the inland valley and leads the water down to the pondfields. This system was not studied, but it is reported that several farmers operate it.

THE OPERATIONAL REQUIREMENTS OF MODERN IRRIGATION

This section discusses the five aspects of irrigation which may require centralized management. As described in Chapter 4, these are construction, maintenance, reconstruction, warfare, and the distribution of water. It will be shown that the modern systems function with only a minimum of suprafamily organization and centralized control. Because of the technological similarity to the traditional systems (cf. Chapters 6 and 7), it suggests that the traditional systems also did not require management. Possible changes both increasing and decreasing the scale and complexity of modern systems will be discussed.

Construction of Irrigation Systems

Construction is now handled entirely by the individual initiative of the farmers involved. Seldom is a system created anew; usually an old system is either put back into production or extended a few patches at a time. Although mass labor is not used, major capital investments are required for hiring mechanical equipment. For example, new or refurbished pondfields are cleared and leveled by tractors. It is clear that the labor requirements of a traditional system have been superseded by the capital requirements of the modern system. The differences between modern and traditional systems in terms of construction are so radical that it should be impossible to extrapolate labor requirements of the traditional system from the present data.

Maintenance of Irrigation Systems

If it can be shown that the technological design of modern systems is similar to traditional designs, the maintenance requirements also should be similar. I will now discuss two major aspects of maintenance — ditch cleaning and water control — to show that contemporary Hawaiian irrigation systems are designed to minimize maintenance requirements.

In all irrigation systems, silt and intrusive roots must be regularly cleaned out in order to maintain sufficient water flow. Farmers generally agreed that a ditch should be cleaned every six months, but the observed intervals between cleanings are considerably longer, about a year. For the ditches studied, silt was not a problem. Cleaning consisted primarily of cutting away the roots of the hau which grows along most of the ditches. Using steel sickles, a kilometer of ditch requires about one-hundred man-hours to clean of roots. Without steel tools, this task would be more labor intensive, but the problem could be solved by keeping the banks free of hau. Presently, ditch cleaning does not require large labor crews. For example, the two part-time farmers on System 14 together maintain a joint head dam and 1.5 km of ditches. The pattern of cooperation between farmers sharing a ditch is informal and based on self-interest. The bottom man on the irrigation system initiates the cleaning because he is the one who first experiences water shortage. The bottom man on System 26 referred to himself as the "anchor man" which means he has to "hustle more." This bottom man would start cleaning just above his patches and work upwards towards the source. As he arrived at another farm, he would try to cajole his neighbors into helping him. This leadership by initiative is not always a successful means of recruitment and the bottom man can end up cleaning the whole ditch himself. Two Hawaiian informants described the identical form of ditch cleaning among the Hawaiians farming System 14 in the early twentieth century. They emphasized that a farmer never would refuse to help his neighbor then, but this ideal reconstruction may or may not represent past reality.

The informal nature of the organization of ditch cleaning depends on the relatively low labor requirements, as previously described. This low labor requirement of Hawaiian irrigation results from the technological design of the systems. In a statement of general irrigation engineering, Zimmerman describes the situation as follows:

> It should always be kept in mind that water at every velocity has a specific bed-load and silt-carrying capacity: the faster the flow the higher the carrying capacity and the coarser the material it will convey. The water will erode and pick up earth particles only until it has reached this saturation. Thus if the flow is kept in this equilibrium condition the canal will remain reasonably stable. However, the water will continue to erode or settle out materials if the velocity is respectively increased or decreased. [1966:276]

The most important factor is not absolute velocity but *relative* velocity. The ideal system, therefore, retains a similar velocity throughout.

The first critical situation is to keep the relative velocities between the stream and the irrigation ditch as close as possible. Because natural stream flow in Halelea's rivers is variable, the easiest solution is to regulate the velocity of the *river* by use of a percolation dam. River stones (20-120 cm) are piled between large in situ boulders to form a loose stone dam stretching across the stream (cf. Systems 14, 15 and 18). The purpose of the dam is not to stop natural river flow but to slow and regulate the flow. There is always an attempt to minimize an alteration of the patterns of natural flow by placing the dam in either a natural rapids or bend where there is already resistance to flow.

By slowing water flow before it enters the ditch, silt is deposited in the stream channel behind the dam rather than in the upper sections of the ditch. In some situations silt deposits could be a problem, but regular flash floods wash out the dam and scour the sediment build up. In essence, it is easier to rebuild the stone-mound dam after floods than it is to clean out the silt collected behind it and in the ditches!

During its entire course, water flows through the system by simple gravity. A constant velocity of flow is maintained by constructing the primary ditches with a near constant slope. Comparison between irrigation systems shows a wide range in average ditch slopes, as a response to different topographic conditions, but within a system, slopes are carefully controlled.

Observations of ditch slopes in System 15 present an analytical example of how this is accomplished. Along the ditch, seventeen measurements of slope were made. Twelve of these measurements fall within a suggested goal range of .002 to .009. The five measurements which are conspicuously higher are found below small diversion dams. These dams act to divide the ditch into sections with suitable gradient (cf. Brown 1920:177).

A second problem of maintenance is the regulation of water flow so that excess water does not flood the patches. Excess water is eliminated before entering the patches by simple design features of the irrigation systems. First, the gross amount of water entering the primary ditch is controlled by the height of the head dam. As volume of water in the stream increases, the head pond rises until it simply tops the dam. Any additional water simply flows unrestricted over the dam, or in the case of flash floods, the water will actually break through the dam and circumvent the system. At intervals along the course of the main ditch, there is also a series of spillways to lead excess water back to the main stream. A stone and earth dam normally stops all water loss from the ditch; however, when the water rises above the height of the spillway dam, excess water escapes freely over it. In some cases, a restricted-orifice device is placed just below the spillway dam to back up water until it overflows the spillway dam.

In sum, regular maintenance of these irrigation systems is greatly simplified by their technological design. There is no evidence that the modern systems require, or, by extension, the traditional systems required, labor crews for maintenance.

Reconstruction Following Natural Disasters

River flooding and tidal wave damage are two periodic disasters which affect the Halelean irrigation systems. Major flooding is not an uncommon localized disaster to agricultural production. Unusually heavy rainstorms in the mountains cause flash flooding which inundates the low-lying agricultural fields in a valley. Because the flat alluvium in the valley bottom is the main area for irrigated taro, such flooding will affect most production within a given ahupua'a, but destruction seems to be localized to only one or two ahupua'a during any given storm. A typical pattern is illustrated by the winter flooding of 1974. Although several valleys experienced minor damage, only Wainiha was severely affected. All agricultural fields in Wainiha were inundated and part of the crop was destroyed outright. With the stone head dams washed out and the ditches clogged with debris, all irrigation was temporarily interrupted. Also, massive numbers of weed seeds were introduced and by the following summer it was difficult to see the taro in amongst the grass. As a combined result of these factors, production was cut by perhaps twenty-five percent and the established cycle of production was broken. Since taro takes twelve to eighteen months to mature, the long-term effects are pronounced, for it takes more than a year to reestablish normal production. In 1974, the flood was not particularly severe and similar floods might be expected every ten to twenty years for a given valley. The effects on the Wainiha community were mitigated by extensive governmental aid in rebuilding the irrigation systems and by the part-time nature of taro income. Other disasters have been more severe. In the 1950's, a mud slide during a heavy rainstorm completely obliterated the intake and upper section of System 16's primary ditch (cf. Fig. 5.2). Although about 4.3 ha were then in production, no attempt was made to rebuild the ditch system and the agricultural area was abandoned.

Tidal waves were also disastrous to irrigation systems in coastal areas. Twice in this century, tidal waves have done extensive damage to the coastal systems in the district. An agricultural system hit by a tidal wave can be completely destroyed. In order to put it back into production, the overburden of intrusive sand must be removed and the affected ditches and pondfields rebuilt. The abandonments of several Halelean irrigation systems can be tied directly to tidal wave damage.

In order to reconstruct a system that has been heavily damaged by either river flooding or tidal wave, large amounts of capital are now required for the mechanized equipment used in rebuilding. This is suggestive that mass labor might have been required in similar situations before mechanization. Modern Halelean farmers are heavily dependent on governmental disaster relief in order to maintain production.

Warfare

Warfare is not presently a threat to Halelea. Although it is perhaps trivial to mention the fact, the United States government is responsible for maintenance of external defense. The situation is, of course, in no way comparable to traditional patterns of warfare and defense, and it is mentioned here only for completeness.

Water Allocation and Settlement of Disputes

The contemporary pattern of water allocation is highly decentralized. Ditches and associated water rights are considered the property of those who own land which historically was used for irrigation. The rights to water and ditch easements are part of the rights of ownership in irrigated *(lo'i)* land.[4] The actual amount of water, is, however, left unspecified and there is no institutionalized way to establish this. Each farmer simply diverts the water which he considers necessary for his fields by cutting openings through the bank of the primary ditch. Neither measuring devices nor scheduling are presently used to distribute water. This pattern of water distribution is highly traditional in the sense that the size and number of intakes tend to remain stable, and any alterations are carefully scrutinized by all interested parties.

This decentralized form of distribution stems, in part, from four existing conditions: (1) the small number of farmers on each system; (2) the high degree of system stability; (3) the simple diversion techniques; and (4) an abundance of water. First, there are only thirty farmers on Halelea's eight modern systems. With the exception of System 22, all systems have fewer than six participating farmers. Second, taro is a declining industry in Hawaii (Anderson, Barron, and Mardus 1972:63) and the present sizes of most irrigation systems are declining. Water should, therefore, be becoming more available to the surviving farmers. Third, the pattern of distribution is made simple by the structuring of irrigation ditches. Each farm has direct access to a primary ditch from which it receives water. Farmers who are the bottom men on their system divert water directly into their patches from the main ditch; but those who are higher on the primary ditch try to simplify their diversion by using secondary ditches so that the equity of their share may be clearly visible and indisputable. Finally, and perhaps most important, preliminary measurements indicate that water available in a primary ditch greatly exceeds the amount of water needed by that system (Earle

---

[4]The definition of *lo'i* land goes back to the 1850 land records.

1973). For example, in System 15 (four farmers; 4.07 ha of taro), only 7% of the water diverted from the stream was actually required for the taro. It is, therefore, not surprising that the farmers interviewed on this system expressed no concern for water shortage.

Despite these conditions, disputes are not unheard of among farmers on an irrigation system. Most disputes are handled by simple self-help whereby the farmer who feels shorted individually attempts to rectify the situation.

> While working at the Agricultural Experimental Station of the University of Hawaii in Wailua [which is on a drier side of the island], Kauai, it was noted by the employees that water flow in the main ditch was sluggish and would be inadequate for the taro pondfields. It was thought that the ditch needed cleaning since it had been neglected for over one year (usually cleaned every six months). After one and a half days of cleaning, the real cause was discovered. A small wooden dam had been built by one of the farmers higher on the ditch to increase his water flow during this relatively dry period. The dam was destroyed but no other action taken. [Earle 1972]

No one knew what would happen if such water stealing resulted in an open dispute, but farmers expressed the feeling that it could be taken to court. The state legal structure, therefore, is seen as a possible course of litigation, but, because of costs and other difficulties, it is avoided. The only documented court cases of water disputes involved either extensive rice operations or sugar plantations.

SUMMARY

Modern taro cultivation in Halelea operates without centralized management, and the only critical aspect of irrigation requiring a centralized governmental apparatus is the infusion of capital for disaster reconstruction. The modern systems are changed in many ways from the traditional ones and several factors may be important in determining the low requirements of management. First, a modern cash economy has various ways to amass the necessary capital for building irrigation systems. Traditionally, how could capital be amassed? Second, modern taro cultivation is only a part-time activity. Traditionally, were there also alternative forms of subsistence income? Third, for all intents and purposes, warfare is not significant in terms of daily production decisions. What would the importance of endemic warfare have been? Finally, water is apparently not scarce in modern systems. Would this have been critical traditionally? In the next two chapters, these questions will be addressed by examining the archaeological and historical data available on Halelean irrigation.

CHAPTER VI

ARCHAEOLOGICAL RESEARCH ON IRRIGATION

A lush tropical tangle of guava, java plum, and hau engulfs the valleys of Halelea and gives to them a sense of unconquerable wilderness. This is a false impression for it belies the district's history of extensive cultivated taro fields which once covered the valley bottoms and side streams. The dense vegetation hides a terraced landscape stepping down the valley slopes toward the sea. During his early reconnaissance survey of Kaua'i, Wendell Bennett noted that "remains of agricultural terraces are very extensive and quite well preserved" (1931:19). Seemingly, wherever he went recording religious shrines and house sites, he also found associated agricultural terracing. Some of the terracing came down almost to the sea, while in other places terraces were located as far into the valley interiors as he was able to penetrate (about 14 km from the sea in the Waimea valley).

The archaeological remains indicate a considerable range in the size and complexity of irrigation systems.[1] The largest and most complex systems were located near the sea, on the extensive alluvial plains which are still farmed today. These sites have many relatively large pondfields and intricate ditch complexes. In contrast, along the narrow interior valleys and along minor streams near the coast, terraced sites are found wherever pockets of alluvial soils have developed and could be irrigated. Characteristically, these small sites have only a few dozen fields and a short irrigation ditch.

The archaeological research reported in this chapter was *not* designed as a complete archaeological survey of Halelea. Because of the heavy vegetation and large area of the district, such general purpose research would require a massive project. Rather, this present archaeological project was designed to coordinate with the historical and

---

[1]For a recent report containing excellent comparative material, see Kirch and Kelly (1975).

ethnographic research on irrigation. As discussed in Chapter 7, after archival research had identified tracts of irrigated taro land in 1850, a field reconnaissance survey was made of these areas. Although modern land uses have completely altered many areas, several major terraced sites were identified and the detailed mapping of these sites yielded valuable data on the technology of traditional Halelean irrigation systems.

The objectives of this chapter are threefold. First, the archaeological features associated with these agricultural sites are described in sufficient detail to be usable in future comparative studies both within Hawaii and with other societies. Second, the archaeological data in conjunction with the ethnographic material, presented in Chapter 5, are used to construct a preliminary typology of Hawaiian irrigation. This typology is then used in Chapter 7 to assist analysis of the historic irrigation systems for which actual archival data are quite sketchy. Third, the archaeological evidence is examined according to the criteria discussed in Chapter 4, which are of possible significance for the evolution of centralized management.

SITE DESCRIPTIONS OF IRRIGATION COMPLEXES

In the initial phase of field research, the areas of historic taro cultivation were investigated, and eight well preserved agricultural sites were located. These sites were then mapped with mountain transit and alidade in sufficient detail to record data on the design and physical dimensions of all irrigation features, including dams, ditches, pondfields, and fishponds. Mapping was the primary research technique used in the archaeological project and the data presented in this section are derived from site maps. The typical mapping strategy is as follows: a pondfield was identified as a discrete, nearly flat terrace which could be described by mapping its periphery and elevation; then, it was a simple geometry problem to calculate the size, natural land slope, and grading required during construction. A total map of an irrigation system shows the association between pondfields and ditches, making it possible to determine the probable irrigation scheme used. Detailed sketching, note taking, and excavation were limited because the time required for these tasks would have reduced the area covered by the project.

A major difficulty in studying Hawaiian irrigation features is to determine their age. Virtually no temporally diagnostic artifacts are associated with irrigation features, and datable materials, like carbon or basaltic glass, are rare. Although other researchers, notably Yen et al. (1972), have recovered datable materials during extensive excavations, test pits excavated in Halelea sites were unsuccessful for obtaining samples with reliable associations.

The problem of dating is overcome by the limited scope of the present project. Since the year 1850 was used as a temporal base line, only sites known to have been in production at that time were studied in detail. As I have argued elsewhere (Earle 1973:182), these sites should represent accurately aboriginal irrigation technology. Except in areas of local urban growth like Honolulu, a general population decline made major new constructions of irrigation systems unlikely between 1778 (first contact) and 1850. There is, however, one major difficulty in using a sample of 1850 period sites; namely, that the population decline from 1778 to 1850 surely resulted in the abandonment of many sites. For example, by 1850 many of the small inland sites were apparently already abandoned.

It is also important that many of the sites in production in 1850 were not abandoned until the twentieth century. The introduction of draft animals, metal tools, and some aspects of Oriental (Chinese and Japanese) technology may have altered these systems. Although this possibility was carefully considered, the specific sites under investigation were relatively isolated from major changes.

The site descriptions below include data on the following subjects: general description of site location and topography; overall design of irrigation; specific description of irrigation features (dams, ditches, pondfields, fishponds, other related features); and the evidence for post-1850 change.

Ka-D5-4

The site Ka-D5-4 covers roughly 8.0 ha of the western portion of the alluvial fan at the mouth of the Limahuli stream, Ha'ena. About 0.5 km from the sea, the stream emerges from a narrow, mountain valley onto a coastal plain. Between the overhanging mountain cliffs and the sea, this gently sloping land was extensively terraced for pondfields, which were in 1850 the main agricultural fields for Systems 1 and 2 (cf. Fig. 6.1). Since then, however, all taro production has been abandoned and parts of the two systems have been destroyed by road construction and other activities. Figure 6.2 illustrates the existing features of site Ka-D5-4. Sections "a" through "f" of this site were part of System 1 and Sections "g" through "j" were part of System 2 (cf. Fig. 6.3).

80 ORGANIZATION OF A COMPLEX CHIEFDOM

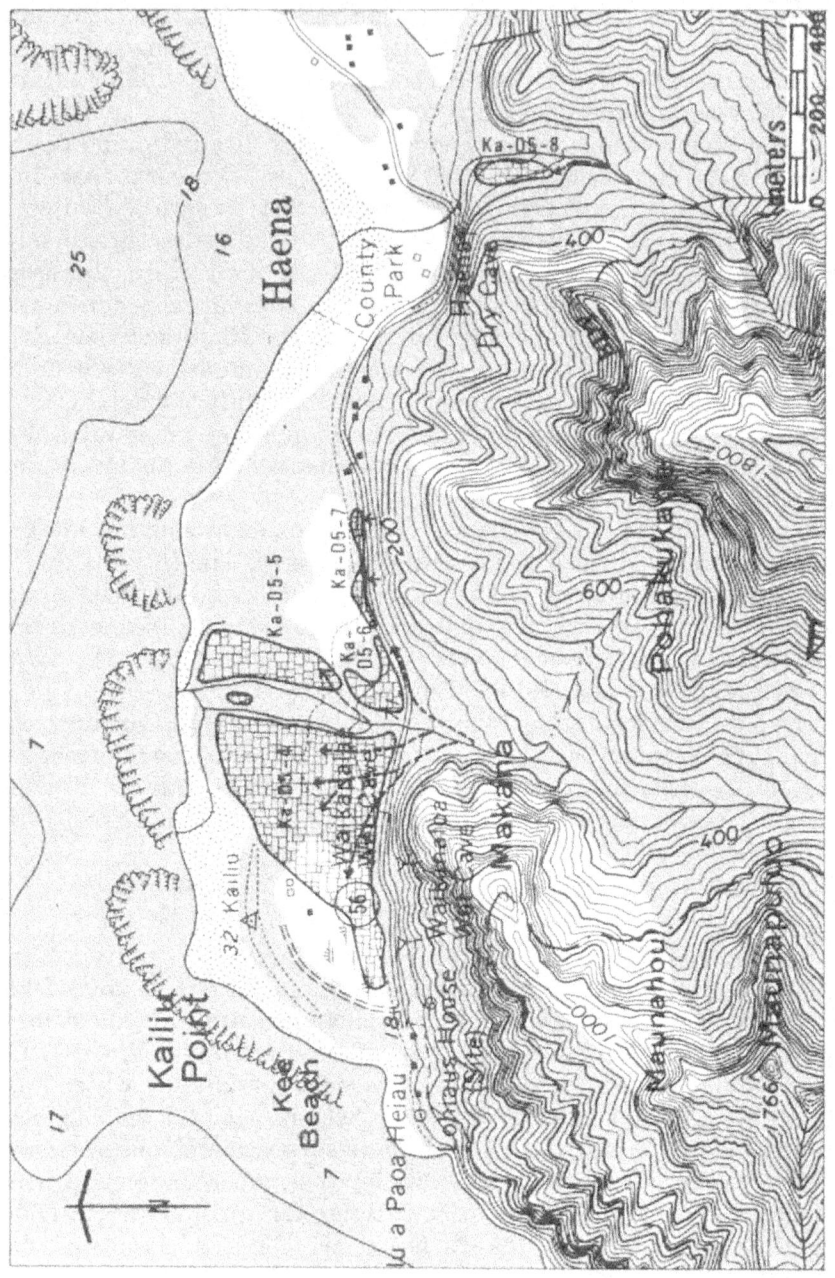

Fig. 6.1 Ha'ena, Kaua'i. Enlargement of United States Geological Survey map for the coastal section of Ha'ena indicating the archaeological sites described in the text.

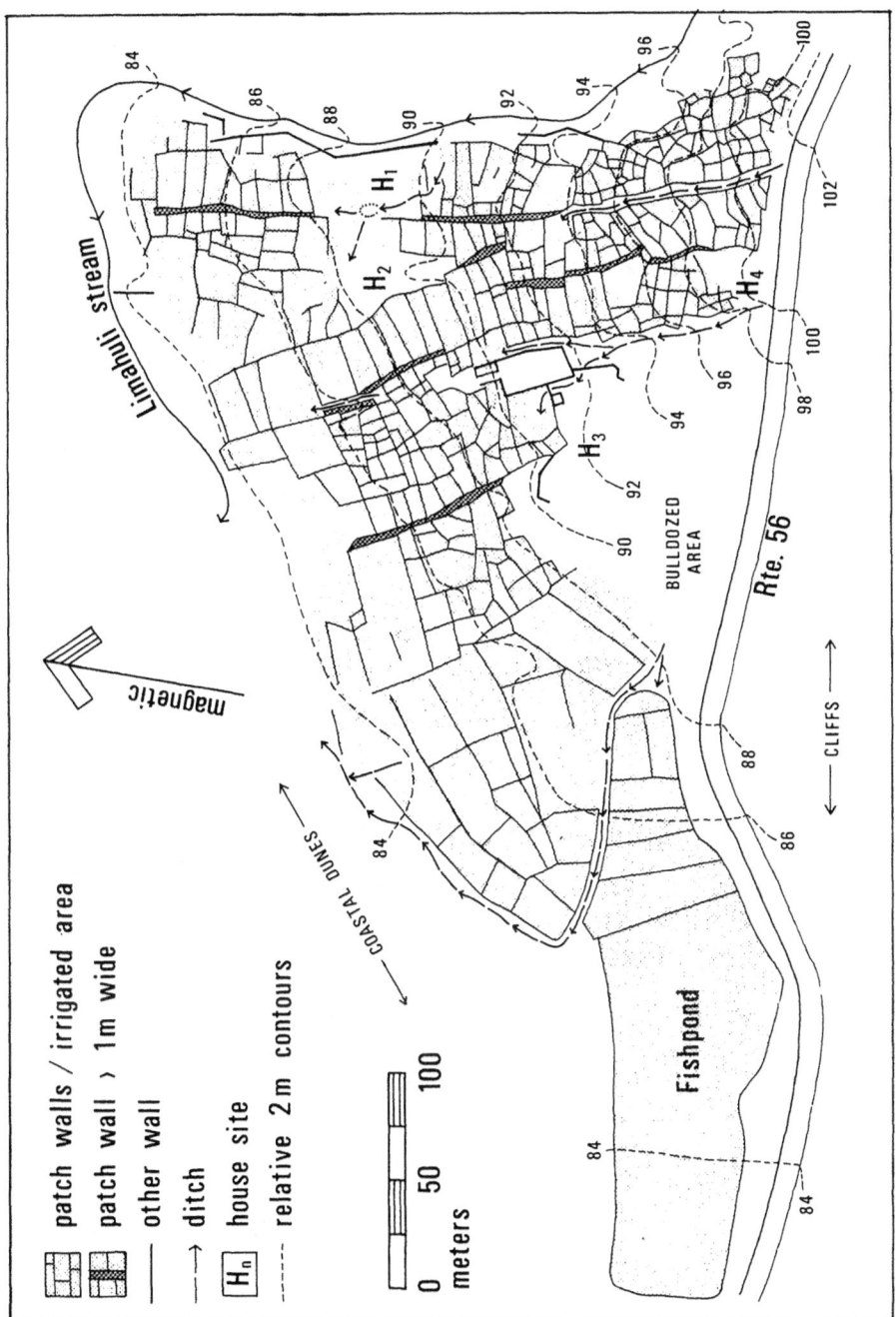

Fig. 6.2 Site Ka-D5-4, Ha'ena, Kaua'i. Extensive irrigation complex on coastal alluvial plain with variable topography.

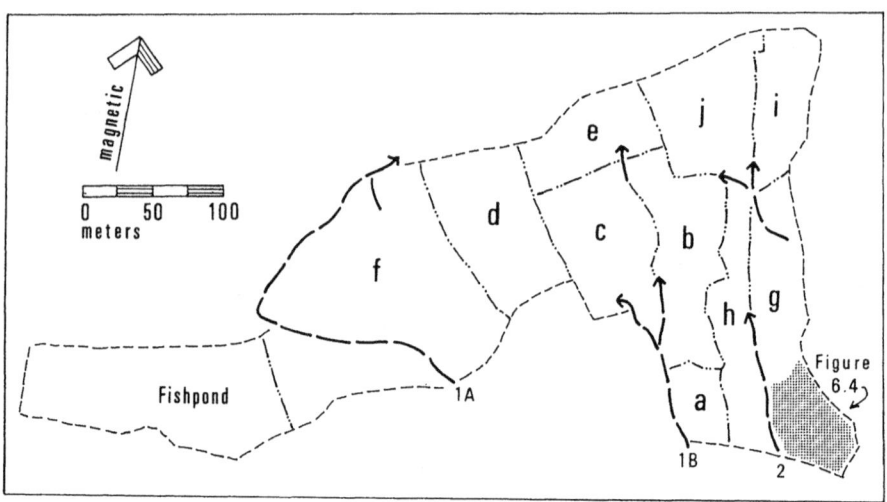

Fig. 6.3 Site Ka-D5-4, Ha'ena, Kaua'i. Representation of the site showing the divisions into sections (a-j) used in the text for descriptive purposes. Heavy dash lines indicate irrigation ditches. Insert is Fig. 6.4.

The site slopes north towards the sea and west away from the Limahuli stream. Three natural topographic areas are identified. The first, including site sections "a," "h" and "g," is at the top of the site and just below the modern road. This area has a fairly steep gradient (.070) and an irregular land surface littered with boulders and small cobbles. Section "g" slopes steeply (.103) down to a branch stream of the Limahuli (cf. Fig. 6.4). The second area, including sections "b," "c," "d," "e," "j," and "i," has a more gently sloping topography (.040-.070) and is less rocky. It is transected by shallow natural drainage swales which run parallel to one another and perpendicular to the site's contours. Finally, a third area, section "f," is located at the extreme westerly end of the site. This area is gently sloping (.030) and nearly free of stones. It is the lowest section of the site and bounded by higher sand dunes to the northwest. In general, the site becomes less steep and more regular away from the Limahuli stream and the mountain cliffs.

Dam and Ditch Complexes

The site was irrigated by two ditches which originated in the narrow Limahuli valley before it enters onto the coastal plain. The higher ditch (System 1) ran along the base of the mountain ridge until it split

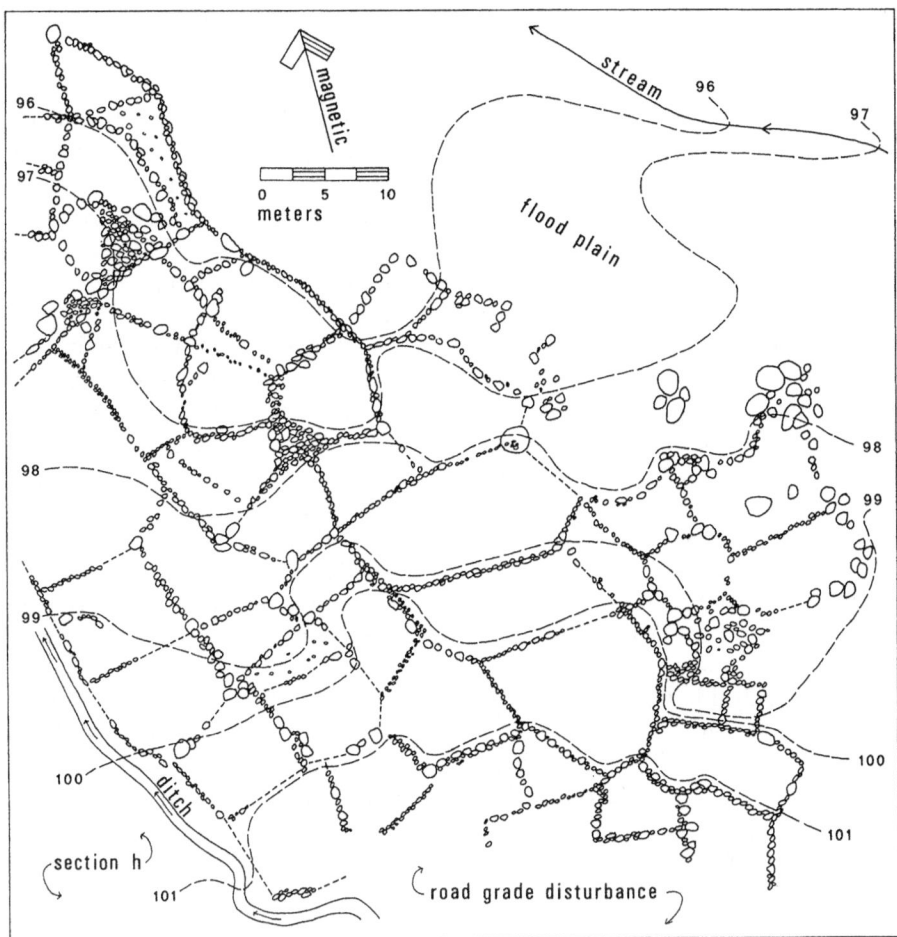

Fig. 6.4 Section g, Site Ka-D5-4, Ha'ena. A detail showing the layout of irrigated terraces in an area of steep and broken topography. Location indicated as insert in Fig. 6.3.

into two segments just above the present road. The western segment (1A), which irrigated section "f," has been mostly destroyed by bulldozing, but the lowest part is still traceable. This ditch turned sharply northeast along the bottom of section "f" where it would have drained exhaust water. The eastern segment (1B) has been badly eroded but its path is discernible. It bordered section "a" and then split around a stone enclosure with the left fork disappearing into section "c" and the right into section "b." Below an eroded area, a segment of the right fork is shown above section "e."

The second ditch complex (System 2) comes off the Limahuli stream about 80 m below the first intake. The primary ditch ran directly down the slope and into sections "g" and "h" where it apparently terminated. Below these sections, an isolated segment of ditch is located so that it would have drained exhaust water from the upper sections and, in turn, fed this water to sections "i" and "j." As can be seen in Figure 6.2, a branch stream of the Limahuli cuts across the bottom of sections "e," "i," and "j" where it would have drained exhaust water.

The design for these ditches was very simple. From the stream, the ditches maintained a minimum slope (almost parallel with the contour) until reaching the top of the site. At this point, the ditches ran perpendicular to the contours and through the pondfields. The slopes of these ditch segments approximate the natural slope of the fan — System 1A, .016; System 1B, .063; System 2, .063. The ditches were often stone lined and measure, typically, 1 m wide and .8 m deep.

There were several critical points of water division at site Ka-D5-4. Within System 1, water was divided between ditches 1A and 1B, and then between the two forks of 1B. Within System 2, there were no major diversions to the primary ditch but water in the subsidiary, isolated ditch was divided between sections "i" and "j." For most of these divisions, water flow was controlled by a combination of ditch size, ditch slope, and stone diversions, but a unique device divided water in the subsidiary ditch of System 2. Exhaust water from sections "g" and "h" emptied into an oval, stone lined pool (3.2 by 8.9 m). Two cuts in the pond's banks then fed water alternatively to sections "i" or "j." Although it seems likely that this pond had additional uses (such as for wash water), it would also have stopped the forward velocity of the water and allowed for an accurate division.

Pondfields

Variability in pondfields (Table 6.1) within site Ka-D5-4 is closely related to the topographic differences. In upper site areas corresponding to a steep and broken topography, the pondfields were small — section "a," 56.5 m^2; section "g," 43.9 m^2; and section "h," 87.0 m^2 (Fig. 6.4). Here each pondfield was an individual terrace with stone retaining walls, often over a meter tall. The retaining walls were constructed of roughly faced subangular basaltic stone (10-150 cm) built up between in situ boulders. In order to minimize changes to the natural topography, the

TABLE 6.1

CHARACTERISTICS OF TARO PONDFIELDS FOR ARCHAEOLOGICAL SITES IN HA'ENA AND WAINIHA

		Minimum Number of Patches	Mean Patch Size in Meters	S.D.	N	Site Slope	Mean Number Intermediary Patches
Ka-D5-4,	a	23	56.5	41.9	15	.082	3.6
	b	27	148.1	107.6	27	.063	2.9
	c	71	96.9	71.5	44	.061	4.8
	d	27	123.1	77.3	26	.048	4.6
	e	6	505.3	188.4	6	.043	8.5
	f	26	389.6	246.8	17	.029	1.1
	g	71	43.9	31.9	57	.103	1.9
	h	70	87.0	72.2	53	.072	2.1
	i	9	196.4	82.5	7	.054	3.7
	j	17	135.3	105.1	16	.046	2.9
Total		347	121.7	122.7	268	.069	3.0
Ka-D5-5		59	278.1	325.1	35	.044	5.0
Ka-D5-6,	a	41	96.2	47.4	19	.107	—
	b	47	37.4	29.3	42	.084	—
Total		88	55.7	44.9	61	.091	—
Ka-D5-7,	a	42	50.0	36.5	14	—	—
Ka-D5-8,	a	33	85.2	70.4	30	.140	8.3
Ka-D6-11,	a	37	292.0	258.1	35	.024	1.0
	b	41	409.0	283.6	31	.018	4.1
	c	36	194.9	111.3	23	.021	5.6
Total		114	307.7	251.6	89	.021	3.3

terraces were highly irregular in form and each small depression or ridge formed a separate pondfield series. The smallest patches (less than 15 m²) were probably not true pondfields, but would have received water seepage from higher patches.

In lower parts of the site, where there is a more even and gradual topography, the pondfields were larger — section "b," 148.1 m²; section "c," 96.9 m²; section "d," 123.1 m²; section "e," 505.3 m²; section "f," 389.6 m²; section "i," 196.4 m²; and section "j," 135.3 m². As noted previously, these areas are transected by parallel drainage depressions separated by low ridges. Typically, the terraces were constructed across these depressions to create an isolated pondfield series stepping down the site. The front of the terrace, running across the depression, was reinforced by a straight retaining wall built of subangular basalt (10-100 cm). These walls were usually 40 to 100 cm high and roughly faced. Section "f" is distinctive; due to its gentle slope and scarcity of rock, the pondfields were constructed on low terraces usually without stone reinforcing walls.

Distribution of water among pondfields would have been handled either directly by the ditch network or indirectly by patch to patch flow. In sections ("f," "g," and "h"), where a ditch ran through the patches, there was direct access to water. In other sections, a ditch terminated at the top of the section and water would have been fed from one patch to the next down the slope. These sections can be identified in Table 6.1, by a relatively high mean number of distributary patches (2.9-8.5). This latter situation would have required careful control to insure that all patches received the correct flow of water.

Fishpond[2]

In the area of lowest elevation, a fishpond (11,344 m^2) called Ke'e, is now indicated by an expanse of marshy grassland. The perimeter of the feature is defined on the east by a retaining wall (1 m high) of a higher pondfield and, on the other three sides, by a dirt embankment rising to the surrounding natural land surface. It appears that the pond was a natural depression which then was artificially leveled and enlarged. The fishpond would have received water not from surface irrigation, but from subsurface groundwater. In other words, the pond was dug down to groundwater, which was raised by seepage from the irrigation system above. Informants report that during this century the pond, although not itself still in use, held water as long as the pondfields above it were in production.

Other Features

Four house sites are scattered among the pondfields on high unirrigated ground. Three of these sites date to the historic or modern period: H_1, wood frame house still standing; H_2, square rock foundation for wood frame house; H_3, paved house foundation (1.9 by 6.4 m) and paved lanai (2.3 by 3.9 m) for grass house. Both H_2 and H_3 are associated with late nineteenth and twentieth century glass bottles and other historic artifacts. House site H_4 has various aboriginal artifacts (adz, adz blank,

[2]Recent archaeological work indicates that this feature was subdivided by internal walls at some point in the past (Griffin: personal communication).

sharpening stone) associated with it. This last house site was constructed on a small knoll (11 m across) above the surrounding agricultural terraces. The top of the knoll was partially paved with subangular stones, mostly less than 10 cm in diameter (Earle 1973:202).

Near the center of Ka-D5-4, there were two stone wall enclosures. The larger of these (16.7 by 31.1 m) was surrounded by a double-faced and rubble-filled wall standing over a meter high and 0.8-1.2 m wide. The second, smaller enclosure (3.9 by 4.3 m) was surrounded by a core wall about 0.8 m high and 0.6 m wide. The two enclosures are joined by a double-faced wall with a stone-capped culvert allowing passage of an irrigation ditch. Historic artifacts associated with these features date to the late nineteenth century. They probably served as animal enclosures for pigs, horses, and/or cows. Other sections of freestanding wall are found in the same area, around H_3, and to the eastern extreme of the site.

As already described, the middle and lower parts of the site are transected by broad drainage depressions running down the slope. The low ridges which separate these depressions are marked by double-faced and rubble-filled or earth mound walls greater than 1 m wide. From evidence in the nineteenth century land records (cf. Chapter 7), these walls appear to have marked boundaries between different farms.

Evidence for Change

Informants report that much of site Ka-D5-4 was in taro production during this century. Aerial photographs confirm that section "f" and small areas of sections "b" and "h" were still active in 1952. The continued use of the site raises the possibilities of substantial change in the irrigation system, but there is little actual evidence for such change. First, the basic layout of the ditches and pondfields correspond well to the available historic data for the site. Second, there is no evidence of modern technological devices like flumes and cement weirs. Finally, all irrigation features were constructed of native materials and used designs consistent with known aboriginal sites. The most likely change is an increased size of pondfields, reflecting changes in cultivation practices. Several of the most recently abandoned pondfields appear larger than would be expected in aboriginal sites of similar topography. The extent of this change is, however, hard to determine accurately.

The most obvious changes from traditional patterns are found in nonirrigation features. For instance, the large walled enclosures are not typical of aboriginal sites and probably were used for large domesticated animals.

Ka-D5-5

Site Ka-D5-5 (Fig. 6.5) covers roughly 1.4 ha of the alluvial fan east of Limahuli stream and across the stream from Ka-D5-4. In 1850, Ka-D5-5 was the pondfield area for System 6, but the eastern portion of the system has been destroyed by bulldozing (cf. Fig. 6.1).

The site slopes to the north, parallel with the stream and toward the sea. The slope (.044) is fairly constant, and the land surface is regular and somewhat rocky. The site is bounded on the west by the Limahuli stream, on the north by a small stream separating the site from the coastal dunes, to the west by a driveway, and to the south by terrace remnants of site Ka-D5-6.

Dam and Ditch Complex

From its intake at a natural bend in the stream, the ditch ran at an angle across the top of the pondfield area. For its total length, 140.6 m, it was nearly straight and without lateral branches. The ditch was unlined, 1 m wide by 0.5 m deep, and its average slope was .052 (range .037-.062). The only distinctive feature was a stone culvert under the freestanding wall down the center of the site.

Pondfields

The pondfields were a continuous series of terraces between the ditch and the small stream at the bottom of the site. The pondfields were regular, rectangular terraces averaging 278 m² in area (Table 6.1). The front of these were reinforced with stone retaining walls usually about 0.5 m high, and the stones, subangular basalt (10-80 cm), were roughly faced during construction.

The distribution of water among the pondfields was handled by interpatch flow for which the water, fed directly into the highest patches, was distributed from patch to patch down the slope. As seen in Table 6.1, the mean number of distributary patches was high (5.0).

Other Features

Historic occupation is indicated by various features on the western side of the site. A stone foundation, some lumber, and metal roofing mark the site of a recently collapsed house. To the southeast are three small roughly paved areas and an oval mound probably indicated a grave. To the north is a large enclosure (11.9 by 38.4 m) with a double-faced and rubble-filled wall. Informants refer to this as a pig pen. Down

ARCHAEOLOGICAL RESEARCH ON IRRIGATION

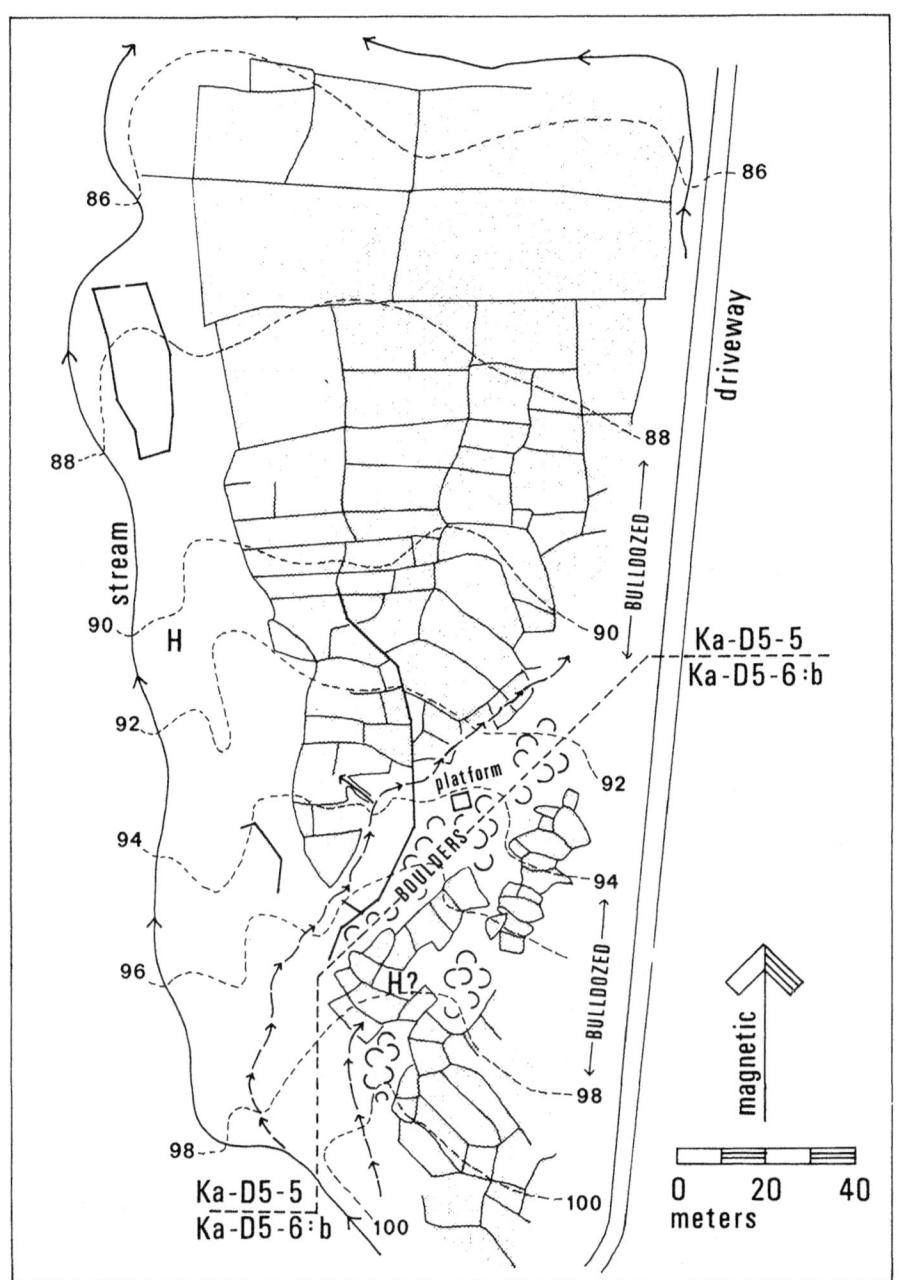

Fig. 6.5 Sites Ka-D5-5 and Ka-D5-6, Section b, Ha'ena, Kaua'i. Legend same as Fig. 6.2.

the center of the site, a freestanding, double-faced and rubble-filled wall probably marked a historic boundary similar to those in Ka-D5-4.

An enigmatic rectangular platform of unknown date is located above the ditch line. It measures roughly 40 by 45 m, is 50 cm in height, and is outlined in stone. Local stories refer to this feature as a grave or a shrine (heiau).

Evidence for Change

Much of site Ka-D5-5 was in taro production during this century. An informant described how his grandfather lived there during the early 1900s: he raised taro in the pondfields, kept pigs and cows near the stream, and had a fish trap on the reef off shore. The historic features probably date to this period and later.

There is, however, very little evidence for change in these pondfields. Although the lowest fields were still in use as late as 1952, their construction was largely traditional. With the exception of a concrete pipe used to channel water between two patches, all irrigation features were made of traditional materials and correspond to traditional designs. There may have been some enlargement to patches as noted for Ka-D5-4.

Ka-D5-6

Site Ka-D5-6 is located on the alluvial fan east of the Limahuli stream, Ha'ena, and just south of Ka-D5-5. In 1850, Ka-D5-6 was part of the pondfield area for System 7, but much of it has been destroyed by road construction and other alterations (cf. Fig. 6.1). Only two separated pondfield sections now remain. Section "a" is strung out directly below the main road and east of a private driveway. Section "b" is to the west of the driveway. Although both sections were mapped, only section "b" is illustrated (Fig. 6.4) because of the fragmentary condition of the archaeological features.

The site slopes fairly steeply to the north away from the mountain ridges which loom overhead. Section "a" is steep (slope .107) but the land surface is relatively even and only moderately rocky. A natural marsh, caused by high groundwater below the cliffs, borders this section to the north; the upper part of this section is truncated by the road. Although Handy and Handy (1972:419) reported that swampland taro was produced in the marsh, agricultural features are not discernible there.

Section "b" is less steep (.084) but the land surface is very irregular and rocky. Large boulder areas are intermixed with narrow pockets of alluvial soil. To the southeast toward section "a," the land becomes more regular but recent disturbances have obscured the arrangement of pondfields. To the north and west is site Ka-D5-5.

Dam and Ditch Complex

The intake for System 7 was on the Limahuli stream near the intakes of Systems 1 and 2. The head dam and upper part of this ditch are now used for an ornamental garden above the road. The ditch originally led water along the valley side and around the ridge front to section "a." It has been destroyed by the road, which apparently was constructed over the original ditch course. No lateral ditches were found, but it seems likely that one may have led water down to section "b."

Pondfields

Section "a" is a long (180 m) and narrow (13 to 54 m) area with about forty pondfields. The narrow pondfields form one to seven tiers of terraces wrapping around the contour of the fan. Although poorly preserved in many places, the front walls of these terraces were reinforced with stone retaining walls identical to those described for Ka-D5-4. The terraces are regular in form but closely fitted to the natural topography. They average 96 m^2 in size. No estimate of distributary patches could be made as the ditches were destroyed. The lack of secondary ditches indicates that water was fed into the top patches and then flowed down the terrace tiers.

Section "b" is an irregularly shaped remnant (roughly 42 by 117 m) of about forty-eight pondfields (Fig. 6.5). These pondfields consist of small terraces (mean size 37 m^2) constructed in pockets of alluvial soil in amongst massive boulders. The alluvial soil is found in narrow drainage channels transecting the site. Irregularly shaped terraces were constructed across these natural channels to form a long descending string, only one or two terraces wide. No estimate of distributary patches was made, but it is evident from the absence of secondary ditches that water was fed to the top patches of a series and then flowed in order to the lower patches.

Other Features

Section "a" has no other features.

In section "b," two small nonagricultural terraces are located on the edge of a boulder area. These terraces are paved with small, subangular stones (less than 20 cm), and they may have supported small structures. No midden was noticed during the survey.

Evidence for Change

The pondfields were abandoned at least by 1930 when the present road was built over the ditch. No informants knew when the pondfields were last in use. The absence of any historic features indicates that it is most likely aboriginal in design and technology.

Ka-D5-7

Site Ka-D5-7 is an area of terraces located in Ha'ena, just east of Ka-D5-6. It is positioned on the lowest slopes of the mountain ridges which face the sea. There are a series of small permanent springs along the base of these ridges which feed into the large fresh water marsh backing onto the shore dunes. In 1850, these springs were the sources for Systems 8 (section "a") and 9 (section "b") which include the area of site Ka-D5-7 and the marsh below (cf. Fig. 6.1). The upper part of the site has been destroyed by road construction and the lower part merges with the unconsolidated marshland.

The site slopes fairly steeply to the north away from the mountain ridges. The land surface is regular and moderately rocky with several clusters of large boulders. The soil is alluvial and kept constantly moist by seepage from the springs.

Dam and Ditch Complex

The upper part of the site has been destroyed, but the present locations of springs indicate that the spring water was fed directly into the highest patches of the site. No ditches were noted in the preserved sections of the site.

Pondfields

The terraces of Ka-D5-7 are poorly preserved, but they appear to have been more rectangular than those in Ka-D5-6. Section "a" is a long (157 m) and narrow (13 to 38 m) area of perhaps thirty-five pondfield features which formed one to five tiers of terraces between the road and marsh. The average size of the terraces is only 50 m^2. The terraces were originally reinforced with stone retaining walls constructed of subangular stones (10-100 cm), but only small sections are still extant. In situ boulders were occasionally incorporated into the wall design.

Section "b" is a separate fragment of terraces located just east of "a." Due to dense, thorny vegetation this section was not mapped in detail. The terrace area was approximately 22 by 71 m, with perhaps a dozen pondfields very similar in construction to section "a."

For both sections, the lack of preserved ditches made it impossible to estimate the number of distributary patches. It seems probable that water was fed into the first pondfield tier and then to lower tiers in order.

Other Features

A nonagricultural terrace, located in the center of section "a," is roughly paved with small, subangular stones. Such paved terraces often supported structures. The terrace is about 6.6 m long but the original width is unknown because it is partially buried by road fill. The terrace is directly above a spring and pondfield.

Evidence for Change

An informant mentioned that one or two of the pondfields were used for watercress during this century, but the site has not been used for taro within memory. All features appear to be of aboriginal materials and design.

Ka-D5-8

Ka-D5-8 (Fig. 6.6) is a small (.8 ha) but well preserved site in the Manoa Valley, Ha'ena. The site is particularly interesting because it shows the relationship between both irrigation and nonirrigation features in an aboriginal context. In 1850, the site included System 10 (Fig. 6.1).

The site is located on an alluvial terrace which stands more than 5 m above the Manoa stream. The west side of the site rises sharply to the ridge bordering the valley and rocks from the talus slope litter the land surface. To the east, the site drops off to the stream bed. The dominant slope (.140) of the site parallels the stream.

Dam and Ditch Complex

The head dam is no longer extant, but it was located just above a natural steep section of the Manoa stream where a stone percolation dam probably diverted water into the primary ditch of System 10. Although poorly preserved, the ditch has been traced 120.6 m from intake to the main terraces. Near the intake, the ditch followed along the contour of the slope for about 36 m and was retained here by an earthen embankment. The ditch then ran down the steep and rocky alluvial terrace until it reached the top of the pondfields. The average slope of the ditch was .105. Due to poor preservation, it was impossible to reconstruct the ditch's cross section, but apparently it was a simple earthen channel, stone lined at points.

Pondfields

In the major pondfield cluster, there are thirty-three well defined terraces (total area, 2409 m^2) and another 5583 m^2 which may have been irrigated. The main terraces form a narrow stairlike series of tiers with one or two pondfields per tier (Pls. 4 and 5; Fig. 6.6). The stonework is of angular to subangular basalt (10-100 cm), roughly faced. The walls, up to 1.2 m high, are nearly straight and parallel to the site's contours. For strength, the walls are battered 10-30° off the perpendicular. Considering the fairly steep slope (.140), patch size is relatively large (85.2 m^2).

As can be seen in Figure 6.6, the ditch line becomes indistinct below the top patches. Most of the water for the pondfield series appears to have been fed directly to the top patches and then to have flowed down the pondfield tiers. The mean number of distributary patches is, therefore, very high (8.3).

About 36 m from the ditch's intake, two small clusters of nine terraces are located on relatively flat (slope .077) areas just below the ditch line. These terraces are very small (18.4 m^2) and irregular in shape. Because of their size, it seems possible that these were not true pondfields but instead received seepage from the adjacent ditch.

Associated Features

In addition to the irrigation features, there were various dry farming, habitation, and cermonial features associated with the site. Features which strongly suggest dryland farming are located along the periphery of the pondfields. Two areas of unirrigated pocket terraces can be seen in Figure 6.6 — (1) at the top of the site, east of the ditch line; and (2) at the center of the site, west of the pondfields. These pocket terraces are defined by rough semicircular retaining walls which were constructed by piling stones in mounds between larger boulders. These retaining walls created small pockets of relatively rock-free alluvial soil, which could have served as a planting zone for unirrigated crops. In

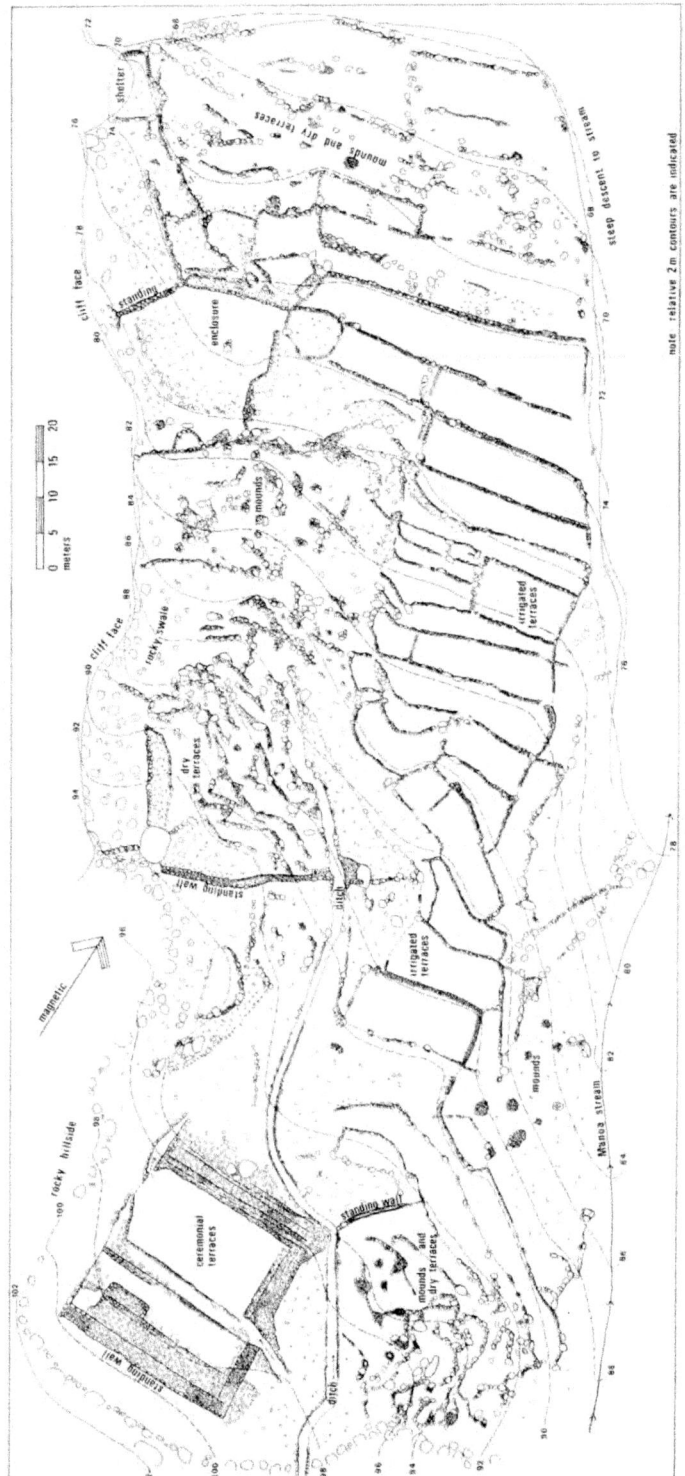

Fig. 6.6 Site Ka-D5-8, Manoa Valley, Ha'ena. Shows relationship between irrigated terraces and other features in a particularly well preserved site.

addition, the alluvial slope between the pondfields and the stream shows evidence of stone clearing perhaps for dryland crops. The stones have been piled in various mounds and rough linear alignments.

Not illustrated are two complexes of dryland agricultural features located to the west of the mapped area. First, on the steep (.170-.320) hillside which hangs above the site, there is an irregularly scattered series of about sixty to seventy-five unirrigated terraces. These terraces, varying in size from 1 by 3 m to 6 by 16 m, are defined by rough retaining walls of angular basalt which were not faced. A relatively flat soil zone is retained behind the walls. Second, in an intermittent water channel on the hillside, there are five small terraces (2 by 3.2 m to 3.6 by 5.3 m) which were constructed by building retaining walls across the water channel. These walls are of rough construction, similar to the hillside terraces. Dryland crops, requiring additional water, could have been planted in the small pockets of soil trapped behind the walls.

To return to the main archaeological complex, a rough enclosure is defined by a freestanding core wall constructed against the cliff to the north west of the site. These walls enclose 397 m^2 which may have been used for penned animals.

The only definite habitation feature is an unpaved terrace constructed under a cliff overhang in the extreme northwestern part of the site. The front of the terrace is reinforced by a stone retaining wall over a meter tall. Without excavation, it is difficult to determine the extent of this feature, but the lack of paving or associated artifacts indicate that it was a field shelter.

Finally, a complex terraced feature of probable sacred significance is located above the ditch and pondfields at the top of the site. There are two main terraces in this feature which were constructed across a natural depression. The front wall of the lower terrace is very impressive; it stands 3.5 m high and had four definite tiers. The east and south walls are thick (2.0-2.7 m), double-faced, rubble-filled walls. These walls are beautifully constructed of angular basalt with careful facing (Pl. 6). They are freestanding and enclose the terraced area. Along the rear of both terraces are narrow secondary terraces at the base of the rear wall. As seen in Figure 6.6, the unusually fine construction and internal complexity of the design indicate a ceremonial use for the terraces. The feature was probably a small heiau (religious shrine). The lower terrace was once irrigated by a cut in the east wall made after the wall itself was built. This could indicate either that the shrine held a sacred field or that it was used for agriculture after abandonment as a shrine.

Evidence for Change

The site has not been used within informant memory. All features appear to be of aboriginal materials and design.

Ka-D6-11

Ka-D6-11 (Fig. 6.7) is located on an island in the Wainiha stream about 2 km from the sea. The site is roughly 3.7 ha in area. Wainiha is a braided stream which creates several narrow islands ideal for taro pondfields. Two of these islands are still in production (cf. Systems 14 and 15, Chapter 5) but a third, System 13, is now abandoned and it is described below (cf. Fig. 5.2).

The site's island is long (540 m) and narrow (145 m). The natural channel which cuts across the top of the island is now dry because of hydrologic changes in the valley but it once joined a secondary channel back to the main stream. The dominant slope (.021) of the island is parallel with the stream. In addition, the island is humpbacked in cross-section — high along a central ridge and sloping down on either side to the stream channels bordering the site. The island's land surface is even and only slightly rocky. The soil profile shows a deep, moderately rocky alluvium.

Dam and Ditch Complex

The head dam was placed on a secondary, natural channel of the stream just upstream from a natural falls created by several large in situ boulders. The well-preserved dam is 6 m long, about 2 m wide, and 0.4 m high. River cobbles have been piled up to create a long mound typical of the percolation dams described in Chapter 5. Several pieces of corrugated sheet metal were added to the dam to inhibit percolation.

Below the intake, the ditch was a simple earth channel which ran 100 m from the head dam to the first patches. Then it ran along the middle of the island with patches to either side. Above the patches, the ditch slope is gentle (.006), but it became steeper (.016-.021) as the ditch ran among the patches. There was also a change in construction of the ditch in these two segments. In the upper segment, the ditch was a simple unlined channel dug perhaps 1 m below the natural land surface (Fig. 5.3). Near the top, it was over 2 m wide but it narrowed to about 0.4 m in the bottom. The cross section of the ditch in the lower segment was quite distinct. It was rectangular, 90 cm wide and 40 cm deep, and stone lined. The ditch was separated at several points from the bordering

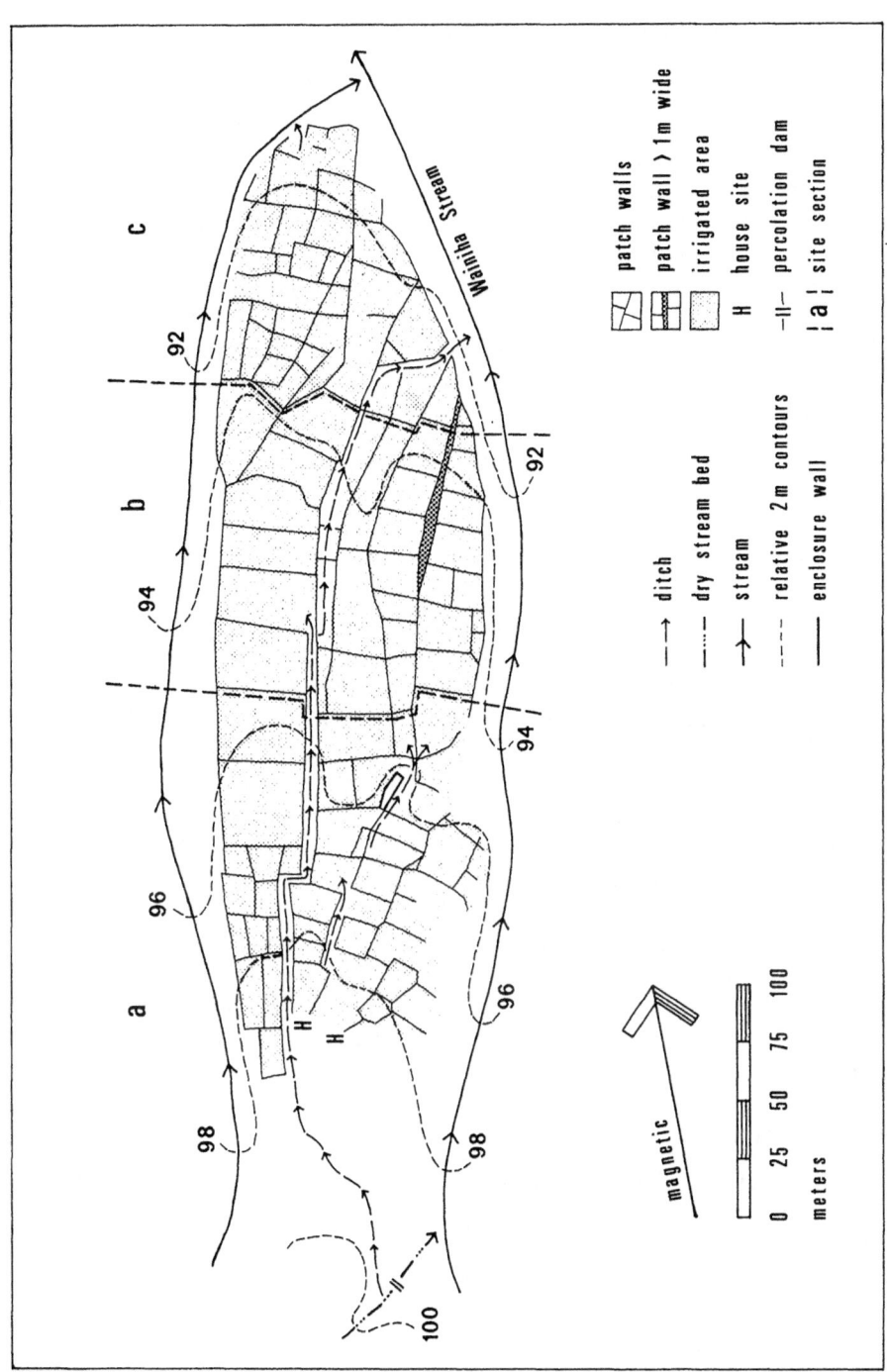

Fig. 6.7 Site Ka-D6-11, Wainiha, Kaua'i. Site divided into sections a-c for descriptive purposes.

patches by a double-faced and earth/rubble-filled wall, 80-150 cm wide and 35-45 cm high (Fig. 5.3).

Because of poor preservation, secondary ditches were difficult to trace but two segments were partially discernible. A fragment of secondary ditching in section "a" east of the primary ditch would have irrigated the patches in the southeast portion of the site. Another secondary ditch was indicated by a branching of the primary ditch in section "b."

The lowest segment of the primary ditch which ran along the base of section "b" is a deep depression, well below the elevation of the surrounding patches. This would have functioned as a drainage ditch for the site by leading excess water back to the main stream.

Pondfields

The pondfields were distinguished by surrounding embankments of earth and stones. Apparently, the stones were not generally used as facing for the embankment but were simply incorporated into the embankment as a way to clear them from the agricultural fields. In some cases, the embankments were reinforced with stone retaining walls. Stones were rounded and smaller (10-50 cm) than those used in Ha'ena and, as a result, facing was not usually evident. In two places in section "a," the lower embankment wall on a pondfield was faced on both sides.

The mean patch size was 307.7 m^2 but it varied markedly by section — "a," 292.0 m^2; "b," 409.0 m^2; and "c," 194.9 m^2. These differences are not easily explained because they do not correlate closely with such obvious factors as differences in slope. It seems likely that the larger size for section "b" can be explained by modern alterations. The grass vegetation in this section indicates that its fields were most recently abandoned. The other sections were forested.

The number of distributary patches also varied by section — "a," 1.0; "b," 4.1; and "c," 5.6. Because of the difficulty in locating secondary ditches, these figures are not highly reliable, but there is an obvious trend toward a more complex distributary pattern in the lower section of the site.

Other Features

In section "a," a small enclosure (5 by 17 m) stands about 50 cm above the surrounding patches. A solid core wall 1 m high enclosed the area which may have served as an animal pen.

Two habitation sites were discovered at the top of the system above the patches in section "a." A crumbling wooden frame building indicated

ARCHAEOLOGICAL RESEARCH ON IRRIGATION 99

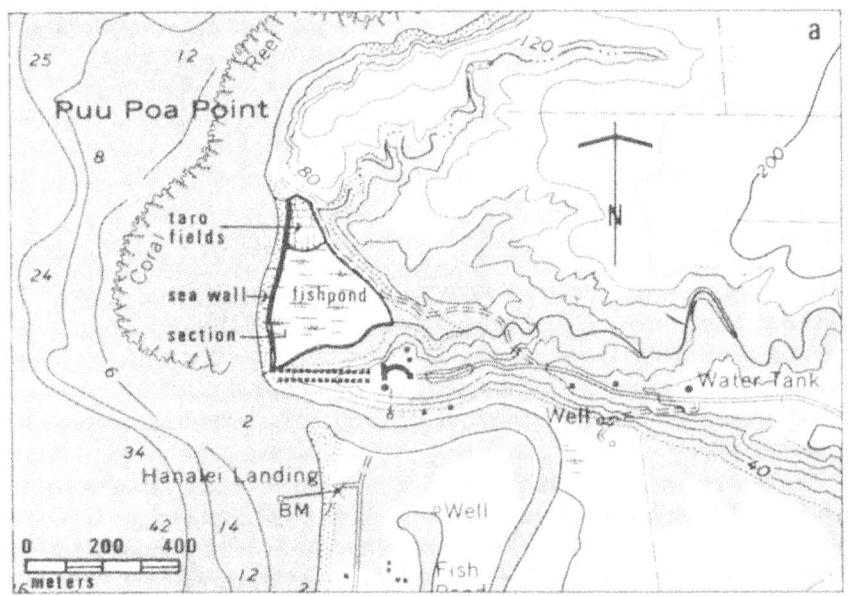

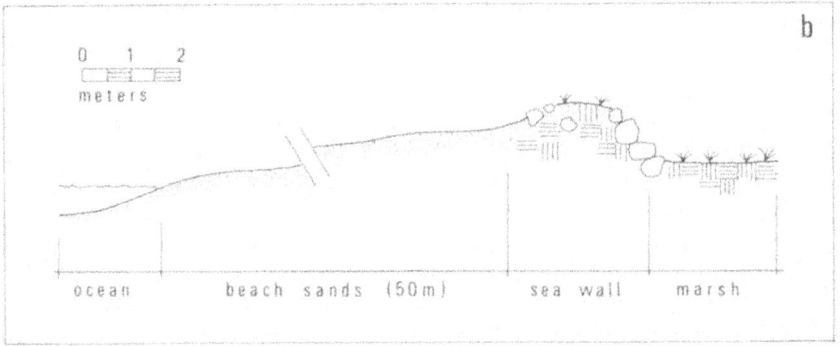

Fig. 6.8 Site Ka-D10-9, Hanalei, Kaua'i. (a) Enlargement of United States Geological Survey map showing location of fishpond; (b) Schematic representation of the cross section of the fishpond seawall.

that these were of recent construction. According to informants, these structures were taro shacks used for tools and occasional sleeping.

Evidence for Change

Informants stated that the island was used for taro until fairly recently (1950s). This probably accounts for an increase in average patch size, especially in section "b," and for certain changes in construction, such as the scarcity of stone retaining walls. The only obvious nontraditional features were the metal sheeting in the head dam and the wood frame structure.

Ka-D10-9

Site Ka-D10-9 (System 30) was a fishpond located at the mouth of the small Waileia stream, Hanalei (Fig. 6.8). This stream descends through a narrow gulch before entering a flat marshy area in back of the sand beach. As shown in a nineteenth century sketch map (Land Court Application #1729, 1956), a sea wall was constructed across the mouth of the valley to create a 1.64 ha fishpond. A small area of taro was also cultivated to one side of the pond, and coconut and breadfruit trees grew along the edge.

Presently, the site is distinguished by a marsh and fragments of the old sea wall. As seen in cross section (Fig. 6.8), the sea wall was an earthen mound about 1 to 2 m high and 2 to 3 m wide. This mound can be identified as artificial by the basaltic stones, not naturally occurring in this area, which are strewn along the mound's edge. A short section (6 m long) of wall is still intact. Rounded stones (30-100 cm) were roughly set to form a stone facing 1.1 m high for the inside of the embankment.

Ka-D10-10

Ka-D10-10 is an irrigation site (System 32) located just east of the Anini stream, Hanalei (Fig. 6.9). The topography of the site is unique. As the narrow Anini valley approaches the sea, it runs parallel to the shore before bending at a right angle to itself and opening directly onto the sea. In other words, a ridge divides the valley from the seashore.

Dam and Ditch Complex

The ditch is the only feature preserved at the site. It was a contour ditch (slope of .009) which formed a U-shaped line around the ridge. Water diverted from the Anini stream was channeled around the base of the ridge and along the ridge facing the sea. The ditch was retained against the ridge by a stone-faced earth embankment (Fig. 5.3). In sections, the ditch was lined with large subangular basalt.

Pondfields

The pondfields, although no longer preserved, were below the ditch line and facing the sea. As the land slopes away from the ridge and

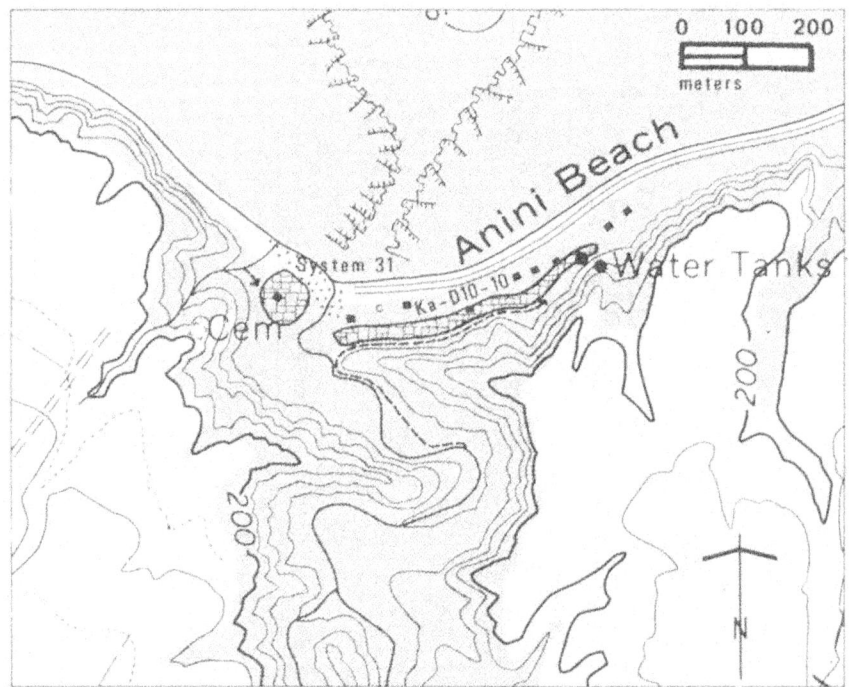

Fig. 6.9 Site Ka-D10-10, Anini, Hanalei. Enlargement of United States Geological Survey map showing the contour ditch and pondfield area (not preserved) for System 32. Location of System 31 (not preserved) is also indicated.

toward the sea, the soil becomes more sandy. Apparently, the pondfields were constructed almost down to the shoreline; however, they were destroyed during a tidal wave in the 1950s.

TYPES OF HALELEAN IRRIGATION

A rough typology of Halelean irrigation emerges from the sixteen[3] modern and archaeological systems which have been described in considerable detail in Chapters 5 and 6. Because of problems with preservation, this sample is opportunistic and too small to describe the total variability in Halelean irrigation. A tentative typology is considered useful, however, to identify the salient features of Halelean irrigation and to show how these features vary.

In the following subsections, a four-part typology of irrigation systems is presented based primarily on variation in natural topography. The requirements of any irrigation system are a permanent water

[3]These systems are: 1 (Ka-D5-4, a-f), 2 (Ka-D5-4, g-j), 6 (Ka-D5-5), 7 (Ka-D5-6), 8 (Ka-D5-7, a), 9 (Ka-D5-7, b), 10 (Ka-D5-8), 13 (Ka-D6-11), 14, 15, 18, 22, 23, 26, 30 (Ka-D10-9), and 32 (Ka-D10-10). Systems 17 and 29 were not historically described.

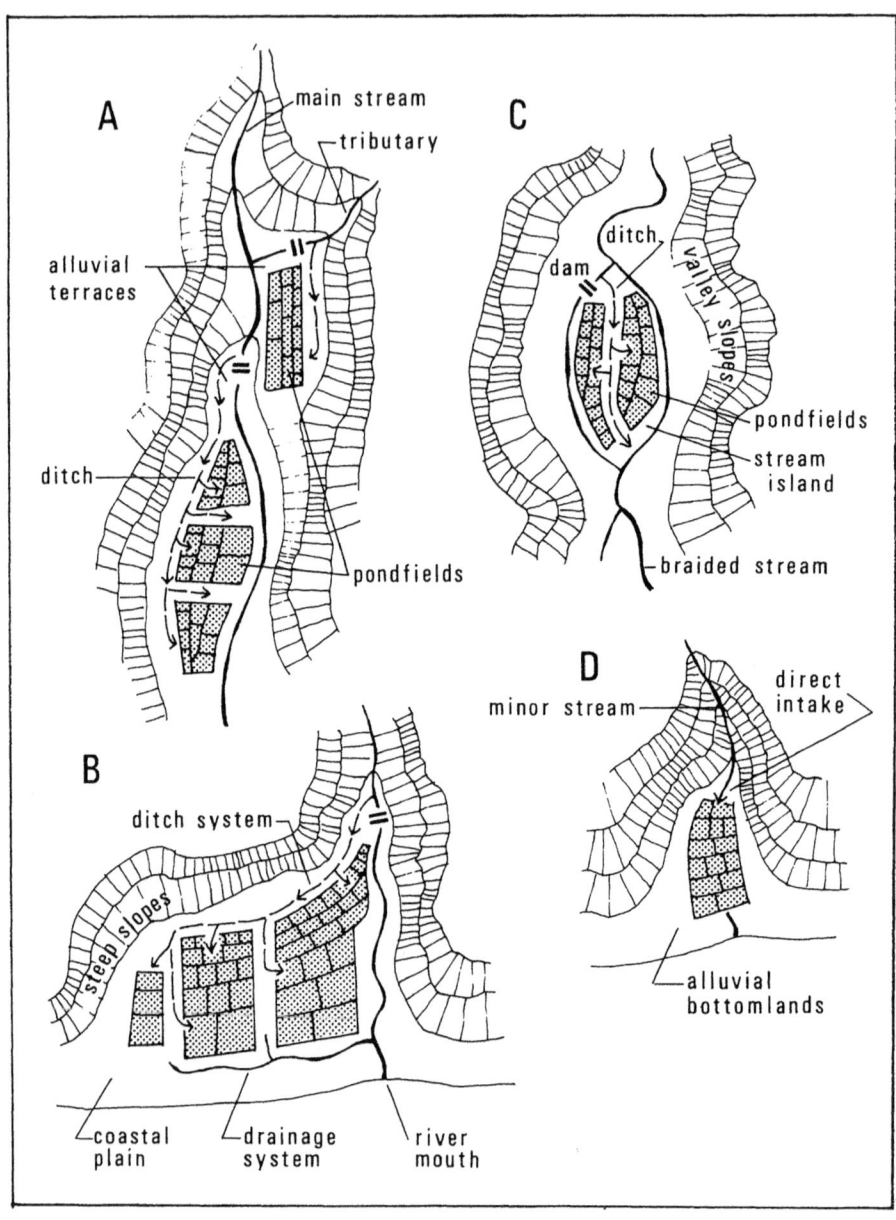

Fig. 6.10 Typology of Halelean irrigation systems. Type A, Alluvial Terrace (showing alternative sources, main stream and tributary stream); Type B, Alluvial Coastal Plain; Type C, Alluvial Island; Type D, Alluvial Bottom.

source and access to gently sloping agricultural land. Variability in water source (main stream, side stream, independent small stream, spring), slope of agricultural land, extent of agricultural land, and distance from source to agricultural land are the major factors determining the type of irrigation. In turn, the type of irrigation affects the possible requirements for management.

Type A: Alluvial Terrace

Type A irrigation systems (Fig. 6.10, A) are found on the alluvial terraces which flank permanent streams. There are two variants of Type A related to source — either central stream or tributary stream. If the primary ditch taps a central stream, the minimum distance required to gain the necessary height advantage is quite long. If, however, the source is a tributary stream or if the main stream has a steep slope, the distance from intake to agricultural fields may be much shorter. The primary ditch continues to run along the ridge slope above the fields until it terminates at a natural barrier like a cliff or lower tributary. In the lower sections of valleys, such ditches may be over a kilometer long but they are shorter on interior or small valleys. Patches step down the slope below the ditch line. The agricultural zone grades from a moderately steep (.08-.20) strip of taluvial soils along the lower ridge slope into a gently sloping (.04-.10) area of alluvial soils bordering the stream. Although limited in the narrow valleys, these soil zones become more extensive in the lower valleys of the major streams. The top patches are fed directly from the primary ditch and then from patch to patch down towards the stream. Secondary ditches are unnecessary except where the distance from ditch to stream is more than about eight terrace tiers. Drainage is not a problem because excess water can easily be led back to the central stream. Examples of Type A irrigation systems include Systems 10 (Ka-D5-8), 14, and 23.

Type B: Alluvial Coastal Plain

Type B irrigation systems (Fig. 6.10, B) are found on the coastal plains at the mouths of streams. Because the primary ditch taps the main stream before it enters the plain, the upper sections of these systems are identical to Type A systems. However, the ditch extends around the ridge face so that it runs above the alluvial plain parallel to the sea. The ditch gradually loses its height advantage over the plain and finally enters the plain. The ditch then travels through the plain as far as the irregular marshy terrain permits (cf. System 22). Springs are occasionally an alternative water source for Type B systems. Since these springs form point sources in a line along the lower slopes of the coastal ridge, the need for a primary contour ditch is eliminated. The patches are located below the primary ditch or springs. The agricultural zone starts as moderately steep (.06-.20) taluvial soils and then levels out into the alluvial plain (slope .001-.070) which extends down to the coastal sand dunes. The terraced patches near the ditch are fed directly from the ditch but the patches in the plain require secondary and often tertiary ditches to distribute water. Drainage is a major problem for the flat alluvial plain. There is usually either a drainage ditch or small natural stream running along the base of the system. Traditionally, poorly drained sections were converted into fishponds, but today elaborate drainage networks are used. Examples of Type B are Systems 1 and 2 (Ka-D5-4), 6 (Ka-D5-5), 7 (Ka-D5-6), 8 and 9 (Ka-D5-7), 22, 26, and 32 (Ka-D10-10).

Type C: Alluvial Island

Type C systems (Fig. 6.10, C) are found on the islands of permanent streams. At the top of the island, the primary ditch taps a secondary channel of the braided stream, and the ditch line runs down the central ridge of the island. Patches usually begin within 100-150 m of the intake. The agricultural zone is on either side of the ditch, between it and the two bordering stream channels. The dominant slope of the island is usually gentle (.004-.020) and parallels the direction of stream flow. The island is also humpbacked in cross section with a high central ridge. The pondfields to either side of the ditch are fed either directly or through short secondary ditches. Because these islands are narrow, the distance from primary ditch to patch is never long. Drainage is not a problem because excess water can be easily led back to the bordering streams. Examples of Type C are Systems 13 (Ka-D6-11) and 15.

Type D: Alluvial Bottom

Type D irrigation systems (Fig. 6.10, D) are found in the alluvial bottom land of a small stream, where the whole valley is converted to a single agricultural complex by damming the central stream. The only example studied is System 30 (Ka-D10-9) which was primarily a fishpond. There are, however, historical examples of Type D systems which were pondfield complexes.

ARCHAEOLOGICAL EVIDENCE FOR THE MANAGERIAL REQUIREMENTS OF HALELEAN IRRIGATION

At this juncture, I wish to distinguish between the overall scale of an irrigation system and the technological complexity of its constituent parts. The historic documentation on forty-two systems, as analyzed in the next chapter, includes data on size, ditch length, and number of farmers. These data permit an evaluation of scale but provide little information on the internal complexity which can be better studied in the archaeological sites. Although irrigation systems are usually only partially preserved in the archaeological record, the specific features of technological elements like dams, ditches, and pondfields are often intact and will be discussed below.

Construction of Irrigation Systems

Two aspects of irrigation technology which could have promoted organized management are the sophistication of design and the required schedule of labor investment. In the first instance, it is often argued that the technical sophistication of some hydraulic devices requires a knowledge of engineering not possessed by the individual farmer (cf. Wittfogel 1957). For Halelean irrigation, this was clearly not the case. The technology was based on only the most basic hydrologic principles — water flows downhill along the line of least resistance. This knowledge can easily be derived by empirical experimentation, which requires little overall planning. There are no sophisticated aboriginal hydraulic devices like measuring weirs or siphons and there are no unusual feats of engineering like massive head dams or high terrace walls.

The simplicity of technology is evident throughout the irrigation complex — head dam, irrigation ditch, diversion devices, and pondfields. The head dam was an unreinforced mound of river cobbles piled between in situ boulders, and it was of modest size — 1-2 m wide, 0.4-0.6 m high, and 6-50 m long. By placing this head dam at a natural bend, rapids, or falls, the inherent resistance to water flow was increased and a percentage of the water was shunted into the primary ditch. The irrigation ditch was a narrow earthen channel (1-3 m wide, 0.5-2 m deep) which was occasionally lined with stone. Water diversion was controlled by a combination of the size of cut in the ditch bank, the relative slope between primary and secondary ditch, and the number of rocks placed in the primary ditch as a crude dam. The pondfield itself was a level basin surrounded by an earth bund. The terraces used to support the pondfield were not large because of the avoidance of steep slopes (usually less than .100) and the small field sizes. The front retaining wall was normally not more than 1 m high. There is no evidence that the construction of such irrigation systems would demand specialized, technical knowledge beyond the practical proficiency of the subsistence farmer.

The layout of the ditch network is a specific example of the simplicity of design represented by Halelean irrigation systems. A primary ditch should maintain the minimum possible sustained slope in order to maximize the area irrigated. As the slope of a ditch decreases, there is an increase in the potential agricultural land; however, a ditch of minimum slope requires accurate preliminary surveying of the ditch line. Because Hawaiian ditches had relatively steep slopes, a ditch could have been laid out without a preliminary design and later extended to its technical limit. The "contour" ditches were in fact quite steep (about .008) and did not really approach a level slope; other ditches simply ran down a site almost perpendicular to the contours. Without the use of gradually sloping, maximum elevation ditches, the engineering problems of design were lessened; however, as a consequence of the relatively steep slopes, aboriginal Hawaiian irrigation systems used only a fraction of the available alluvial land. The total area of irrigated land in 1850 is estimated to have been 115 hà. In comparison, by using longer ditches with lesser slopes, the Chinese rice farmers had an estimated 526 ha in production at the turn of this century.

With respect to labor scheduling for construction, the aboriginal irrigation technology was characterized by low and divisible labor requirements. Labor investment was minimized by altering the natural topography as little as possible and by using only local materials. For example, pondfields were constructed by cut-and-fill whereby the level terrace was built up with earth excavated from the rear of the terrace to fill in the terrace front. The stone retaining wall was constructed with rock most probably uncovered during this excavation. Even within a site, such as Ka-D5-4, the size and angularity of the stones used in retaining walls vary according to the materials available in the immediate vicinity. Pondfields were arranged to correspond closely to natural topography and thus minimize the amount of earth moved during construction. As can be seen in Table 6.1, as slope increases the size of a patch tends to decrease. This is a direct result of the energetics of terrace construction. For a pondfield of constant size, the volume of earth moved in construction increases geometrically with the natural slope of the land. By decreasing the average size of a terrace on steeper slopes, however, the volume of earth moved for a given area may be held constant. As the size of a pondfield decreases, however, the percentage of land area devoted to bunds dramatically increases. A "mini-max" solution to these opposed principles is therefore required. In any specific area, larger pondfields increase the percentage of area in production. Since larger pondfields require larger labor investments, it is reasonable to suggest that their construction might require large work crews with related recruitment and management responsibilities. This, however, is not necessarily true. A large pondfield can be constructed in segments and thus the labor required may be broken into small staged units; as an example, an area may first be terraced as four separate pondfields in succeeding stages and then, later, converted again in stages into one large pondfield. As discussed in Chapter 4, the critical factor is the time available; large crews are required only if large terraces must be built quickly.

In sum, evidence suggests that the Halelean irrigation systems were built slowly by accretion. Because the irrigation ditches were not designed to maximize productive area, no overall design was necessary. Instead, ditches were probably gradually extended to their limits as more land became necessary. Similarly, the pondfields were often built in stages by combining smaller terraces. In fact, there is no evidence for massive construction in any parts of the Halelean systems; rather, a process of slow extension and intensification seems indicated.

Maintenance of Irrigation Systems

Because of the similarity between modern and archaeological technologies, the general conclusions regarding the low maintenance and self-regulation of modern systems seem applicable to traditional systems as well. The design of archaeological ditches (ditch cross section and slope) is comparable to the modern ditches described in Chapter 5. There was considerable variability in the length of primary ditches described for the archaeological sites; type A with main stream sources and type B systems generally required longer ditches than type A with side stream sources, type C, and type D systems (see Chapter 7 for a larger sample size). In all cases, however, the archaeological ditches were shorter than their modern counterparts. In sum, archaeological evidence indicates that maintenance requirements for traditional irrigation would not have been extensive.

Reconstruction Following Natural Disasters and Warfare

There is no archaeological evidence of the possible effects of natural disasters and warfare; therefore, the possible significance of these factors cannot be evaluated with these data.

Water Allocation

Archaeological data on water allocation are limited, but two important points should be made. First, the pattern of ditches was very simple. With the exception of System 1 (Ka-D5-4), the primary ditch continued the length of the system without major branching. Secondary ditches were usually small and watered only restricted areas of pondfields. System 1, as typical of Type B systems, however, indicates some complexity in water distribution in the large alluvial plain systems. System 22 (Chapter 5) is a modern example of such a system but no major disputes have been described ethnographically.

Second, the archaeological systems have fewer secondary ditches than their modern counterparts; thus the number of distributary patches is higher in archaeological sites. As discussed in Chapter 5, as the number of distributary patches increases, the intricacies of water distribution increases. The historical data presented in the next chapter, however, will show that the pattern of land tenure neutralized this potential source of conflict.

SUMMARY

The archaeological data from Halelea offer little support for Wittfogel's suggestion that the technology of Hawaiian irrigation resulted in the evolution of centralized management. For construction, the rudimentary technology would not have required special technical knowledge unavailable to the individual farmer. Specific features like dams, ditches, and pondfield terraces were not massive and show no evidence of preliminary overall design. The conclusion is that the systems were constructed largely by extension and gradual intensification. Maintenance tasks, especially ditch cleaning, are shown by analogy to modern systems to be of minor importance and certainly not to require organized labor crews. Finally, although somewhat equivocal, the allocation of water is seen as comparable to modern Halelean irrigation systems which apparently function without major disputes. Because the archaeological evidence is not complete, I will now analyze the archival data on historic irrigation systems, which provide a larger sample and better information on the overall scale of traditional Halelean irrigation.

CHAPTER VII

HISTORICAL RESEARCH ON IRRIGATION

The historical research on Hawaiian irrigation was directed toward describing traditional practices of taro cultivation and investigating the possible evolutionary significance of these practices. The five lines of investigation summarized in this chapter are outlined below:

(1) Descriptions of taro pondfield systems found in early explorer accounts are synthesized. These accounts provide excellent personal observations on the irrigation technology and physical layout of the agricultural fields. At contact, extensive irrigation complexes were reported for the Hawaiian Islands and in scale and technology they are basically similar to the archaeological data described in Chapter 6.

(2) The practices used in the irrigated cultivation of taro are synthesized from traditional histories, explorer accounts, and ethnographies. In addition to a qualitative description of the operation of irrigation agriculture, the traditional organization of labor in agriculture is documented.

(3) A specific and quantitative description of historic irrigation in Halelea is presented from information derived from the archival records of land allotments issued to the Hawaiian commoners (1848-1854).

(4) From this historical data base, the irrigation technology in Halelea is compared to similar irrigation systems in four other societies. This section is a preliminary test of Wittfogel's notion that the complexity of irrigation results in centralized management. A basic similarity in technology is shown to have little relationship to the organization of labor and the complexity of political development.

(5) In the final section, the probable evolutionary significance of Hawaiian irrigation is reviewed and the *scale* of the irrigation system is generally rejected as an important factor in the evolution of centralized management. Other aspects of irrigation, *not* related to scale, are indicated as deserving further analysis.

EXPLORER ACCOUNTS OF IRRIGATION

Because the early explorers who visited the Hawaiian Islands were in search of provisions for their ships, their accounts invariably give descriptions of the local agriculture. Captain James Cook, the British expeditionary credited with the "discovery" of the Hawaiian Islands, first landed at Waimea, Kaua'i in 1778. Here he described "Plantations which were chiefly of Tara, and sunk a little below the common level so as to contain the water necessary to nourish the roots" (Beaglehole 1967:269). Although brief, this account clearly describes taro pondfields at time of first western contact, and later accounts expanded on this initial description. The next major expedition, headed by the Britishers Portlock and Dixon, stopped at Waimea in 1786.

> ...the greatest part of [these plantations] are made upon the banks of the river, with exceedingly good causeways made with stone and earth, leading up the valleys to each plantation; the taro-beds are in general a quarter mile over, dammed in, and have a place in one part of the bank, that serves as a gateway [for water]... [Portlock 1789:191]

Although Portlock described accurately the pondfield complex, he failed to identify the ditch network and stated that patches were watered by periodic flooding of the stream. This error was corrected during the 1792 expedition commanded by George Vancouver who penetrated farther inland to where the primary irrigation ditch emerged from the narrow Waimea canyon. The expeditionary's botanist, Archibald Menzies, described the scene as follows:

> We walked to the conflux of these two streams [which form the Waimea River], and found that the aqueduct which waters the whole plantation is brought up with much art and labor along the bottom of the rocks [cliff] from this northwest branch, for here we saw it supported in its course through a narrow pass by a piece of masonry raised from the side of the river, upwards of 20 feet and facing its bank in so neat and artful a manner as would do no discredit to more scientific builders. Indeed the whole plantation is laid out with great neatness and is intersected by small banks conveying little streams from the above aqueduct to flood distant fields on each side at pleasure, by which their esculent roots are brought to such perfection, that they are the best of every kind I ever saw. [1920:28-29]

During the fifty years following initial contact, excellent descriptions of the taro irrigation complexes were made for Waimea, Kaua'i (Vancouver 1798:170-71), Waikiki and Honolulu, Oahu (Vancouver 1798:163-64; Menzies 1920:28; Kotzebue 1821:340; Meyen 1913 [1834]), and Lahaina, Maui (Menzies 1920:105, 112; Arago 1823:119-20; Macrae 1922: 8, 11; and Stewart 1830: 142, 183).[1] These accounts offer consistent statements on the aboriginal technology of taro irrigation. Early

---

[1] The accounts refer to visits on the following years: Vancouver and Menzies, 1792; Kotzebue, 1816; Arago, 1819; Macrae, 1825; Meyen, 1831; and Stewart, 1823-1825.

taro "plantations" were similar in general layout to, but differed in detail from, the modern taro systems (cf. Table 7.1). The taro was

TABLE 7.1

QUANTITATIVE DATA ON TARO PONDFIELDS AS DESCRIBED
IN EARLY EXPLORER/TRAVELER ACCOUNTS

	Average Patch Size	Water Depth	Bank Width	Bank Height
Portlock (1789:179,191)	—	6 inches; 1.5-2 feet	—	—
Dixon (1789:131)	—	—	2 feet	—
Vancouver (1798:164,170)	—	—	"narrow"; "where only one person could pass"	—
Arago (1823:118)	—	—	—	2-4 feet
Campbell (1822:115)	Usually less than 100 yards square	18 inches	—	6 feet
Kotzebue (1821:340)	160 feet square	2 feet "6 inches for planting"	3-6 feet	—
Macrae (1922:8)	—	2-2.5 feet	—	4 feet
Meyen (1834:17-22)	Average 40-50 feet square	2-3 feet	narrow	—
Stewart (1830:142,183)	Average 60-90 feet square— "few yards" to "half an acre"	—	—	2-3 feet
Whitman (ms.)	—	3-5 inches	—	4 feet
Paulding (1831:214)	40 feet square	1-2 feet	—	—
Range	40-360 feet square	3-36 inches	2-6 feet	2-6 feet
Average	80 feet square	18.5 inches	—	4 feet

cultivated in small water-filled basins surrounded by an earth and stone embankment. These observers recorded the typical patch size as 40 to 160 feet square (12.2-48.8 m^2), which is smaller than both the average archaeological terraces (mean 142 m^2) and modern pondfields (mean 530 m^2) described in this monograph. The bunds were apparently earth reinforced with stone retaining walls as described for the archaeological sites (Chapter 6). The width of the bunds was 1-2 m and their height about the same. In addition to retaining the ponded water, the bunds served as pathways to the fields and as unirrigated planting areas for crops such as banana, sugar cane, and ti.

The pondfields were watered by a ditch complex which tapped a stream or spring. The most detailed description of a primary ditch was recorded by Vancouver for Waikiki: " . . . near a mile from the beach . . . was a rivulet five or six feet wide, and about two or three feet deep, well banked up, and nearly motionless . . . " (1798:163-64). Within the pondfields, several observers (cf. Arago 1823:119-20; Campbell 1967 [1822]:115) mentioned an intricate pattern of secondary ditches criss-crossing the field area. As described by Kotzebue (1821:340) below, water was then distributed among the pondfields by "sluices" cut in the pondfield bank. For a pondfield itself, the typical water depth was recorded as varying from 3 inches to 3 feet (7.6-91.4 cm). This is considerably deeper than the modern practice of flooding to only 10 cm. The greater depth may have been necessary for raising fish in the pondfields (Kotzebue 1821:340; Macrae 1922:8).

I shall now quote several of the more comprehensive descriptions at length to give an appreciation of the detail included in these accounts.

> The mode of culture is extremely laborious, as it is necessary to have the whole field laid under water; it [taro] is raised in small patches, which are seldom above a hundred yards square; these are surrounded by embankments, generally about six feet high, the sides of which are planted with sugar-canes, with a walk on top; the fields are intersected by drains or aqueducts, constructed with great labor and ingenuity, for the purpose of supplying the water necessary to cover them. [Campbell 1967 [1822]:115]

> The artificial taro fields . . . excited my attention. Each of them forms a regular square of 160 feet, and is enclosed with stone all around like our basins. This field, or rather this pond, for such it really may be called, contains two feet of water, in the slimy bottom of which the taro is planted, as it does not thrive except in such a wet situation; each pond has two sluices, to let in the water on one side, and out again at the other, into the next field, and so on. The fields are gradually lower, and the same water which is led from an elevated spring or rivulet, can water a large plantation. . . . In the spaces between the fields, which are from three to six feet broad, there are very pleasant shady avenues, and on both sides banana and sugar-canes are planted. The taro fields afford another advantage; for the fish which are caught in distant streams thrive admirably when put into them. [Kotzebue 1821:340]

These early accounts demonstrate the basic similarity of the Hawaiian irrigation at time of contact to the archaeological evidence for later (1850) historic systems (Chapter 6) and to modern systems in Halelea (Chapter 5). The early accounts typically describe Type B irrigation systems (cf. Chapter 6) which, because of their location on the alluvial flat land near the sea, were most prominent to visitors. The only major difference between the contact systems and those described archaeologically is an increase in patch size; modern systems continue this trend toward increased patch size and have narrower bunds and shallower water.

TARO CULTIVATION

In this section, traditional practices of irrigated taro cultivation are compiled from diverse historical sources. The discussion focuses on the organization of labor in agriculture and the use of cooperative labor teams. As reported in Chapter 5, in modern taro farming, labor is organized primarily within the household unit. This aspect of taro cultivation is unusual in small scale agricultural societies where interhousehold work teams are a common way to organize certain productive activities (cf. Malinowski 1922; Sahlins 1962; Bennett 1968). Because agriculture is often closely synchronized to environmental cycles (e.g., temperature and rainfall), labor activities peak at planting and harvest times. In contrast, irrigation largely removes water as a limiting factor in Hawaii and so taro production can be continuous. By staggering the schedules for individual pondfields, a farmer's labor needs are kept relatively stable through the year and there is little need for labor outside the household. As is shown in this section, although there is a basic similarity in production scheduling between modern and traditional taro cultivation, group labor was used extensively in the traditional period. The reasons for these group work teams are discussed as they relate to the Wittfogelian notion of labor management.

Information is drawn from three types of sources — traditional histories; explorer/traveler accounts; and ethnographies. (1) As discussed in Chapter 2, various Hawaiians (e.g., Kamakau, Malo, Ii. and Kepelino) wrote extensively during the nineteenth century on their native culture and its history. These accounts, which were compiled from personal observations and informant interviews, are a comprehensive synthesis of many aspects of Hawaiian culture including agricultural activities. These personal narratives are vivid and comprehensive, but they are heavily idealized and somewhat biased. Particularly, the historians, who themselves were of high social status, emphasized activities associated with the elites. (2) The explorer/traveler accounts, in contrast, describe specific activities observed by the authors while they journeyed around the islands. These descriptions tend to concentrate on conspicuous or unusual activities and so many aspects of cultivation are ignored. A major difficulty in assessing the accuracy of these accounts is that later statements frequently are copied from earlier ones. (3) For our present purposes, the most salient ethnographic summaries of traditional Hawaiian agriculture are the monographs by Handy (1940) and Handy and Handy (1972). In addition to the traditional histories and explorer/traveler accounts, Handy collected detailed information from informants who, in the 1930s, either practiced or remembered traditional methods. Although the informant data are excellent, they refer to a period over a hundred years after contact and so their applicability to a reconstruction of aboriginal methods must be viewed with caution. In general, Handy's work is flawed by a presentation of an idealized description of taro cultivation which does not distinguish adequately the sources used for specific statements. In order to alleviate this problem, I use a standard format to synthesize sources. Because the traditional histories are the most comprehensive, I present these descriptions first with comments on internal consistency. Then, to correct for bias and various gaps, the explorer/traveler accounts and the ethnographies are briefly summarized.

Construction of the Irrigation System

The only comprehensive account of ditch construction was written in the late nineteenth century by Nakuina, Commissioner of Private Ways and Water Rights, District of Kona, Oahu. To summarize her article (Nakuina 1894:79-84), new ditches were dug by a cooperative labor force supervised by the konohiki of the land division(s) involved. Labor was recruited from the farmers who would benefit from the construction, and the amount of labor which they contributed determined their water allocation. Nakuina asserted that the ditch was excavated from the farming area upwards to the source and that this task required planning and supervision. After the ditch was completed, the konohiki provided pigs and fish for a feast by the workers and the gods. After the feast, a dam of loose stones and earth was built to divert water from the stream.

Following the initial construction of the dam-ditch complex, pondfields were constructed. Kamakau's narrative is the most detailed traditional account, but it should be noted that the following quotation describes the construction of a large pondfield for a chief or other prominent individual (cf. Kamakau 1976:33).

> ... when the soil was thoroughly soaked, "food" and "fish" were brought to the scene of labor ... When the men had gathered — perhaps ... several hundred — most of them were lined up at the lower bank of the patch. If the patch were 40 *anana* [40m] in length, they were perhaps in two or three rows. Along the two shorter sides there might also be two or three rows [of men].
> Then the embankments, the *kuauna*, were raised by heaping up dirt from below. Two or three meters away from each bank they dug down for three or four feet and, leaving the dirt of the bank to make a solid foundation, they heaped up the dirt to raise the embankment ... They stamped the sides facing the *lo'i* [pondfield] with their feet to straighten them, then beat in sugar cane tops ... [and] coconut stems, *ha niu*. To make firm the foundation underneath, they pounded in large flat rocks ... [Finally], they covered [the banks] with fine soil, trash, and grass to prevent them from cracking in the sun.
> After that the *lo'i* itself was dug out. This digging took from a month to some years to complete. [Kamakau 1976:34]

Malo's description corroborates Kamakau's, although it does not mention group labor.

> Banks of earth were first raised about the patch and beaten hard, after which water was let in, and when this had become nearly dry, the four banks were reinforced with stones, coconut leaves and sugar-cane tops until they were water tight. [Malo 1951 (1898):204]

Ii describes a specific situation at which group labor was used to construct pondfields under orders from the paramount chief, Kamehameha. Kamehameha had recently conquered the island of Oahu and was apparently reconstructing/intensifying its agricultural base by using corvée labor crews. "The men, scattered systematically ... , dug and beat on the banks with dried coconut leaf stems" (1959:68). The beating of the bank must have been an impressive sight, for it is also mentioned in several western accounts (Corney 1896 [1818]:108; Whitman ms.; Stewart 1830:142; Paulding 1831:214).

Soil Preparation

The next stage was the preparation of the planting surface. Prior to treading, the patch was dried and the soil was broken up before letting water in (Malo 1951 [1898]:204). Kepelino (Beckwith 1932:152) described that weeds were incorporated into the soil, which was then mounded up. Ii described the use of group labor for this activity at Nuuanu, Oahu, under direction from Kamehameha (see above).

> ... innumerable people [were] all over the farming area ... The bullrushes ... were cleared away in a single day. Some men cut the rushes, some dug them out, some

built mounds, and others covered the mounds with the rushes. Much food was provided for the noonday meal ... [Ii 1959:68]

As described in the early western accounts, the two ways to prepare the pondfield surface were leveling and mounding. Campbell, for example, describes the tilling and leveling of a field while the farmers sat "squatting on their hams and heels" (1967 [1822]:115). Alternatively, Macrae describes that after an old pondfield was harvested, it was allowed to dry for several days before earth mounds "about two feet high and seven to eight feet in circumference [were heaped up] at short distances from each other" (1922:9). Whitman (ms.), Stewart (1830:142) and Corney (1896:108) mention that before planting, vegetable materials were incorporated in the soil, probably as a means of fertilization.

After the pondfield was leveled and/or mounded, water was let in and the soil puddled to inhibit seepage. In Kamakau's description, a ceremonial party treaded the newly flooded field:

> On the day of treading the lo'i was filled with water, and the owner of the patch made ready plenty of "food" (poi), pork, and "fish." It was a great day for men, women, and children ... [who] bedecked [themselves] with greenery and worked with all [their] might ... This treading was done so that the water would not sink into the soil, and to allow the taro to grow. [Kamakau 1976:34]

Both Malo (1951 [1898]:204) and Ii (1959:68) mentioned, but did not describe in detail, the treading. Of the Western observers, only Campbell (1967 [1822]:155) mentioned the treading.

Planting

Aboriginally, cuttings were similar to the planting material presently used (Malo 1951 [1898]:205; Beckwith 1932:152; Macrae 1922:8; Campbell 1967 [1822]:115; Stewart 1830:142; Whitman ms.). Cuttings were selected both by variety[2] and healthiness (Kamakau 1976:34; Handy 1940:39-40), and, as is the case among modern planters, cuttings from sucker plants were preferred (Whitman ms.).

Considerable confusion exists about the pattern and method of planting. Malo stated that "A line was stretched to mark the rows, after which the *huli* [cuttings] were planted in the rows. Sometimes the planting was done without the rows being lined in" (1951 [1898]:205). Planting in straight lines, apparently in the puddled soil, is corrobo-

---

[2]The whole complex of native taro varieties is extremely interesting and deserves further study. Handy gives a list of 346 taro variety names among which he was able to decipher sixty-seven varieties with distinctive characteristics (1940:17-34). Variability in colors of corm and petiole are primary distinctive features. Secondarily, variability in planting location (wet vs. dry, for example), maturation time, and yield are important characteristics associated with varieties.

rated by Stewart (1830:142), Corney (1896:108), and Whitman (ms.). Distances between plantings are listed as 1.5-2 ft (Stewart 1830:142), and 4 ft (Whitman ms.). Macrae (1922:8) and Tilley (1861:330) also report planting in raised mounds. In all probability, the patterns of line planting in a flooded soil and clustered planting in mounds were alternative aboriginal techniques. One late nineteenth century traditional account (Queen Emma ms.) recorded that line planting was used when a patch was first planted but as soil became exhausted mounding was used. This seems quite likely because the aerobic conditions created by mounding would have permitted rapid decay of organic materials and thus increased nutrient availability. Mounding may also have been used in the lowest sections of irrigation systems where periodic draining and aeration of the soil was impossible.

After planting the pondfields, the farmer planted the surrounding banks with banana, sugar cane, and ti (Kamakau 1976:34; Kotzebue 1821:340; Corney 1896:108; Macrae 1922:8; Meyen 1913 [1834]:17-18) and stocked the water with fish (Kamakau 1976:34; Kotzebue 1821:340; Macrae 1922:8; Corney 1896:108).

Nurture

Although critical for crop growth, the actual procedures of flooding are seldom described in the traditional accounts. Malo simply stated that after planting "Water was then constantly kept running into the patch" (1951 [1896]:205). The western observers took a greater interest in this process. Whitman (ms.), Stewart (1830:142), and Paulding (1831:214) stated that the taro was planted dry and later flooded. Kotzebue (1821:340), on the other hand, said that the taro was planted in 6 in. of water which was later increased to 2 ft. Most observers mentioned only that the taro was kept constantly flooded (cf. Table 7.1 for depths). A detailed schedule of flooding depth was compiled by Handy (1940:44) from his informant data.

The primary activities of plant nurture described by Kamakau were weeding and care of the cuttings:

> When the taro was growing vigorously the weeds were pulled out and the *huli* pressed firmly into the earth from one side of the patch to the other. [1976:35]

After a brief prayer to the god Ku, the patch was then tabu until the plants were mature (Kamakau 1976:35). Kepelino also mentioned that after the plants were in leaf, weeds were pulled up and "stamped down into the soil again and allowed to decay and to enrich the soil" (Beckwith

1932:152). Weeding was mentioned only rarely by western observers (cf. Macrae 1922:8).

Harvest Procedures and Scheduling of Crops

According to Kamakau (1976:36), the yellowing of the leaves and slackening of growth were the primary signs of crop maturity. Maturation time for taro was described variously as "a few months or perhaps a year" (Kamakau 1976:36); twelve months (Malo 1951 [1898]:205); six to nine months (Whitman ms.); nine months (Corney 1896:108; Campbell 1967 [1822]:115); and six to twelve months (Handy 1940:45). The plants, however, could be stored in the field up to eighteen months after maturity (Whitman ms.).

As discussed for modern taro cultivation, pondfield practices permitted a nonseasonal, continuous production of taro by the staggering of individual patches: "On land supplied with running water agriculture was easy and could be carried on at all times" (Malo 1951 [1898]:204). Macrae corroborates this point: "They . . . have no particular season for planting or for taking up the taro, but go on using the large roots as they occasionally want them for food from the ponds that are most forward . . ." (1922:8). The two major implications of this are that the continuous production of taro largely eliminated the need for storage facilities and minimized the periodicity of labor in agriculture.

Discussion of Traditional Cultivation of Taro

A comparison of aboriginal methods of taro cultivation to their modern counterparts (cf. Chapter 5) shows a general similarity in pattern. The taro plant remains unchanged and its basic requirements for water, nutrients, rooting medium, etc. are the same. In addition, the scale of production has not been substantially altered; family farms, with little mechanization, are larger than their traditional counterparts but not radically changed. In all the tasks of taro cultivation (the construction of patches and ditches, soil preparation, planting, nurture, and harvest) are comparable if not identical. Perhaps, most significant is the general similarity in scheduling. Traditional taro cultivation, like its modern counterpart, was nonseasonal and geared to a continuous production schedule by the staggering of individual pondfields.

There are, however, several significant differences between traditional and modern methods, which relate to basic changes in the goal of production, the method of fertilization, and the use of technology. Traditionally, agricultural production was geared to the subsistence needs of the community, and irrigated taro fields produced a wide range of useful products including fish and dryland crops. The greater water depth and wider bunds, in comparison to the modern specialized fields, allowed for these multiple uses. Fertility was maintained traditionally by the application of green manures. To increase nutrient availability, the soil surface was dried and broken up before planting, and mounding was used to increase aeration. Finally, the modern use of metal hand tools and horse drawn equipment as well as the recent use of bulldozers and hand tractors have obvious altered the labor requirements of cultivation.

The most salient difference between traditional and modern practices is in the organization of labor. In contrast to the modern situation, group labor teams were used aboriginally for a variety of tasks including construction of irrigation ditches and pondfields and the preparation of planting surfaces. An obvious explanation for this difference would be that higher labor requirements existed aboriginally for these tasks. This is certainly true in part. Mechanization has reduced labor requirements for construction of irrigation features and the preparation of field areas, and the use of chemical fertilizers has reduced labor requirements for soil preparation, especially moundings. This change in labor requirements is, however, only a partial explanation, because two factors would have restricted labor requirements for the traditional taro farmer. First, the size of a family farm was considerably smaller in 1850 than at present; in other words, mechanization has resulted more in an expansion in the scale of production than in a reduction in absolute labor requirements. Second, archaeological data (Chapter 6) indicate that construction was in most cases a gradual process whereby labor investment was spread over a considerable period of time.

The traditional use of group labor in Hawaiian agriculture was related most likely to the organization of the productive process. As described in Chapters 8 and 9, the chiefs were the owners of all lands and much of the agricultural production was geared explicitly to their demands. Group labor was directed by the konohiki who was the land manager for the ahupua'a chief. The large work teams described in the traditional and explorer/traveler accounts were engaged most probably in corvée labor for the chiefs. For example, the pondfield for which Kamakau (1976) describes the use of group labor was 40 m long (estimated area 800-1600 m^2). Such a large pondfield could only have been built by a chief, a "prominent" man, or another individual with extensive kin ties (cf. Kamakau 1976:33). The group labor activities described by Ii (1959:68) were apparently organized by the paramount chief himself as a means to increase an area's productivity. It seems that the emphasis on group labor in the ethnohistorical accounts may represent a bias in the historical accounts for the unusual, conspicuous activity. In summary, the traditional use of group labor was less a requirement of the agricultural tasks themselves than it was an aspect of the production process which was organized as a capital investment (income source) for the elites.

THE LAND RECORDS OF 1850

The Hawaiian government records associated with the land division of 1848-1854 are an extremely valuable source for quantitative data on the scale of traditional irrigation systems. As described in Chapter 2, the paramount chief, as focal individual of the reconstructed chiefly conical clan, was owner of all land. He distributed his land to his chiefs who in turn allocated subsistence plots to commoners. The aboriginal pattern of land tenure was hierarchical and overlapping. The explicit goal of the nineteenth century Hawaiian land reforms was to separate these rights so that individuals would hold land in fee simple similar to English or American land tenure laws; theoretically, one-third of the land was to be granted to each of the following: government (the paramount), landlords (chiefs), and tenants (commoners) (*Indices of Awards* 1929:3).

The legal process of land allocation was recorded in three sets of documents: (1) Native Register; (2) Foreign Testimony and Native Testimony; and (3) Land Commission Awards and Royal Patents. To be eligible for an award, a commoner had to be living on the land and working it for his subsistence and he had to have filed a claim (Native Register) before February 15, 1848. Subsequently, two local residents came forward to verify the legitimacy of the claim and this testimony was recorded in English (Foreign Testimony) and in Hawaiian (Native Testimony). Then, if the claim was granted, the plot was surveyed and a Land Commission Award issued to the claimant who, upon the payment of surveyor and legal fees, was issued a Royal Patent giving him fee simple title.

The most valuable documentary source is the Land Commission Awards (LCA) which include relatively detailed, consistent, and quantitative information on local land use. In the descriptions of each section *(apana)* of an award *(kuleana)* are the surveyor's metes and bounds, the area of the section in acres, an outline sketch with adjacent land units identified, and a short description of land use. Other records provide valuable checks on accuracy and contain scattered social and economic information.

From these land records, it was possible to describe the approximate area devoted to each land use in an apana. Each apana is described as a unit by a set of native terms for land use. These native categories are made on three hierarchical levels of contrast. On the upper two levels, distinction is made by the presence or absence of characteristic features and overlap between categories is minimal. First, land is used for a residence (*pahale* or houselot) or for subsistence (*'aina* or agricultural land). Second, agricultural land is categorized on the presence or absence of irrigation. Nonirrigated land is *kula*. It may be cultivated, fallow, or grazed but there are no named subcategories. Irrigated lands are an unnamed inclusive category. Third, irrigated lands are divided into three overlapping categories: *loko* (fishpond), *loko kalo* (taro pond), and *lo'i* (pondfield). It is important to understand that fish were grown in pondfields and that taro was grown in fishponds. These last three native categories divided a continuum of relative importance of taro and fish production. The loko emphasizes fish production; the lo'i, taro; and the loko kalo is intermediate. Reflecting the fact that there were apparently no sharp definitional boundaries between these categories, a specific apana is often assigned alternatively to different categories in different documents.

An apana is characterized by one or more of these land use classifications. For the cases in which a single land use is listed for an apana, its total area is assigned to the appropiate use. If multiple land uses are listed, it is necessary to estimate the relative importance of each. This is done first by examining apana with single land uses. Because isolated pahale (houselots) averaged 0.32 acres (0.13 ha), for a multipurpose apana with pahale, that area was estimated as residential. Similarly, it was possible to estimate that apana with kula and with "some" kula represent, respectively, a 20% and 10% allocation to dryland farming. Using these calculations, the land area devoted to each land use was estimated.

The next step in analysis was the association of apana with irrigated land use into irrigation systems. In the original land division mapping, the apana were not located regionally on a base map or identified as to irrigation system. The regional mapping of apana was made around the turn of this century when private surveyors were hired to map the larger land holdings of the district, and this information was then incorporated in the county tax maps. Between initial granting and first regional mapping, some apana were "lost" (location unrecorded) and others mislocated. By careful attention to the original boundary descriptions, however, many of these errors and omissions could be corrected during this project. The result is a fairly comprehensive and accurate location of apana and land uses for 1850, based on the State of Hawaii Tax Maps for the district.[3]

From these maps, the outlines for the historic irrigation systems were reconstructed, despite the fact that, with the exception of Wainiha and Ha'ena, actual physical remains were highly fragmentary or nonexistent. After all apana used for irrigation agriculture were identified, these locations were visited during the general reconnaissance survey of the district and the apana locations were described according to topography and potential water source(s). Because the archaeological and ethnographic research had shown that there were several consistent patterns for Halelean irrigation systems, it was a fairly straightforward procedure to determine the probable layout of primary ditches and thus to associate the apana into irrigation systems.

For each irrigation system identified in the land records, information on the following physical and social characteristics was collected:
Source and length of ditch. The probable water source and length of primary ditch were estimated from topographic information collected during reconnaissance survey.
Net size. The net size of an irrigation system was calculated by summing the area of irrigated land granted to farmers within the system.
Gross size. The gross size of an irrigation system was estimated from the area of potential irrigated land within the system's perimeter (line enclosing all irrigated apana of the system).
Net number of farmers. The net number of farmers was the actual number of farmers receiving irrigated apana within a system.
Gross number of farmers. In many instances additional farmers who did not receive grants were mentioned in boundary descriptions. The gross number of farmers was calculated by adding these extra individuals to the actual grantees; this figure is often given as a range because it proved difficult to distinguish personal names from named land units.
Number of communities. The communities serviced by an irrigation system were determined by the number of ahupua'a territories included

---

[3]Although the documents on the 1850 land division yield detailed information on settlement pattern, there are several major weaknesses in the data. For reasons of either ignorance or restraint, many individuals did not file for land even though they were eligible. In one ahupua'a studied, there were no applications despite evidence of a sizeable population. There are also probably many inaccuracies due to poor surveying and recording. Most of the surveyors were foreigners who could have misunderstood the situation or have been purposefully misled. Finally, only the holdings of the commoners were recorded in detail. Lands in production for the chiefs or the crown were not described directly. Location of these lands can be determined only from boundary descriptions accompanying the commoners' grants and quantitative information is thus unavailable.

within a system's boundaries. In other words, were the apana of an irrigation system within one or more ahupua'a?

The following subsection describes the historic irrigation systems in Halelea according to these six basic characteristics. The apana associated with each system are listed in Table 7.2 and Maps 1 and 2 show the systems' locations. The summary data for all historic systems are presented in Table 7.3. These summary descriptions will be used to compare the Halelean irrigation systems with those from other societies.

Sources

The probable sources for all historic systems have been identified (cf. Earle 1973) and are classified here into four basic categories — main stream (M), side or tributary stream (S), small independent stream (I), and ground water (G). The type of source indicates the difficulty involved in water diversion. Main streams, with sizable water flow rates, require relatively large diversionary dams in comparison to the smaller tributary and independent streams. Ground water sources, including springs, require no head dams. For Halelea, the distribution of source types is as follows: main stream, 18; side stream, 6; independent stream, 12; and ground water, 6. In terms of percentage of gross irrigated agricultural area, the dominance of the main streams becomes clear: main streams, 70%; side streams, 6%; independent streams, 12%; and ground water, 12%.

TABLE 7.2

LIST OF LAND COURT AWARD NUMBERS FOR APANA ASSOCIATED WITH THE HISTORICAL SYSTEMS ANALYZED IN THE HALELEA DISTRICT

System	Number	LCA Numbers
Ha'ena	1	7949/5477:2; 7996; 7998; 8200C:1; 10674; 10941
	2	7943:1; 10223; 10940
	3	8200B:2; 8200C:3
	4	10940
	5	7946
	6	7942; 7949/5473:3; 9179
	7	7942; 7945
	8	10562:1; 10965
	9	8262; 9140; 10396
	10	7967:1

124 ORGANIZATION OF A COMPLEX CHIEFDOM

TABLE 7.2 (Continued)

System	Number	LCA Numbers
Wainiha	11	11069:1
	12	9170
	13	9801:1; 9802; 9803; 9804:1; 9805
	14	9171:2,3,4,5; 9169; 9796; 9798; 10329/3894; 10586:1; 11062; 10063
	15	9076; 9207; 9215; 9267; 10586:2; 11031:2; 11053:2
	16	9117; 9117B; 9184:1; 9266; 9268; 9269; 9270:1; 9271:1; 10334:1; 10697
Waipa	18	235N:2; 3917:4; 7918:1; 9832:1; 10661; 10663:1
	19	3781:1; 7918:3; 9118:1; 9277; 10171:2
	20	9832:2; 10076:1
	21	3781:3
Waioli	22	1001B:2; 3917/10305:2,3; 4025/9280:1,2,5; 8037; 8124:2; 8261; 9069; 9070:1; 9070B:2; 9079/3817:1; 9080:2; 9139:1; 9182:2; 9261:1,2,3; 9273:3,4,5; 9274; 9275:1,2,3; 9276:2; 9278:2; 9833B:1; 10074:2; 10096:2,3; 10308:1,4,5; 10315; 10316:1,3; 10317:1; 10564:1,2; 10593:1,2; 10594:2,3; 10915:1; 10956:1; 10959:2,3; 11059:2; 9072:2
	23	8196:1; 9070:2; 9072:3; 9081:1,2; 9152; 9833; 9833B:3; 10074:2; 10317:2; 10659; 10959:1
	24	7670; 8124:1; 8124B:2; 9136; 10309:1
Hanalei	22	4076:1; 4080:2; 8125:1,2; 8263/8268; 10081:1; 10325:1; 10676; 10691:1; 10955
	26	4076:3
	27	2660:2; 7944:2; 10954B:1
	28	3816/10648:1; 3819:2; 4073/9078:2,3,4; 4083/9137:1; 9279; 9284
	31	10328
	32	7671; 8224:1,3; 9956; 10720
Kalihikai	33	9129:1,2
	34	11253:1,2; 11254; 11255:1,2
	35	7585:2; 8266:3; 11245:2; 11247:2
	36	8266:1; 11244:1,2; 11246:2; 11248:2; 11249:2; 11250:3
Kalihiwai	38	8129; 9071:1; 9128:1; 9148:2; 9221:2; 9260:2; 9262; 9281; 9285:1; 10075; 10078:2; 10079; 10090:1; 10091:1; 10318:1; 10434:2; 10647:1; 10958:1
	39	10072
	40	9260:1; 9840:1; 11030:1
	41	10596
	42	8127:1; 10434:1
	43	11065
	44	9221:3

TABLE 7.3
SUMMARY OF DATA FOR THE
HISTORICAL IRRIGATION SYSTEMS IN HALELEA DISTRICT

	System Number	Type	Source	Length in Meters of Irrigation Ditch Total	Length in Meters of Irrigation Ditch Initial Segment	Area in Hectares of Irrigation System Net	Area in Hectares of Irrigation System Gross	Number of Farmers on Irrigation System Net	Number of Farmers on Irrigation System Gross
Ha'ena	1	B	M	480	275	4.11	7.39	6	10
	2	B	M	300	175	1.52	4.15	3	5
	3	-	G	0	0	0.41	0.41	2	2
	4	C	M	?	?	?	?	1	1
	5	A	M	?	?	0.16	0.16	1	3
	6	B	M	140	55	1.45	2.19	3	3
	7-9	B	MG	540	435	3.19	8.20	7	14
	10	A	I	120	35	0.72	0.72	1	1
Wainiha	11	A	S	?	?	0.50	0.50	1	1
	12	A	S	?	?	1.05	1.05	1	1
	13	C	M	420	50	2.54	4.49	5	5
	14	A	M	1725	435	4.26	9.35	8	13-19
	15	C	M	490	135	3.29	6.46	7	8
	16	A	M	1120	385	3.27	4.83	10	14-17
Waipa	18	B	M	1095	400	2.56	5.18	6	8
	19	B	M	875	745	1.80	1.80	5	9-10
	20	D	I	0	0	0.33	0.33	2	2
	21	-	G	0	0	0.36	0.36	1	1
Waioli	22*	B	M	905*	120	11.49	14.20	34	48-54
	23	A	S	315	105	3.63	3.63	11	14-17
	24	A	M	?	?	1.27	1.27	5	6
Hanalei	22*	B	M	695*	-	4.89	4.89	9	11-14
	25	-	G	0	0	-	2.62	-	-
	26	B	M	3745	190	0.69	0.69	1	6
	27	-	G	0	0	4.82	4.82	3	3
	28	?	?	?	?	2.76	2.76	6	8
	30	D	I	0	0	-	1.64	-	-
	31	B	I	25	25	0.31	0.31	1	1
	32	B	I	520	240	1.00	1.54	4	5-7
Kalihikai	33	A	I	160	80	0.32	0.32	1	3
	34	B	I	335	115	1.32	3.73	3	5
	35	B	I	300	120	0.93	1.32	4	8-10
	36	B	I	360	35	1.37	2.49	6	8-9
	37	B	I	155	70	0.12	0.12	2	2
Kalihiwai	38	A	M	565	15	4.98	7.48	18	23-31
	39	A	S	25	25	0.44	0.44	1	1
	40	A	M	415	235	1.32	1.32	3	5
	41	A	S	60	60	0.34	0.34	1	2
	42	A	S	135	135	0.52	0.52	2	3
	43	D	I	0	0	0.80	0.80	1	1
	44	A	I	85	85	0.37	0.37	1	1
Number				36	36	39	39	40	40
Mean				447	133	1.93	2.84	4.7	6.0

*System 22 listed in two parts but calculated as a single system. Ditch length for Hanalei 22 is additional to service that section.

Length of Ditch

Length of the primary and major secondary ditches was estimated for thirty-six historic irrigation systems (Table 7.3)[4]. The average length is 447 m with a range from 0 to 3745 m. Nine of these systems (3, 8, 9, 20, 21, 25, 27, 30, 43) functioned without ditches by tapping groundwater sources directly or by terracing across a valley as described for Type D systems (Chapter 6). Only five systems (14, 16, 18, 22, and 26) used ditches longer than 1 km; these systems contained 34% of the total gross irrigated are.

As discussed in Chapter 4, only the initial segment of ditch before the first major diversion is usually the responsibility of all farmers on the system. In Halelea, this initial section was usually short, averaging 133 m with a range from 0 to 745 m. Only five systems (7, 14, 16, 18, 19) had an initial length of more than 300 m.

In terms of actual maintenance responsibilities associated with these ditches, the length of ditching per farmer can be calculated by dividing the ditch measurements by the minimum gross estimate for farmers on a given system. For the total length of major ditches,[4] there is a mean of 66 m per farmer with a range of 0 to 137 m. For the initial section only, the mean is 20 m per farmer (range, 0-85 m). The ethnographic research (cf. Chapter 5) indicates that a ditch required about 0.1 man-hours per meter per year. The labor investment per farmer on the historic systems would thus have been on the order of 6.6 hours per year for all ditches and two hours per year for the initial segment.

As discussed with respect to potential conflict, the pattern of ditch branching defines points of likely disputes (cf. Chapter 4). In thirty-seven of the forty-two historic irrigation systems, potential conflict was minimized by a simple ditch network lacking major branches. The primary ditch conveyed water the full length of the agricultural system and gave farmers direct access to this water. Direct access to the primary ditch was guaranteed by the layout of individual land holdings within a system. For example, the primary ditch of a Type A system runs along the lower slopes of a flanking ridge. The apana were positioned below the ditch line, extending from the ditch down to the stream. Similarly, in Type C systems, apana were laid out perpendicular to the ditch, either across the ditch or between the ditch and the bordering stream. In Type B systems, the upper apana were arranged as in Type A systems; after the ditch of a Type B system entered the coastal plain, apana straddled the ditch or were located to either side.

---

[4]Systems 25 and 30 not included.

Major secondary ditches, servicing more than a single farmer, were only necessary where the distance across an alluvial flat was longer than about 200 m. This was the case for larger Type A (Systems 23 and 38) and Type B (Systems 1, 22, and 26) systems. Only System 22 appears to have had more than one major branching. In general, major secondary ditches were relatively infrequent in historic irrigation systems.

Net and Gross Area of an Irrigation System

Historically, the irrigation systems in Halelea were for the most part small in size. From the irrigated lands actually granted, the mean net area of these systems was calculated to be 1.93 ha (range, 0.1-16.38 ha).[5] Only System 22 had land grants totaling more than 5 ha in area; sixteen systems had less than 1 ha in irrigated land grants. The gross area of possible irrigated lands within these systems was somewhat higher — mean, 2.84 ha (range, 0.12-19.09 ha).

Net and Gross Number of Farmers on an Irrigation System

A typical Halelean irrigation system was used cooperatively by only a limited number of farmers. The mean number of farmers receiving grants within an irrigation system was 4.7 (range 1-43). Four systems (16, 22, 23, and 38) were used by ten or more farmers receiving grants; while the farm lands in thirteen of the systems were granted to single farmers. The mean number of total farmers using the irrigation systems was six (range, 1-64).

Number of Communities

The historic irrigation systems of Halelea were virtually all community level projects. Because the territorial communities (ahupua'a) were usually physically isolated from each other by ridges, a given ditch network serviced the agricultural lands of a single community.

There was only one case where a ditch network crossed an ahupua'a boundary; historically, System 22 serviced lands within the two ahupua'a of Waioli and Hanalei. This exceptional case, however, may not represent an aboriginal condition, because there already had been severe economic disruption in this area by 1850. In 1842, a major portion of the alluvial bottom land of Hanalei was leased to a foreigner, J. Bernard, as a coffee plantation. Although the lease specifically excluded

---

[5]The two fishponds (Systems 25 and 30) which were not granted as kuleana have been eliminated from these calculations. Also, because the area of System 4 could not be estimated, it too was not used in the calculations.

the taro patches, Bernard proceeded systematically to destroy the taro fields and to evict the Hawaiian farmers (Land Commission Foreign Testimony Vol. 1:54-55). At this time several dispossessed farmers received land in Waioli systems, and it seems probable that System 22 was expanded into Hanalei at this time. As described in Chapter 3, Waioli and Hanalei shared access to a large alluvial plain which was partitioned more or less arbitrarily between the two ahupua'a. The extension of System 22, therefore, was technologically a simple matter. By 1850, the community distinction between Hanalei and Waioli was blurred as indicated by individuals receiving apana in both ahupua'a. Of the thirteen cases of inter-ahupua'a kuleana, eleven were between Hanalei and Waioli.

Evidence, therefore, clearly indicates that irrigation systems were historically contained within the jurisdiction of a single community. This restriction would have minimized the potential managerial difficulties involved in the irrigation systems.

CROSS-CULTURAL COMPARISONS

Cross-cultural comparison of irrigation-based societies is hampered by a paucity of detailed ethnographic descriptions of the physical characteristics of irrigation systems and the social organization of their operation (cf. Hunt and Hunt 1974). The lack of this comparable material precludes any thorough evaluation of the hydraulic theory which would require, for adequate testing, quantitative data on both technological and social variables. Suggestive material is, however, available in several good ethnographic accounts of societies practicing irrigation agriculture. It is the purpose of this present section to compare the Hawaiian data with societies using similar irrigation technologies.

For this analysis, a pragmatic three-part typology will be used: (1) interregional systems; (2) regional, intervillage systems; and (3) local, village systems (cf. Wolf and Palerm 1955). This typology is based on two interrelated variables, size of system and number of dependent sociopolitical units. An *interregional system* is typically a massive complex of interconnecting canals which service communities in politically differentiated regions. These megasystems are common in many modern states and they were characteristic of the ancient civilizations of Egypt, Mesopotamia, and China. The *regional, intervillage system* is more modest in scale and services several communities within a single political region. There are excellent discussions of such multivillage systems for peasant societies in Mesoamerica (Millon, Hall, and Diaz 1961; Lees 1973), Japan (Eyre 1955; Beardsley, Hall and Ward 1959), Indonesia (Geertz 1959, 1963, 1972), and elsewhere. The *local village irrigation system* is restricted to a single community, and it often services only a portion of that community's farmers. Frequently a community may control a number of irrigation systems with separate water sources.

The historic irrigation systems of Halelea may clearly be classified as local village irrigation. With the exception of System 22, all irrigation networks were contained within the boundaries of a single ahupua'a community. The scale of the Hawaiian systems in terms of irrigated area, length of ditch, and number of farmers is also consistent with this last category. The historic Halelean systems will now be compared to the irrigation systems from four well documented societies which also use village level irrigation. These examples are the Sonjo, Tanganyika (Gray 1963 and personal communication), the Ifugao, Philippines (Barton 1919, 1922; Conklin 1967, 1972, 1974), Moala, Fiji (Sahlins 1962), and Pul Eliya, Sri Lanka (Leach 1959, 1961). I first compare the physical irrigation systems from the five societies to document the similarities in scale and complexity; then I analyze the social organization of production, the specialization of management, and the centralization of authority. If these social variables are determined by the technological characteristics of irrigation agriculture, similarities in the irrigation systems should result in similarities in the social organization.

The Irrigation Systems

Halelea

The dominant sources of irrigation systems were the main streams, but smaller streams and springs were also important. In all but one case, both sources and ditches serve single ahupua'a communities. The average length of primary ditches was 447 m, with a maximum length of 3745 m. A community controlled multiple sources but the main streams of the ahupua'a predominate. The gross size of the irrigation systems averaged 2.8 ha with a maximum of 19 ha. The number of farmers averaged six with a maximum of sixty-four.

Sonjo

For irrigation at the community of Kheri (Gray 1963:49), the dominant source is a stream with additional water provided by three springs. Irrigation ditches are used exclusively by a single community and they vary in length from very short to about one mile (1.6 km) (Gray: personal communication). The Kheri community uses three irrigation systems all on the same stream – spring source but no estimate of area is given. The village size varies from 120-300 houses (Kheri, about 180) which is an approximate measure of the number of farming units.

Ifugao

The preponderance of pondfield areas are watered directly from springs, but ditches also tap the local streams (Conklin 1972). In the twelve complete "agricultural districts" mapped from aerial imagery (Conklin 1972, 1974), approximately fifty-six "major ditches" are recorded but only ten are longer than 400 m. Most ditches are contained within the boundaries of an "agricultural district," but four ditches cross district boundaries. The longest ditch complex services three districts (Kinnākin, Pu'itan, and Bagnina) and consisted of approximately 8 km of primary and secondary canals. Within a district, the reliance on spring water appears to give a very high source diversity. Since a pondfield area may be fed both by a major ditch and numerous springs (Conklin 1974), it is impossible to isolate separate hydrologic systems. No size data for systems are available. Although number of farmers per system is also unavailable, the Conklin (1972) maps record roughly an average 200 (range about 50-650) structures per district. The structures, both houses and granaries, are clusters in multiple hamlets scattered through the district.

Moala

On Moala, Fiji, irrigation farming is of secondary importance to dryland cultivation of yams, and the irrigation technology used is "rudimentary and limited in scale" (Sahlins 1962:43). Sahlins describes two contrasting patterns of irrigation, using as examples the villages of Nuku and Keteira. At Nuku, three separate irrigation systems tap a single stream source (Sahlins 1962:Diagram 2). The largest of these irrigation systems is described as consisting of a stone percolation dam (8 ft long by 2-3 ft wide by 5 ft deep; 244 x 61-91 x 152 cm), an unlined primary ditch (1 ft wide by 2 ft deep; 30 x 61 cm), and a secondary ditch leading water among the fields of nine farmers (all of a single named kin group). The irrigation complex as a whole was not mapped but "it is of the magnitude of a few hundred yards in length and about the same width [perhaps 5 ha]. Not all of this is cultivated" (Sahlins 1962:44). At Keteira, six springs and a small stream are used to irrigate the farm plots of nine farmers. Dams are not used and ditches are said to be unnecessary except to circulate water among the various fields. As in the Ifugao system, the multiplicity of small sources makes it impossible to identify separate irrigation systems. From the diagram (Sahlins 1962:Map 3), it appears that the bottom lands of four small valleys have been converted to low agricultural fields. For both Nuku and Keteira, the irrigation systems are restricted entirely to the village. In 1954-1955, Sahlins (1962:67) estimates the population of these villages to be 66 and 115 respectively.

Pul Eliya

For the Nuvarakalāviya district, Leach states that there are two categories of irrigation systems — "the small reservoirs (tanks) associated with individual villages and the very much larger central reservoirs and feeder canals which now, as formerly, are under the control of the central government" (1961:17). Pul Eliya and its neighboring villages depend entirely on the village level tanks. In an aerial photograph of the environs of Pul Eliya, thirteen tanks are identified. These tanks are owned variously by the central government, by the temples, and by individuals. The map of Pul Eliya irrigated fields (Leach 1961:44) shows four tanks owned by the government (Main Tank and Kumbukwewa Tank), the temple (Temple Tank), and presumably a private individual (Kana-hiti-yawa). The canals from these tanks form an intertwined pattern of irrigation systems but water from the main tank is clearly dominant. From all tanks, there are about 9.8 km of primary and secondary ditches which irrigate Pul Eliya's agricultural area (about 58 ha). Since the land lies directly below the tanks, the initial section of ditching is short and most ditches are used to distribute water among farm plots. All farmers have direct access to a section of a primary or secondary ditch and this, theoretically, insures equal division of water within a section. There is an elaborate pattern of ditch junctioning in which wooden weirs with traditionally established dimensions are used for water division (cf. Leach 1961:161-64). In Pul Eliya, there are thirty-nine family heads representing approximately the same number of farming units on the irrigation complex.

Conclusions

Although there are certain specific and possibly meaningful differences between the irrigation technologies of these five societies, they all may be classified unambiguously as local, village irrigation. The predominance of irrigation systems are contained within the community boundary. The systems are relatively small in terms of ditch length, irrigation area, and number of farmers. In addition, most communities utilize multiple sources which they control exclusively.

Social Organization

Sonjo (Gray 1963)

The Sonjo were basically a segmental society composed of small, politically autonomous villages when they were described by Gray. *Within* the community, a stratified social structure defined an elite *wenamiji* who, as a group, controlled access to irrigation water. They had prior claim to water and acted as patrons to others in the village requiring water. They were true managers, discussing operations of the irrigation systems in meetings, allocating positions in water schedules, and calling out group labor for cleaning and repairs. This "council of ruling elders" settled disputes involving both water and other village matters.

> These elders are believed to understand the irrigation system better than other people, and thus to be best qualified to control and regulate water. They were also regarded as the guardians of sacred tradition. Thus the welfare of the village and its very existence is thought to depend on them, not in the sense that there is a mystical bond between the *wenamiji* and the village, but because the irrigation system would collapse in chaos if it were not strictly regulated and if the proper relations between the village and supernatural powers were not maintained through proper ritual. [Gray 1963:143]

Village labor, consisting of all able-bodied males except smiths, was called out yearly to clean and to repair the ditches and dikes after the rainy season (Gray 1963:55). Additional corvée labor was called out only in the case of severe damage by a later storm.

Ifugao [6]

The Ifugao were highly decentralized and politically acephalous. Social relationships were determined largely by kindred networks. Amity – enmity relations were determined by social distance, and war-

---
[6] Description is of traditional Ifugao social organization as described by Barton (1919, 1922).

fare between valleys was endemic. However, there was a defined social stratification based on wealth. The elites' *(kadangyany)* wealth depended largely on the irrigated rice lands which were privately owned. Rights to water were also privately owned and could be sold. The construction or maintenance of an irrigation ditch was, therefore, not a community affair but involved the individual allocation of capital by the owner(s). Since rice was the traditional medium of exchange, irrigated rice production generated capital which was then reapplied to extending an individual's production capacity by hiring labor to construct terraces and ditches. Management was not a political matter, but a matter of individual investment and profit oriented production.

Moala (Sahlins 1962)

Before Moala was incorporated into the Tongan state and later the British Empire, it was composed of primarily village level chiefdoms. Each village was traditionally composed of various kin based corporate groups which were ranked with respect to each other. The highest ranking individual of the dominant group was the principle village chief *(Tui)*. This chief held a general leadership role with respect to the village and he was responsible for convening the village council, for maintaining public peace, and for organizing village labor. The Tui held no special responsibilities in the irrigation systems and in fact his role in irrigation was very limited. The irrigation systems were owned by an individual corporate kin group which was often not that of the chief. In this situation, the chief had no explicit managerial functions, for it was the "owners of the water" who were responsible for "equitable flow" to all farmers (Sahlins 1962:284). The chief handled cooperative labor for the construction of new fields and he settled public disputes over water, but both of these responsibilities were minor and handled similarly to other cooperative activities and village disputes. Although the chief was involved in the operation of irrigation, this was merely one aspect of his generalized leadership responsibilities for village matters.

Sahlins notes a significant difference in the distribution of land holdings in irrigation systems. At Nuku where irrigation was based on canal irrigation from a single stream, holdings were distributed with respect to the dual principles of ownership and rank. As Sahlins states, "these diversion structures [dams and ditches] literally open the possibility of inequitable water distribution and demand, therefore, social regulation of access to land and water . . ." (1962:286). In contrast, at Keteira where a number of separate springs formed multiple, diverse sources, there was no such defined structure of land holdings.

Pul Eliya (Leach 1961)

During Leach's fieldwork in 1954, Pul Eliya was an agricultural village in the North Central Province of the British colony of Ceylon. Governmental authority in the village rested in the Vel Vidāne (irrigation headman) who was elected by the village but who reported to higher level bureaucrats on agricultural and legal matters. Internally, the Vel Vidāne's major responsibilities were related to irrigation. He was responsible both to his village and to his government for the equitable division of water from the main government owned tank. As Leach noted, "operation of the sluice [used to divide water between different ditches] is an exclusive prerogative of the Vel Vidāne personally" (1961:64). Leach, however, emphasizes that this division was largely determined by traditional rules unalterable by the Vel Vidāne (Leach 1961:164-65). The Vel Vidāne was also responsible for compiling a list of the irrigated area held by each farmer. This list was then used by higher level bureaucrats to assess corvée responsibilities on the main tank. The colonial government retained a strong control over irrigation affairs through its ownership of the water source, and it took responsibilities for repair to the tank and for equitable distribution of water.

In his evaluation of Wittfogel's theory, Leach (1959, 1961) emphasizes that the day-by-day operation of the irrigation system depended on established tradition more than centralized decision making. Although this is apparently true, the overarching state authority was still critical. It established many operational rules and its regional courts were used indirectly to settle intravillage disputes (Leach 1961:70-71,165-66). Irrigation was also an important aspect in retaining wealth stratification within the village. Although the Vel Vidāne was compelled by traditional division of water within established irrigated areas, when *new areas* were opened up, the Vel Vidāne, as representative of the most powerful and wealthy kin group, was in a position to enhance this differentiation.

> Compound groups A_1, A_2, B_1 and Dx acquired all the wealth and influence, while compound groups C and D_2 came to form an opposition faction which contained most of the genuine poor peasants in the community. It is remarkable that down to 1954, *despite the supposed purposes of the Land Development Ordinance*, not a single member of the underprivileged opposition had succeeded in getting a title to *badu* [newly irrigated] land.
>
> The basic reason for this was not official corruption or inefficiency, but the more elementary fact that it was the Vel Vidāne's faction which controlled all the main irrigation channels. In these circumstances it was a waste of time for the opposition even to apply for land. [Leach 1961:230]

This situation was only alleviated by direct governmental intervention to renovate an abandoned tank for use by the "underprivileged families" (Leach 1961:230).

Conclusions

Two conclusions may be reached from this brief comparison of societies relying on village-level irrigation systems. First, there is a full range of variability in types of political organization represented. These four societies represent everything from politically acephalous tribes like the Ifugao or Sonjo, to the village chiefdoms of Moala, to the state dominated village of Pul Eliya. In all cases, specific managerial roles seem largely unrelated to the technical requirements of irrigation; rather, these roles are largely determined by the greater social context of the community. This is similar to Lees' conclusions:

> the range of variations [in societies practicing "small-scale" irrigation] is extremely wide, and the source of variation lies in the fact that the organization of water control in each case is embedded in the larger social setting. [1973:119]

The simple fact that societies (Sonjo, Ifugao, and to a lesser extent Moala), practicing irrigation comparable to Halelea's irrigation exist effectively without a regionally centralized managerial apparatus is sufficient to reject the more simplified versions of Wittfogel's hypothesis as related to Halelea. Second, however, all four societies show at least incipient tendencies towards *social stratification of wealth* apart from any specific political structure. This latter point seems critical and I will return to it in Chapter 9. Basically, irrigation as a capital investment and as a structured access to a strategic resource is a major cause of social differentiation in society. The concept of irrigation's inherent possibilities for inequality of access to water has been discussed by Sahlins (1962) and Lees (1973). The importance of capital investment in irrigation is, however, less well discussed despite the fact that it seems essential to understanding the importance of irrigation in social evolution.

THE SIGNIFICANCE OF IRRIGATION IN HAWAII

As suggested by Wittfogel, the complexity and scale of an irrigation system should determine the requirements for management and, in turn, the development of centralized organization. Five basic aspects of irrigation — construction, maintenance, dispute settlement, natural disasters, and warfare — were set forward in Chapter 4 as possibly requiring centralized management. In this section, these five aspects are evaluated to see if the scale or complexity of traditional Hawaiian irrigation was sufficient to cause political centralization. This evaluation is only preliminary because it is impossible to test rigorously the theory without more detailed, comparable data from other societies. The results, however, strongly suggest that the complexity and scale of irrigation were not the critical factors in the evolution of a politically centralized organization in Hawaii.

Construction and Maintenance of Irrigation Systems

There is no evidence that managers were required for either the construction or maintenance of irrigation systems in Halelea. Irrigation features such as dams, ditches, and pondfields were relatively small in size and appear to have been built gradually by extending the irrigation ditch and increasing the size of pondfields (Chapter 6). Maintenance tasks were also minimized by the short length of irrigation ditches and their self-maintenance (cf. Chapter 5). Why then in the absence of required management were konohiki involved in directing construction and maintenance of tasks?

It is possible to argue that management, although not strictly necessary, may still be able to increase the efficiency of group labor. On this assumption, a local population would accept, if not encourage, such management if a centralized political organization already existed. This argument, however, seems inapplicable to Halelea. The increase in efficiency made possible by management would still be related to the size of group labor required and the probable small size of labor crews in Halelea would have minimized the significance of management. Rather, as discussed in Chapter 8, there is some evidence that small kin-based groups were localized on irrigation systems and that such groups would easily have provided the necessary organization for construction/maintenance activities.

Indication of the relatively minor significance of the konohiki in irrigation is also found in the nineteenth century court cases.[7] As I discuss in Chapter 8, the primary function of the konohiki involved the granting of land and water rights in return for corvée labor. Therefore, with the granting of land in fee simple to the commoners, this function was nullified when the system of konohikiship was abandoned. The court cases describe the management of these systems after the

[7] The data on nineteenth century Hawaiian court cases were collected by Jocelyn Linnekin, a student working under Dr. Marshall Sahlins. I gratefully acknowledge their assistance in allowing me full use of this valuable material.

konohiki were removed. As expressed by the farmer Olelo, "Everybody now that he has a kuleana [land grant] of his own is a konohiki" (Sherman Peck et al. vs. Edward Bailey 1866-1867). Associations of farmers on an irrigation system were formed to replace the managerial role.

> Kaamu swears: The Kuleana system commenced, and at that time the authority of the tax collector and also the authority of the konohiki were over. They had no luna [overseer], and were in pilikia [difficulty], so they joined together to keep the ditch in repair. They made the association. There were certain laws made for the regular distribution of water for the different lands. I was the scribe and I also have charge of the book. All the people interested in the ditch went to Kuehelani [tax collector, last government official responsible for water division], and he called together all the people. They consulted with each other what they should do, and they chose a committee of three to frame a law. Then they had another meeting. The law was read to the assembly, that their work was to repair the dam and run the water into the ditch. They were under the committee they themselves had chosen. [Names committee.] They had two duties . . . to distribute water and also to call on the people to come and repair the ditch or clear it out. [Sherman Peck et al. vs. Edward Bailey 1866-1867]

Apparently, the local economy was able to adapt rapidly from the original condition of close supervision by an appointee of the regional sociopolitical system to a local, democratic system of controls based on committee-directed irrigation associations. There is good evidence that this committee functioned effectively as a replacement for the konohiki (cf. Willfong et al. vs. William H. Bailey et al. 1873).

Allocation of Water and Settlement of Disputes

There is little evidence that disputes over water allocation were either common or severe in traditional Hawaiian irrigation. The restricted number of farmers on the Halelean irrigation systems and their containment within community boundaries would have minimized the likelihood of severe disputes. In addition, the simplicity of irrigation patterns (few major diversion points) and the diversity of water sources would also have combined to mitigate conflict situations.

Important for determining the probability of conflict would also have been the relative abundance of water. In Halelea, water would seldom have been a limiting factor because of the restricted extent of irrigation and because of the high year around rainfall. This point is clearly substantiated by the dramatic extension of irrigation for Chinese rice cultivation.

For the drier leeward coasts, however, this constant sufficiency of water is less clear. In various court cases, traditional systems of water allocation by quantity and time (day/night) are described for Wailuku,

Maui (Sherman Peck et al. vs. Edward Bailey 1866-1867; Willfong et al. vs. William H. Bailey et al. 1873), for Waikiki, Oahu (Liliuokalani et al. vs. Pang Sam et al. 1884), and for Palolo, Oahu (Loo Chit Sam et al. vs. Wong Kim 1884). These locations are on the leeward coasts and thus are susceptible to seasonal and long-term droughts. The testimony makes clear that allocation of water was necessary only during dry periods. For example, "Kapa swears: No division of water during the wet weather, only division during the dry weather" (Loo Chit Sam et al. vs. Wong Kim 1884). During dry periods, the scarcity of water could easily have resulted in disputes.

> Pupule swears: In wet seasons there used to be no trouble, but there was in dry times, when they used to steal from one another. [Liliuokalani et al. vs. Pang Sam et al. 1883]

After the abandonment of the konohiki system, water allocation and dispute settlement were taken over by the local irrigation associations. In the testimony by Kaumu quoted earlier, the first duty of the association's council was said to be the distribution of water. In later testimony, Kaumu described the situation as follows:

> Kaumu swears: All the landholders used to meet every year on the 4th of July, and any matter of dispute was arranged . . . [Willfong et al. vs. William H. Bailey 1873]

At present, it is difficult to evaluate the probable significance of water allocation and dispute settlement by the konohiki. The ability of these roles to be transferred to local associations would appear to deemphasize the significance or at least irreplaceability of the konohiki. The issue of water scarcity, however, is poorly understood. The dramatic decrease in population after 1778 would certainly have reduced water requirements for subsistence production of taro. Counteracting this trend would have been a considerable increase in the use of water to irrigate cash crops. The profit oriented production of sugar cane by the Hawaiian elites and foreigners began early in the nineteenth century. An increased competition between subsistence crops and cash crops is mentioned in the court cases; for example one case described the day use of water for the Wailuku sugar cane plantation and night use for the Hawaiian farmers (Willfong et al. vs. William H. Bailey 1873). How the nineteenth century water conditions described in the court cases relate to aboriginal conditions is simply not well understood.

Reconstruction of Irrigation Systems Following Natural and Social Disasters

Despite the oft-repeated image of Hawaii as a tropical paradise of abundance, famines are recorded frequently in the historic and traditional documents. Famines were the result of a failure in subsistence production following some natural disasters such as flooding, tidal waves, droughts, or eruptions and social disasters such as warfare or unusual corvée requirements (cf. Cordy 1972). For Halelea, the most frequent and fearsome disasters are winter storm flooding and tidal waves.

During the winter months, rain is unusually heavy and regularly results in some flooding and damage to the irrigation systems and taro fields. For percolation dams, farmers each winter expect damage requiring frequent repairs. Examples of such frequent destruction are common in the nineteenth century court cases for other areas:

> Maiau swears: The old dam was made of sods and stones and water ran through [typical percolation dam]. When there is a freshet, in times of high water, the dam was of no consequence. The water would break it up, and we would have to rebuild the dam after every freshet.
> Rev. William Alexander swears: Heavy rains make sudden freshets . . . It washes away the heads. The Kamaauai head has been washed away every winter since I have been here. [Sherman Peck et al. vs. Edward Bailey 1867-1868]

Traditionally, the repairs to both dams and ditches were directed by the konohiki but as discussed earlier these duties were shifted over to locally based associations after the division of land among the commoners. Apparently, these repairs were never so extensive as to require labor outside of those immediately involved:

> Kaumu swears: Every year they had troubles of freshets. All those who owned land adjacent to the watercourse assisted in repairing the dam on those occasions. [Sherman Peck et al. vs. Edward Bailey 1867-1868]

Kaamu, in later testimony, tells how he as "secretary of the water association" at Wailuku would determine when repairs were necessary and then organize the work crew for the job (Willfong et al. vs. William H. Bailey 1873). It therefore seems clear that such frequent, restricted damage could easily be handled on a local basis.

Although less frequent, more extensive damage was caused by major floods and tidal waves. In Chapter 5, I described modern examples of these disasters for particular valleys in Halelea. Historically, extensive flooding is described for the Hanalei Valley, Halelea (Johnson 1844) and the record of tidal wave damage is chronicled for all the islands by Pararas-Carayannis (1969). Although not common, these disasters occur frequently enough (perhaps every twenty to one-hundred years per community) to present a definite emergency situation to which the community economy must be adapted.

Production in irrigation based districts like Halelea is particularly susceptible to such disasters because a heavy predominance of agricultural production is concentrated in the low alluvial zone near the sea. In addition to the direct destruction of capital improvements, the staggered cycle of taro production would have been badly disrupted and would have taken over a year to be reestablished fully. During this reconstruction period, the community would have needed to shift to an alternative food source. The most direct response would have been to increase fishing, and agricultural production of quickly maturing species (like sweet potato), and the collection of wild and feral "famine" foods (cf. Chapter 8). It seems unlikely, however, that simple shifts in strategy would have been sufficient compensation for the loss in taro production.

A social response to such emergency situations would probably have been necessary. In segmental societies, regional networks are utilized in these situations (cf. Dalton 1977), but, in Hawaii, community endogamy would have greatly restricted this kindred network. Historically, a famine in Hanalei, probably resulting from flooding, forced local farmers to purchase taro from the neighboring valleys of Lumahai and Wainiha (Johnson 1844); however, the lack of primitive money (aboriginally) would have restricted this option. It seems likely that the community would in these situations have been dependent on the regional redistribution structure for support (cf. Chapter 9).

Disasters of similar magnitude also afflicted dryland agricultural districts. These disasters consisted primarily of droughts on the leeward coasts like Ka'u, Hawaii (Handy and Pukui 1972[1958]:239) and volcanic eruptions on Hawaii (Handy and Handy 1972:274).

Man-made disasters are also frequently mentioned in the historical accounts. For our consideration of irrigation, destruction during warfare is particularly important. Because of the vulnerability of the irrigation systems to purposeful devastation aimed at ruining a chiefdom's productive capacities, they were often the target of interchiefdom warfare. Broughton (1804:37) describes in detail the devastation of Lahaina, Maui by the invading forces of Kamehameha. Such disruption of subsistence production eliminated an effective base for resistance or rebellion. As discussed in Chapter 4, the vulnerability of irrigation systems might well have increased the dependence of local populations on a regional sociopolitical organization.

CONCLUSIONS

This chapter culminates a three-part analysis of the data sources — ethnographic, archaeological, and historic — on Hawaiian irrigation. The one conclusion which is prevalent in this analysis is that Hawaiian irrigation was small in scale and would not have required management by a regional bureaucratic structure.

Particularly in terms of construction and maintenance activities, Hawaiian irrigation systems were designed to minimize the size of requisite labor crews. The allocation of water and the settlement of disputes seem hardly a pressing reason for regional centralization, although this relationship deserves closer attention. Only major disasters offer a compelling reason for a regional organization, and community exogamy would seem as logical a solution as a political centralized superstructure.

What was it, therefore, which lay behind the evolution of regionally centralized organization and the direct involvement of this organizational superstructure in local production? In the next chapter, two additional theories will be examined and rejected.

Another point (that I will return to in Chapter 9) is that the understanding of management, in general, and the role of the konohiki, in specific, requires an evaluation of the managerial function from a somewhat different perspective. Who are the most direct beneficiaries of the managerial activities? For whom do the managers work? The konohiki were representatives of the chiefs. Their main role was specifically to mobilize and to direct labor in productive activities so as to maximize the income flow of the elites. Irrigation takes on a very different significance in this light. *Regardless of scale,* irrigation is potentially significant because of its seemingly limitless potential for intensification (cf. Geertz 1963). Two possible relationships between irrigation and management are thus suggested. First, the technical complexity of irrigation may require management. For Hawaii, we can reject this because of the technological simplicity of the systems. The second relationship is more involved as it is part of a highly interdependent set of social, economic, and political components. As I shall argue in Chapter 9, irrigation as an opportunity for capital investment was central to the evolution of Hawaiian chiefdoms.

CHAPTER VIII

THE HAWAIIAN COMMUNITY

The principal aim of this monograph is to evaluate three theories which purport to explain the evolution of centralized sociopolitical organization. In previous chapters, the scale and complexity of irrigation technology has been rejected as a major factor in the development of social complexity in Hawaii. This chapter now examines two alternate theories concerning (1) redistribution (Service 1962, 1975) and (2) warfare (Carneiro 1970). These theories stress basic ecological relationships of a local community, namely the specialization of community economies and the scarcity of strategic resources. Central to these theories are assumptions concerning the organization of the local community. This chapter begins with a lengthy discussion of the ahupua'a communities of Halelea, which were organized at the three inclusive levels of the household, the interhousehold association, and the community. At each level, the organizational arrangements and their economic functions are described, and the articulation between the local community and the regional superstructure is indicated. The lack of economic interdependence was pronounced at both the household and the community levels. The specific economic/ecological factors of environmentally determined specialization and resource competition were not well documented and are rejected as adequate explanation for Hawaii's evolutionary development.

SOCIAL AND ECONOMIC ORGANIZATION OF
THE HALELEAN COMMUNITIES

Previous anthropological research has offered two interpretations of the social organization of traditional Hawaiian communities. Initially, Handy and Pukui (1972 [1958]) presented the *'ohana* model in which several extended families within an ahupua'a integrate economically specialized households into separate self-sufficient productive units. Sahlins (1973) argues that the 'ohana model is not applicable because households within an ahupua'a were related by multiple, overlapping kindred networks without formal structure. In the following discussion, the social organization and economic implications of these alternative formulations are outlined and evaluated with the historic data from Halelea.

The traditional historians such as Malo and Kamakau do not describe in any detail the social organization of Hawaiian commoners. Malo (1951 [1898]:66) implies that the basic social unit among commoners was the conjugal pair with their natural and adopted children and that this nuclear family was the basic economic unit, structured on a sharp division of labor by sex. As noted by Kamakau (ms.:172-73), the extent of a commoner's kindred was restricted by the shallowness of his genealogies (cf. Chapter 2).

Relying on ethnographic reconstruction from data collected in the twentieth century, Handy and Pukui (1972 [1958]) present a detailed description of commoner social organization for Ka'u, Hawaii. Their work emphasizes the importance of the 'ohana which was composed of "relatives by blood, marriage and adoption, living some inland and some near the sea but concentrated geographically in . . . a particular location . . . " (Handy and Pukui 1972 [1958]:2). The 'ohana is said to have consisted of several related households *(hale)* which were ranked with respect to each other in a manner similar to the organization of lineages elsewhere in Polynesia. The 'ohana is thought to have been associated with a subdivision of the ahupua'a called the *'ili*. Because 'ili crosscut the environmental zones of an ahupua'a, this would have permitted the 'ohana to encompass economically specialized households exploiting the different resource zones (cf. Earle 1977). The head of the 'ohana is said to have been the *haku,* theoretically the eldest male of the senior line who filled various leadership roles in economic and social activities.

Sahlins (1973) disputes Handy and Pukui's understanding of Hawaiian social organization. In his archival research on the Oahu land records, he found no mention of "any corporate, genealogically ordered local groups" (Sahlins 1973:13) as implied by the 'ohana model. (This lack of named, kin-based groups is in sharp contrast to similar land records studied by Sahlins [1962] in Fiji.) Sahlins (1973:13) points out that 'ili were not apparently associated with 'ohana or other kin groups because an individual grantee often claimed rights in two or more 'ili. In fact, he argues that land rights were not determined on genealogical principles but were simply use rights allocated by the konohiki. Sahlins (1973:14) concludes that 'ohana were not groups per se, but kindred networks. Because of "intense local endogamy prevailing within the ahupua'a land division and among adjacent ahupua'a" (Sahlins 1973:15), a community would have consisted of a complex set of overlapping 'ohana networks rather than several well defined kin groups.

Sahlins (1973:14-15) argues that this commoner social structure was a result of pressure from the elites. First, the maintenance of genealogies was forbidden to the commoners because "the chieftainship would not tolerate an indigenous [commoner based] conception of rank in its face, nor a notion of lineage that would give local groups a solidarity and interest apart from their obligation to the chief" (Sahlins 1973:14). Second, local endogamy was favored by the konohiki as a means of retaining the labor pool of the ahupua'a. The konohiki, responsible for production quotas, would have attempted always to maintain or expand his labor force.

The two models (Handy and Pukui vs. Sahlins) have somewhat distinct economic implications. The more structured organization envisioned by Handy and Pukui is well suited to integrate economically specialized households into self-sufficient productive units. Alternatively, the more informal organization suggested by Sahlins is highly adaptable to numerous political and economic conditions, and there is a greater independence between households. As argued elsewhere (Earle 1977), these two models are not necessarily contradictory; rather, they appear as different organizational responses to contrasting ecological conditions. The extended family ('ohana) model was described for the dryland farming areas of Ka'u where there is a marked spatial separation between resource zones. In contrast, Sahlins' model was formulated for the irrigated farming areas of Oahu where economic resources were concentrated and any need for a structured, extended family would have been minimized. In sum, it seems probable that there may have been variability in Hawaiian interhousehold organization reflecting different organizational requirements.

As will be discussed later, the resources in Halelea were highly concentrated within a few kilometers of the sea. In this context, households were largely independent of each other economically but dependent on the chiefs through the system of land tenure which allocated use rights from the konohiki as representative of the local chief. In the nineteenth century land records, an individual's rights to land were established by an initial claim and then by supporting testimony from other witnesses (cf. Chapter 7). For any specific claim, a witness recited the chain of title resulting in the claimant's purported rights to a piece of land. These rights were based on an initial allocation of the land to some individual, usually within the last twenty years, and then the transfer of land among close relatives. It is clear that rights to land were based on the original allocation from the konohiki and that subsequent transfers were limited and revocable by the konohiki. Allocations were to individuals and transfers were between individuals. Never is there reference to a named or unnamed group with rights to land.

There is furthermore no evidence from Halelea that the 'ili land divisions were associated with kin-based groups. The importance of 'ili in Halelea is questionable in the first place. The presence of 'ili are confirmed in the land records for only three (Wainiha, Hanalei, and Kalihikai) of the seven ahupua'a with land records (Earle 1973:258). For the other four ahupua'a, land units were instead often listed as part of a named *mo'o*. Apparently, a mo'o was a narrow strip of irrigated land along an irrigation ditch. For neither 'ili nor mo'o is there evidence for the long slices of land cutting across economic zones as described by Handy and Pukui (1972 [1958]). Rather, both 'ili and mo'o were restricted in Halelea to a single irrigation system or part thereof and the land immediately adjacent. There are numerous cases of individuals receiving land in more than one 'ili.

An alternative interpretation for the 'ili and mo'o would construe these named land segments as managerial units, because they were restricted to discrete sections of irrigation systems. In the 'ili Ki'ilua, Wainiha, a konohiki was assigned control of the 'ili separate from the ahupua'a (Earle 1973:158).

Evidence from the Halelean land records clearly supports Sahlins' view on the social organization of Hawaiian communities. There are no references to ranked lineages with the rights to ownership of land; rather use rights were allocated to individuals by the konohiki. Land units within the ahupua'a were not associated with social groups but may have served certain managerial functions. In the sections which follow, three levels of organization — the household, the interhousehold cluster, and the community — are described and their economic functions discussed. Although each level of organization is phrased in kinship terms, the historic evidence supports a model of social organization based on a flexible system adjusting to specific political and economic situations.

The Household

Historically, the basic social and economic unit of the commoners in Halelea was the household which resided at a *pahale,* a parcel of land theoretically demarcated by a surrounding stone wall or *pa*. A typical land award consisted of two separate sections: (1) a pahale and (2) a cluster of pondfields with some dryland farming area attached. Such a grant formed the economic foundation for an independent householding unit. Thus, in most cases, each award (kuleana) signified an independent family. The analysis which follows describes first the organization of this household and then discusses its economic activities.

Organization of the Halelean Household.

The size of the household can be estimated by dividing the population of an ahupua'a by the number of awards. Excluding Hanalei and Waioli because of extensive economic disruption, and excluding Waikoko and Lumahai because no awards were granted, the population for Halelea in 1847 was 547 (Schmitt 1966) and the number of awards was ninety-eight. From these figures, the calculated size of a household was 5.58 (range 3.1 for Kalihiwai to 8.1 for Ha'ena). Normally, these figures would be considered well within the size range of a nuclear family but because of severe population decline resulting in a top heavy age-sex pyramid for Halelea (Schmitt 1966), it is quite possible that minimal extended families or stem families were also represented.

Awards were granted not to households but to individuals. In most instances, this individual was a male who acted as the economic focal point for the householding unit. The male role is critical for understanding the domestic economy of the household and its articulation with the political economy of the elites. In Polynesia generally, the male is the focal member for the group, but it is not this structural principle which is operating in Halelea. Rather, because use rights were allocated by the konohiki in accordance with a male's labor contribution to ko'ele land cultivation and other activities, it was necessarily through the male that a household obtained a claim to land.

The critical significance of a male (as corvée laborer) for obtaining a household's rights to land is made clear in the process of land transfer described in land records. As already described, the primary claim to land was based on allocation from the konohiki. After land use rights were granted by the konohiki, however, these rights could be transferred, subject to the konohiki's consent, either as inheritances or as gifts. In order to establish the legitimacy of a claim, an individual and his supporting witness had to describe the chain of title from the original grant.

Seventy-five cases of land transfer between consanguinial and affinal relatives were described in the land records for Halelea. The most frequent were lineal (parent to child, forty-one cases or 55%; and grandparent to grandchild, five cases or 7%). Males were specified as donor in twenty-four cases and females were never specified as donor. As recipient, males were specified in twenty-five cases and females in five cases. There were only four cases (5%) of collateral (sibling) transfers. As donor, males were specified in three instances and females only once. As recipients, males were specified three times but never females. For all consanguinial transfers in which sex was identified, fifty-five of the participants were male and six were female. A male bias is quite evident.

The importance of the male is shown from a different perspective in the twenty-five cases (34%) of transfer between affines. Eleven cases involved the transfer of land from husband to wife upon the death of the husband. Because rights to land rested on corvée labor contribution required of males, it was necessary for a household to include a male and quick remarriage was common. After marriage, the land use was transferred to the new husband (as reported in eight cases) who could then fulfill corvée responsibility attached to the use right.

Another six cases of affinal transfer involved the exchange from brother-in-law to brother-in-law. Since in most cases the transfer probably resulted from a brother's death, the sister should be seen as the initial inheritor who then passed the use right to her husband similar to the cases of remarriage.

Before the granting of the land awards in fee simple, it is apparent that males formed the focal position of the household as "owners" of use rights to houselots and subsistence plots. Evidence that this position was based on the corvée responsibility to the konohiki is demonstrated by a shift toward female ownership and matrifocal households after the abandonment of the konohiki system. In other words, Hawaiian family shifted from a strongly patrifocal organization toward a matrifocal organization with the change in land tenure rules (This shift in family organization is the subject of a qualifying paper by Jocelyn Linnekin, Department of Anthropology, University of Michigan, Ann Arbor.)

The Domestic Economy

In addition to providing information on the organization of the Hawaiian household, the land records provide information on the domestic economy, which was geared to generalized production through a mixed strategy of farming, fishing and gathering. This generalized subsistence strategy contrasts with the model of household specialization presented for the Ka'u 'ohana (Handy and Pukui 1972 [1958]) and can be understood as resulting in part from the concentrated economic resources of the Halelea district.

Economic self-sufficiency for the Hawaiian household required access to multiple areas for farming, fishing, and collecting. Access to these areas was guaranteed by household use rights to specific land units later granted as kuleana (land awards) and by general use rights to unassigned ahupua'a land open to all ahupua'a members with the consent of the konohiki. Each award (kuleana) included a number of separate sections (apana) ranging from one to five (mean 2.0). In the descriptions of the apana given in both the testimony and the awards, land use was described as being one or a combination of the following: houselot (pahale); irrigated agriculture (lo'i, mo'o kalo, or loko); and rainfall agriculture (kula).

In 1850, the Halelean subsistence economy depended extensively on taro, as shown by the fact that 96% of awards included taro lands. The remaining four percent of awards were single houselots restricted to the ahupua'a of Hanalei and Waioli, where Western plantation agriculture disrupted the traditional subsistence systems and offered alternative, cash based economic opportunities. Elsewhere in Halelea, land grants always included irrigated taro lands.

Rainfall agriculture was a secondary form of farming in Halelea. Kula land was listed in 59% of land awards and in most instances (80 of 101 awards with kula) these areas were directly associated with either a pondfield area or a houselot. Rainfall agriculture was important to produce a wide range of crops for food and technology. In most instances, the specific crops were not described in the records but scattered references were made to banana, pigs, 'awa (beverage source), bamboo, koa (a wood source), firewood, and noni (a dye plant) (Earle 1973:125-26). Apparently, kula farming was on the decline because of the destruction of gardens by newly introduced cattle, but dryland agriculture would have served originally as an important supplementary farming technique for most households in Halelea.

Evidence for household involvement in fishing and collecting is indirect and will be discussed at more length in the section on the ahupua'a community. There is, however, documentation that fishing was an important component of the economic strategy in most households. Assuming that distance from a housesite to an economic resource is a rough measure of that resource's significance, the spatial location of pahale may be used to judge the relative significance of fishing as compared to farming. The favored location for housesites (85%) was the sandy strip near the shore positioned between the two primary resources, alluvium for pondfield agriculture and the shallow, inshore waters for net fishing. Table 8.1 compares the straight line distance from pahale to the nearest taro apana of the same kuleana with the distance to the shore line. These measurements are not directly comparable because the former is the distance to a specific area of known exploitation and the latter is the distance to a general area of possible exploitation. In other words, we know precisely where the alluvium was being farmed but only approximately where the waters were being fished. Other things being equal, the former distance would always be longer than the latter. The similarity between the two measurements (572 m to taro apana vs. 397 m to sea shore) would indicate a balance between fishing and farming in the household economy.

TABLE 8.1

MEAN DISTANCES FROM HOUSELOTS TO SPECIFIED LOCATIONS, MEASURED IN METERS

Ahupua'a	1st Taro Apana	Sea	Nth Nearest Pahale			N
			1st	2nd	3rd	
Ha'ena	341	88	141	334	442	10
Wainiha	313	1036	150	350	470	21
Waipa	339	215	108	215	238	8
Waioli	788	293	68	85	163	27
Hanalei	698	238	76	128	190	15
Kalihikai	208	109	103	134	196	11
Kalihiwai	920	275	78	125	162	17
Mean	572	397	100	186	260	
S.D.	262	352	33	106	129	

In some ahupua'a, the relative distances to farming or fishing areas indicate an emphasis on one or the other resource. For example, in Wainiha, many houselots were located above irrigation ditches inland from the sea. Average distance to taro land was therefore shorter (313 m) than to fishing areas (1036 m). The reverse was true in Waioli, Hanalei, and Kalihiwai. Although this may indicate real differences in economic orientation, it is not, I feel, evidence of household specialization. The distribution of houses in Wainiha during the early part of this century supports a model of generalized household economy. Although the primary residences on the original pahale grant were inland, additional structures were built on the shore for use during fishing. Alternatively, in ahupua'a with pahale near the sea, households maintained a second "taro shack" among the pondfields.

The most vivid summary of the generalized household economy is the settlement pattern of the Halelean ahupua'a. This pattern was determined to a large degree by a single environmental factor, the compactness of economically significant zones. Within a kilometer of the beach, the three most important resource areas are found in juxtaposition. For fishing, the richest areas were the reefs and sandy bottoms of the shallow, inshore waters. From the shoreline, a sandy zone of active coral sands extends inland and becomes mixed with alluvial deposits. The housesites and small garden areas were scattered in loose clusters in this locale. Immediately in back of the sandy zone, the coastal alluvial plain slopes gradually back to the lower mountain ridges of the central island. The irrigation systems which started in the narrow interior valleys extended to include this alluvial zone, often down to the edge of the sand. The land use map for Waioli in 1850 is an excellent example of this compact pattern (Fig. 8.1).

Historically, the compactness of diverse economic resources was amplified by the diverse conditions found within the irrigation systems. Although pondfield irrigation primarily creates an artificial hydromorphic environment, it includes as well a diverse set of agricultural conditions. As discussed in Chapter 7, historic descriptions of irrigation systems often noted the use of interpatch bunds for various crops including banana, sugarcane, and ti. An excellent description of the diversity of crops possible in a pondfield system is given in the following quotation describing the island of Molokai:

> Poniohua has a taro patch that has been dug up with large mounds in the center where bananas, sugar cane, sweet potatoes, onions, and so on has been planted, while taro grew in the water. [Kanepu 1867, in Summers 1971:146]

An irrigated set of pondfields presents a gradation from the deep water of the fishpond to the shallow pondfield to the moist soils bordering the water to the dry soils of the fallow fields and bund ridges. Thus within a single irrigation system, there are the full range of soil-water conditions required by the dominant Hawaiian crops.

In sum, the compactness of diverse economic resources resulting from the geography and technology of Halelea offered a wide range of

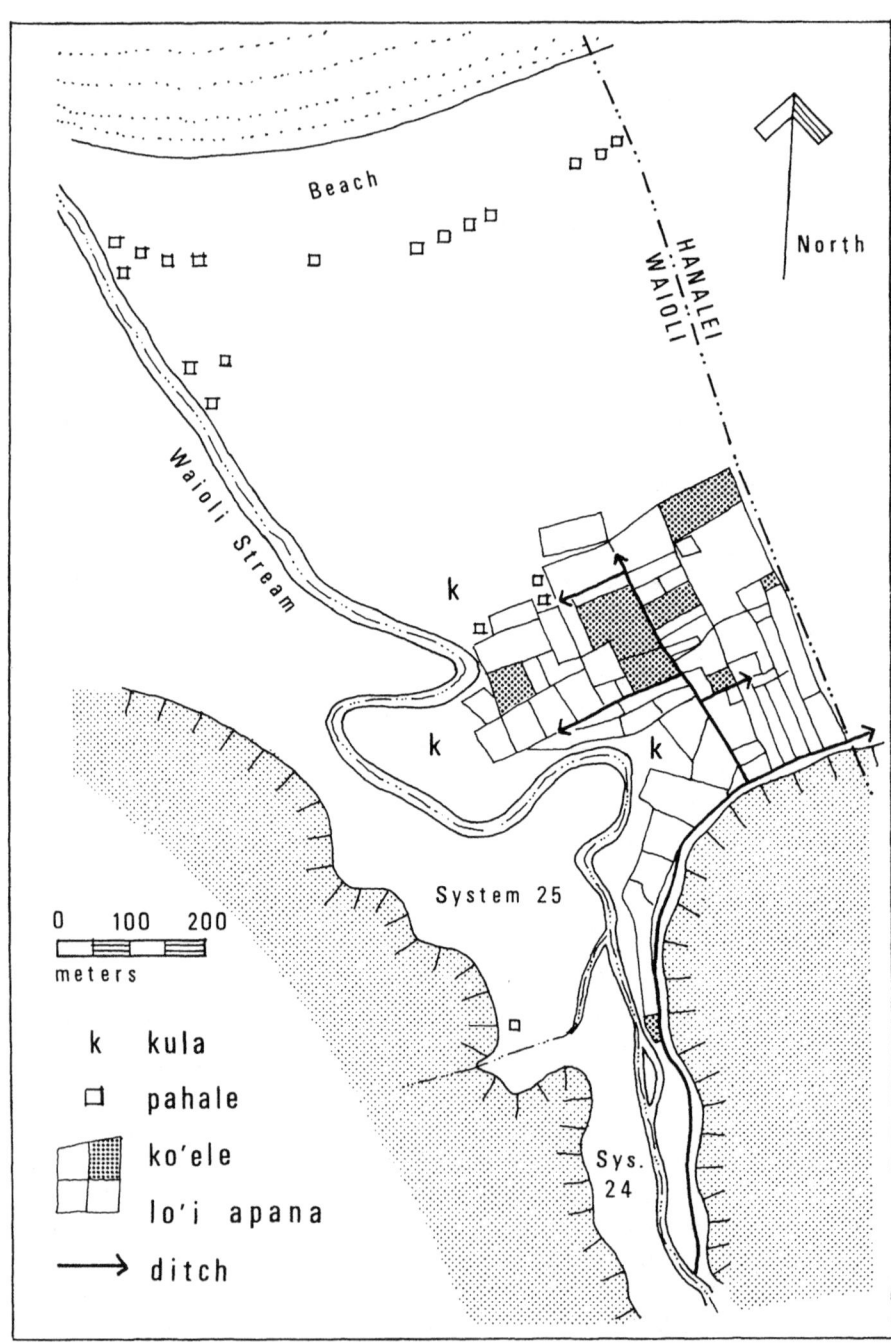

Fig. 8.1 Historical (1850) land use pattern, Waioli, Kaua'i. Reconstruction from land records (1848-1852) and Lydgate map (1912).

subsistence possibilities to the Hawaiian household. Present evidence strongly indicates that the household took advantage of these diverse opportunities to maintain a generalized economic strategy.

The Interhousehold Cluster

Evidence for interhousehold groupings is not common in the land records for Halelea. As mentioned earlier, there is no evidence for corporate, named groups above the household. The land records do indicate the presence of two types of unnamed groups which appear to have functioned as subsistence production units and residential units.

The first type of group is represented by joint claims to taro land filed by an association of two to eight individuals. There were thirteen such joint claims with a mean of 3.2 individuals per group. In all but one case, individual portions of the joint claim were on a single irrigation system.

Although the structure of these groups cannot be documented, I strongly suspect that they were formed on a kinship basis such as brother or brother-in-law ties. A few such links are mentioned in the records but limited kinship data are available. In addition, the joint members of a claim tended to live close to each other. This may indicate kinship relationship or, alternatively, it may indicate only the independent attraction of residential units to the same agricultural resource. Whatever the situation, some form of group was present and it most probably served as a cooperative unit for irrigation matters like maintenance and water allocation. Such irrigation associations would have acted as an organizational alternative to direct management by the konohiki.

The importance of these irrigation associations, however, should not be overemphasized. Spatially, they were restricted to only a few ahupua'a — seven for Wainiha, five for Ha'ena, and one for Waioli. Furthermore, these groups rarely controlled an entire irrigation system (exception: System 13 in Wainiha) but shared their systems with independent farmers.

The second form of interhousehold association was the residential cluster. In the description of awards (136 with houselots), eleven awards noted multiple families living on a single pahale. These houselots were claimed by and granted to a single individual but one to five (mean 2.25) additional families were allowed to occupy them as well. The relationship between these families is not known, but a logical explanation for at least some groupings would reflect the cycle of household development. While 96% of all awards included taro land, a smaller number (79%) included a pahale. This suggests a possible sequence whereby an individual first acquired rights to agricultural land and later acquired a housesite. A young male might first have established his economic viability before establishing an independent household. Informants, describing residential patterns in the early twentieth century, frequently mentioned that a newly married couple continued to live with either the husband's or wife's parents for several years (often including the birth of one or two children). Only then would they build their own house and claim domestic independence.

An additional explanation for residential clusters appears to have involved associations with a politically prominent figure, especially the konohiki (cf. Sahlins 1971 for similar groups on Oahu). In four cases, the multifamily pahale were granted to individuals who either were konohiki in 1850 or who had been konohiki earlier. Often pahale seem to cluster into small groups based on social cohesion. (The alternative explanation, which would see the groups as based on independent attraction to a desired resource, cannot be eliminated at this time.) A good example of such a pahale cluster is the eight houselots bordering the Kanoa fishpond (System 25) in Hanalei. Included in this cluster were the houselots of Namanu and Kahui. Namanu was the brother-in-law of Ka'ainahuna who, after he helped suppress the 1824 rebellion on Kaua'i, was given the konohikiship of Hanalei. The other six houselots were granted soon after 1824 to individuals who were probably the victorious warriors receiving houselots as compensation for services. It seems that these houselots represented a sociopolitical group focused on the warrior-konohiki Ka'ainahuna who himself was dead by 1850.

Corroborative evidence for residential groups associated with the konohiki is found in the missionary records. In the first yearly mission report for Waioli, the missionary, Alexander, described the arrival of the new konohiki Papohaku, at Waioli and the establishment with his followers of a residential cluster:

> Davida [Papohaku], an excellent member of the Waimea Church, accompanied us, as a helper in building up a new station, and with him his train, making in all 75 — They have built a city on the Waioli plain which they call Bethlehem — . [Alexander 1835]

On the evidence that his abandoned pahale was "in Bethlehema" (Foreign Testimony for LCA 10096) Mareko, who later became konohiki of Waioli, was probably a member of this group of followers. Mareko later married Papohaku's widow (Johnson 1848).

In both these cases, the group associated with the konohiki was, like the konohiki himself, foreign to the area. The group would, therefore, have offered valuable local support for the konohiki and may have functioned in various managerial capacities. Some kinship basis for the groups seems to be indicated in the two cases described and the office of konohiki appears to have been transferred within the group.

The Community

Traditionally, the Hawaiian community was based on a territorial unit, the ahupua'a. An individual was considered a member of an ahupua'a if he resided there and, if an adult male, he contributed to corvée labor for the konohiki. People were not tied to land but were allowed to move from one ahupua'a to another. There was, however, a strong incentive for the konohiki to retain the maximum possible population as a labor pool for corvée, and thus the konohiki discouraged emigration either for outside jobs or for marriage. Speaking of the first Kaua'i sugar plantation at Koloa, Jarves described the difficulties obtaining sufficient native laborers:

> ... as the people are held rigidly by the chiefs, who consider their dignity enhanced by the number they control, it was with much difficulty that they [laborers] could be obtained. [1838:71]

As noted by Sahlins (1973), endogamy encouraged by the konohiki was high. The high rate of inmarrying and low rate of emigration must have created a community interconnected by complex overlapping networks of consanguinity and affinity.

Informants describing Wainiha in the early twentieth century referred to it as one "family." Precise relationships were, however, often ignored as it was recognized that one could trace relationships to all community members variously through ties of blood and marriage.

Aboriginally, there were two general ahupua'a patterns on the Hawaiian Islands, reflecting contrasting geographic conditions (Earle 1977). The first, or valley ahupua'a, was located in geologically old areas where major streams had developed through erosion. An ahupua'a ideally encompassed a complete catchment area — one major valley, one ahupua'a. The second, or upland ahupua'a, was found in geologically young areas where major streams were absent. Its boundaries, running perpendicular to the contours, define an arbitrary strip which ran from the mountains to the sea.

The ahupua'a in Halelea were characteristically that of the valley pattern. As discussed in detail in Chapter 3, there were nine ahupua'a identified in the land records. Seven of these ahupua'a circumscribed entire catchment areas for major streams — Ha'ena, Wainiha, Lumahai, Waipa, Waioli, Hanalei, and Kalihiwai. The other two,

Waikoko and Kalihikai, were based on alluvial areas from smaller streams. Territorial boundaries were defined by the intervalley ridges, but, near the coast, the boundaries became more arbitrary as they partitioned small coastal catchment areas, broad coastal plains (Hanalei-Waioli-Waipa-Waikoko), and fringing reefs (Ha'ena-Wainiha, Hanalei-Kalihikai-Kalihiwai).

The Halelean subsistence economy relied on three significant resource zones — (1) alluvial farm land; (2) shallow inshore and reef areas for fishing; and (3) residual uplands and valley interiors for collecting.

(1) As discussed in considerable detail earlier, irrigated taro farming and associated rainfall farming were concentrated on the alluvial bottom land associated with the major streams near the sea. Because of the diverse soil-moisture conditions within an irrigation system, this area produced a full range of products from the fish raised in ponds to in the pondfields to numerous dryland crops on the bunds and fallow fields.

(2) Of equal significance because of their protein contribution, fish and shellfish were obtained from the intertidal and shallow water of the inshore and reef areas. Newman (1970:34-61) summarizes the historical evidence for the importance of fishing in Hawaii. It is his conclusion that fishing in shallow water (less than 15 m) with nets, lines, and other techniques was the dominant strategy for marine exploitation. The inshore fishing zones were partitioned as territory owned by the ahupua'a and rights to this zone were held exclusively by the community.

(3) Collecting in the upland plant communities (cf. Chapter 3) was also important. The soils (regosols, lithosols, latosols, and hydromorphic soils) of these communities are generally heavily weathered and eroded. Although minor irrigation systems (less than 1 ha) and some forest gardens were located here, the primary uses of these zones were collecting and hunting of wild and feral species. The numerous species of these zones provided variety foods (feral bananas; taro and yams; mountain apples; kukui nuts), protein (feral pigs and chickens), fibres (hau, olona), construction materials (bamboo, 'ohia, koa), beverages ('awa), lighting fuel (kukui nuts), ceremonial greenery (ti), firewood, and medicine. (For additional information on wild and feral species see Handy and Handy 1972.) Furthermore, many of these species (especially the feral taros, yams, and bananas; noni; tree fern; and *Pandanus*) were used as "famine foods" reserved for time of need. Once established, these plants required little or no care but were an invaluable source of additional food during failure of normal agricultural production.

The territorial boundaries of the ahupua'a were set so as to define natural, repetitious units. Since an ahupua'a centered on a stream system, it included within a community's territory all the necessary resource zones. All communities included areas of rich alluvium, shallow inshore waters, and rolling uplands/valley interiors. Although varying greatly in total size, each ahupua'a was structurally identical, balancing access to the full range of subsistence resources. The significance of this territorial arrangement was to create a largely self-sufficient economic base for the community (see next section on redistribution).

Land tenure within the ahupua'a consisted of various overlapping precedential rights. The ahupua'a was allocated by the paramount chief to a lower ranked chief for his personal support. The ahupua'a was managed for the chief by his appointed manager, the konohiki. Commoners held rights to land use as members of the ahupua'a community. Specific use rights to farm land and houselots were granted to individuals in exchange for corvée labor, but the vast proportion of all lands were held in common. Fishing areas directly off-shore and in the stream and collecting areas in the uplands and interior valleys were open to exploitation by all community members. The restrictions on these resources were twofold — (1) only ahupua'a members held access rights; and (2) the konohiki, as representative of the ahupua'a chief, held rights of tabu *(kapu)* on specific species. During the nineteenth century land reform, the commoners received their small land plots in fee simple, and the chiefs received residual ownership to the ahupua'a, subject to the traditional use rights of the commoners.

Community territorialism is still strong in Halelea. For example, the Wainiha Bay and Stream are considered the fishing territory for Wainiha families and unrelated individuals are strongly discouraged. An outsider is expected to join in with a local party if he wishes to fish these waters.

Traditionally, the ahupua'a also defined the maximal labor pool used for most economic ventures. The konohiki, as community political leader, organized community oriented activities including everything from the construction of religious shrines to large net fishing endeavors. Because such activities required more labor than was available to the household or household cluster, it was recruited and directed by the konohiki. In this capacity, the konohiki acted in a role directly analogous to the village chief elsewhere in Oceania (cf. Firth 1939; Sahlins 1962).

Summary

The social and economic organization of Halelean commoners was based on principles of self-sufficiency at both the household and community level. There was no corporate lineage structure as found commonly elsewhere in Polynesia, and attempts to minimize specialization in economic production are clear. Households were *not* integrated into extended family or lineage systems and communities were *not* bound by economic interdependence. This pattern contrasts to the local and regional networks of kinship and alliance typical of acephalous societies (cf. Dalton 1977), and it is also very different from the image of chiefdoms as representing "organic solidarity" (cf. Service 1962; Sahlins 1972). Economically, the generalized production of Halelea is segmental — composed of repetitious, structurally identical units. Socially and politically, however, the regional organization of chiefs dominated the local community. Through the system of land tenure, households were dependent on the chief and these differentiated elites performed many of the organizational functions performed by kinship networks in acephalous societies. The organizational significance of chiefdoms will be the subject of Chapter 9.

A CONSIDERATION OF THE THEORY OF REDISTRIBUTION

In a manner analogous to the requirements of irrigation technology, exchange has been viewed as a causal factor in the evolution of centralized organization. All societies are involved in material exchange but the frequency of this exchange varies greatly with the form of economic organization. For segmental societies, the local, structurally identical units produce largely for local consumption. In contrast, with increasing economic specialization, production becomes geared to exchange and the self-sufficiency of the local unit is reduced. Durkheim (1933) characterized this as the development of "organic solidarity" whereby economically specialized social units become bound by the necessity for exchange. Various researchers have postulated ecological theories of cultural evolution which identify specific environmental conditions requiring intercommunity exchange which in turn selects for the evolution of a regionally centralized organization. For example, Rathje (1971) interprets the Maya florescence as a response to the managerial requirements of exchange of nonlocal raw material, especially obsidian. Sanders (1956) has emphasized the importance of interregional exchange of specialized goods as underlying the evolution of state organization in Central Mexico. Specifically for chiefdoms, Service (1962; 1975) has argued that the evolution of centralized organization is a result, at least in part, of the intensification of intercommunity exchange. It is specifically Service's redistributive theory of chiefdoms which I examine in this section.

To summarize Service's (1962:144-52) argument, chiefdoms are redistributive societies with a permanent central agency for coordination, which developed as a consequence of economic specialization and the resulting requirements for exchange. Two conditions result in specialization: (1) "the pooling of individual skills in large scale cooperative production"; and (2) "the regional, or ecological, specialization of different local residential units" (Service 1962:145). In the first instance, the central organization of chiefdoms would evolve as a response to the managerial needs of large-scale cooperative labor activities such as those associated with irrigation systems (cf. Wittfogel 1957). Service, however, believes that the second condition is the most common factor in the evolution of chiefdoms; chiefdoms would develop as a response to ecological diversity. Given a sedentary settlement system, the centralized redistributive hierarchy is necessary to distribute the specialized products procured in the ecologically differentiated areas.

> Most chiefdoms seem to have risen where important regional exchange and a consequent increase in local specialization came about because ecological differentiation was combined with considerable sedentariness. [Service 1962:146]

The Hawaiian islands are an ideal case in which to examine the theoretical relationship between ecological diversity and chiefly organization. Ecological diversity is pronounced — comparable to or more marked than environmental conditions in chiefdoms elsewhere in Oceania, the Americas, and Africa (cf. Service 1962:152-53). Within a single island, microenvironments range from the xerophytic biotic communities with rainfall less than 750 mm per year to the tropical forests with more than 2500 mm of rain per year. As would be predicted by Service, associated with this environmental variability is the regionally specialized, political organization of the Hawaiian elites. Service's argument would suggest that this centralized agency functioned to integrate the economies of locally specialized groups. Such local specialization, corresponding with microenvironmental variability, would result in economic dependence and select for the regional organization.

Evaluation of Service's Hypothesis: Halelea

Central to Service's hypothesis is the notion that redistributive exchange integrated *economically specialized communities*. This was clearly not the case for Halelean communities, which were based on a generalized economy. Ahupua'a boundaries were laid out to include all necessary resources within the territory of a single self-sufficient community. By controlling a full valley, each community was guaranteed access to productive alluvial land with water for irrigation, to shallow water fishing areas, and to extensive upland zones for collecting. As already noted, boundary lines followed natural ridges except near the sea where these lines often deviated from the obvious, natural boundaries to divide areas of critical resources between ahupua'a. This equalizing principle is shown in several cases like the boundary between Ha'ena and Wainiha. A section of small, independent catchments separated these dominant ahupua'a areas, and the coast along this interstitial section is fringed by two major reef areas. The boundary was drawn so as to bisect these productive fishing zones and give one major fishing area (Ha'ena Point) to Ha'ena and the other (Lae o Kaonohi--Kepuhi Point) to Wainiha (cf. Map 1).

To summarize, the ahupua'a territories were structurally similar to each other. The pattern was one of repetition; each ahupua'a community maintained unrestricted access to substantial areas of each of the three subsistence resource zones. However, although structurally similar, the ahupua'a were quite unequal in physical size (range, 0.3 km^2 for Waikoko to 7.5 km^2 for Hanalei). This variability in size was compensated for by the distribution of population.

Theoretically, there is a spectrum in the possible pattern for the distribution of population. At one extreme, population can be distributed such that each community is approximately equal in size. This pattern is characteristic of acephalous societies where communities are politically autonomous and in direct competition. Small communities must either recruit additional members or risk defeat in battle (cf. Rappaport 1967). Without strong community leadership, large communities tend to segment. At the other extreme, population is distributed with respect to resource availability. Because population is closely adjusted to resources, community self-sufficiency is enhanced; however, variability in community population size (according to resource availability) requires an organizational mechanism to guarantee the viability of smaller communities.

For Halelea in the early nineteenth century, there was a marked variability in ahupua'a population and this variability corresponded closely with resource availability. In 1834-1835, the average community size was 188 people with a range from 85 for Waipa to 522 for Hanalei (Waikoko is excluded because no population figure is given). The relationship between population size and various measures of resource availability is shown in Table 8.2. If the correlation coefficient (r) approaches one, population was distributed evenly with respect to the resource; but if r approaches zero, population is distributed independently of the resource. Population figures are obtained from a census taken by missionaries in 1834-1835 (Schmitt 1973). Resource figures are obtained by measuring with a scalar planimeter surface areas from the following maps: United States Geological Survey (1:24,000, Kauai County, Hawaii) and Soil Conservation Service (1:62,500, Kauai). On the most general level, there is a good correlation ($r = .889$) between population size and size of ahupua'a. More specifically, there are high correlations between population and area below 1000 ft (305 m) in elevation ($r = .915$), between population and area of alluvial soil ($r = .925$), and between population and area of shallow inshore water ($r = .556$).

To conclude, the boundaries of ahupua'a territories were laid out to create environmentally repetitious patterns in terms of access to neces-

TABLE 8.2

DISTRIBUTION OF HISTORICAL POPULATIONS AND RESOURCES FOR THE HALELEA AHUPUA'A

Ahupua'a	Population in 1835	Area in Square Kilometers of			Shallow, Inshore Water
		Total Ahupua'a	1000' Elevation	Alluvial Soils	
Ha'ena	116	7.7	3.8	0.6	3.4
Wainiha	216	43.5	14.7	1.3	1.6
Lumahai	119	36.9	11.0	1.8	0.3
Waikoko	—	1.8	1.8	0.3	0.4
Waipa	85	6.8	4.6	0.8	0.5
Waioli	158	14.2	7.4	0.8	0.3
Hanalei	522	68.5	33.7	7.5	3.6
Kalihikai	99	9.9	9.9	0.4	1.5
Kalihiwai	190	35.0	22.3	0.7	1.0

sary resources. In direct contradiction to Service's expectations, the definition of the community territory and the community organization permitted a self-sufficient (generalized) community economy. By minimizing the economic interdependence between communities, the structure of the local community reduced possible economic, integrative functions for a regional socio-political organization. In fact, the effect of the regional organization in Hawaii was to enhance community self-sufficiency. Because the regional organization virtually eliminated intercommunity warfare, the population of communities could vary according to resources, and the need for intercommunity exchange was further reduced. For Halelea, there is no evidence that ahupua'a specialization existed in the subsistence economy, and by extension there is no support for Service's hypothesis that redistribution in chiefdoms functioned to integrate economically specialized communities.

Elsewhere (Earle 1977), I have noted that some economic differentiation existed between districts in Hawaii. Although self-sufficiency was retained to a large extent by stressing a balanced fishing-farming strategy, there was some exchange in specialized products like tapa, mats, and preservable foods. This exchange was *not* handled by the redistributive hierarchy, however; the exchange which did take place was handled by direct barter at small markets (Ellis 1963 [1827]:229-30). Government officials were present to tax exchange and to maintain peace but they were not directly involved in the exchange beyond these activities.

As I will discuss in Chapter 9, the redistributive system in Hawaii was separate from such exchange. Rather than organizing subsistence production, redistribution was geared to provide support for the elite population (ali'i) which was physically removed from subsistence activities. Centralized redistributive collections in Hawaii cannot easily be seen as required by the subsistence economy but were integral to financing the expanding system of social stratification.

POPULATION CIRCUMSCRIPTION AND WARFARE

In a recent statement on the population and warfare theories of state formation, Carneiro (1970) has argued that a main causal factor in state formation is population growth in a circumscribed area where emigration is not a feasible corrective mechanism. Growth in such areas causes competition and eventually warfare over scarce agricultural resources. Warfare in turn requires cooperative military organization and results in the social domination of one group (the conquered) by another (the conqueror). Both the resulting cooperation and stratification would select for state organization.

For the Hawaiian Islands this theory has immediate appeal because the initial condition of a population increase in a circumscribed area is clearly documented. From a small founder group probably consisting of fewer than one hundred individuals, the Hawaiian population grew to about 300,000 in approximately 1200 years. Of greater importance is the fact that the islands are physically circumscribed; their physical isolation in the middle of the Pacific made emigration virtually impossible. Although traditional histories refer to voyaging from Hawaii to other island groups, such trips are reported only for the distant and mythical past and, at contact (1778), such voyaging was not practiced.

It, however, remains to be shown that the population increase caused pressure on agricultural resources, leading to warfare. All population figures for Hawaii at the time of contact are largely guess estimates, but I use the generally accepted figures given by Emory (Schmitt 1968: 42). In 1778, the total population of the seven main islands was 300,000 and had a mean population density of 47 per square mile (18.1 per square kilometer). The range in population density for the various islands was 21 per square mile (8.1 per square kilometer) for Ni'ihau to 103 per square mile (39.8 per square kilometer) for Maui. Kaua'i had a population density of 54 per square mile (20.8 per square kilometer). For a society with extensive irrigation agriculture, this density is not unusually high. Handy and Handy describe the apparent underutilization of resources as follows:

> The statewide survey that was made in the preparation of *The Hawaiian Planter – Volume I* (Handy 1940) made it evident that, at time of discovery by Captain James Cook, the Hawaiian Islands were not completely settled. Only the best of the arable land, capable of cultivation by the gardening methods practiced by the natives, was actually utilized. Compared with areas like Peru and the Philippines which were terraced up to high altitudes, land and water resources in Hawaii were by no means fully developed. [1972:280]

This underutilization of agricultural resources is particularly evident for Halelea. Although extensive areas suitable for rainfall agriculture are present (especially the uplands of Kalihiwai, Kalihikai, Hanalei, and Waioli), only the prime areas of alluvial soils were farmed intensively aboriginally. Even the alluvial soils were greatly underutilized as shown by the later, tremendous expansion in irrigation agriculture for rice. The inattention to kula farming and the restriction of irrigation farming cannot be explained on technological grounds. Rainfall farming was highly developed in areas like Kona and Ka'u, Hawaii and Hana, Maui where stream systems were not available for irrigation. Also, as seen by the cut stone aqueduct in Waimea, Kaua'i, and as seen by the extensive terrace complexes on the Napali coast, Kaua'i, the Hawaiian agriculturist had the considerable technological sophistication necessary to extend irrigation agriculture (Handy and Handy 1972:280-82). Yen (1973:79) emphasizes that Hawaiian irrigation agriculture, in contrast to other Oceanic areas like New Caledonia, was "simple" (nonintensive) on the basis that valley slopes and ridges were not regularly terraced. Since this expansion was technologically possible, it seems reasonable to conclude that it was not necessary. For Halelea and most areas with irrigation, Hawaiian agriculture does not show the intensive development normally associated with population pressure.

It is still possible to argue that warfare was caused by competition over prime agricultural land suitable for irrigation. With irrigation, since there is always a marked difference in land productivity such that only a small percentage of all suitable land is most desirable and therefore well below carrying capacity, there may be competition for the most desirable acreage. In order to show that warfare in Hawaii was primarily a response to competition over prime land *needed for subsistence,* it should be shown that warfare took place between local communities since it is these units which are critical in terms of subsistence production. The outcome of warfare also should be a significant *readjustment of population* — the victors should occupy the conquered lands after largely eliminating or at least dislocating the local population.

For Halelea itself, the evidence for warfare is completely absent. Unlike other areas (cf. Hommon 1972:161-67), there is no ethnohistorical or archaeological evidence for mountain ridgetop retreats or other refuges. The dispersed pattern of residential locations also contrasts with the pattern of nucleated villages often associated with warfare. In Halelea, the housesites are only loosely clustered. For the district as a whole, the mean distance to first, second, and third nearest pahale were 100 m, 186 m, and 260 m respectively (Table 8.1). In Ha'ena and Wainiha, there was almost no clustering of houselots. In these cases, the distance from a pahale to the first taro apana of its kuleana was less than the distance to the third nearest pahale. In other ahupua'a, residential clusters were somewhat larger but they could hardly be called nucleated villages. In many respects, the apparent mutual association between houselots seems rather to be independent associations of houselots with the strategic location of the sandy zone (cf. Fig. 8.1). Handy and Handy (1972:284-85) go as far as to say that Hawaiians had neither a conception of nor a term for villages and that any groupings were fortuitous. At least sources agree that there appears to have been no tight nucleation.

It might be argued either that nucleation had been abandoned after the last war (1824) or that nucleation might not be a logical response to the type of warfare found on Kaua'i. With reference to the first point, the last war had been only twenty-six years before the dispersed pattern described in the land records. Although dispersal may have been quite rapid, there is no indication of nucleation in the archaeological record either. With reference to the second point, since it is known that warfare was present on Kaua'i, it can be concluded that a dispersed settlement pattern is a satisfactory arrangement. Wright (1975: personal communication) has mentioned the possibility that warfare might have developed to such a scale that the logical response for a noncombatant commoner would have been to run for the hills and thus a dispersed settlement pattern would be admirably suited to the situation.

So far there is really no evidence that the local community was structured internally in any way to counter the threat of warfare. In fact, the evidence, already cited, for the very unequal distribution of population between ahupua'a would strongly suggest that warfare *between local communities* was not present. If it can then be concluded that warfare between communities over agricultural land was not practiced, what was the cause of and goal for Hawaiian warfare?

In answer to this question, I will argue in the following chapter that warfare in Hawaii was not between local subsistence units over land but was between regional chiefdoms over the control of those local communities. Warfare will be shown to have functioned *not* as a means to distribute resources as is often argued for acephalous societies (cf. Rappaport 1967) but functioned as a means to expand a chiefdom's redistributive web and thus expand its financial base.

CONCLUSION

In both the traditional histories and early European reports there is evidence that both redistribution and warfare were important aspects of Hawaiian culture. The exact significance of these factors is not well understood, and suggestions that they may have been primary causal factors in the development of complex social organization in Hawaii cannot be verified.

For Halelea, the evidence for redistribution based on economic specialization is negative. Within ahupua'a, settlement patterns would indicate a generalized economy. Because of the extreme compactness of the different ecological zones, a house was at most a few kilometers from all primary resources. There is no indication that there was economic specialization either within or between ahupua'a. Each ahupua'a was structured similarly to the next, and apparently population size of communities served to compensate for differences in resource availability rather than exchange between communities.

The present evidence from Halelea also deemphasizes the probable significance of warfare over scarce agricultural resources. With an underutilization of arable land, population was clearly not approaching carrying capacity as defined by technical potential. There was no direct evidence for warfare. For example, settlement pattern (often used as evidence for warfare) showed a dispersal indicating a distribution dictated by resources and not by defense.

It can be concluded that although some form of redistribution and warfare most probably existed in Halelea, they cannot be explained as a simple reflexive response to ecological conditions of the local community. Both redistribution and warfare may have been critically important in the evolution of complex society in Hawaii, but the deterministic models examined here are too simplistic to offer an adequate explanation of the observed development. In the next chapter, I will redirect the discussion away from the local community to the regional organization of Hawaiian elites. I will try to show that an explanation of Hawaiian social development must focus on the systemic characteristics of the regional organization. In this new context, the significance of irrigation, redistribution, and warfare will be reexamined.

CHAPTER IX

A RECONSIDERATION OF CHIEFDOM ORGANIZATION: HAWAII

Aboriginal Hawaii was socially stratified and politically centralized, in contrast to the simple Polynesian chiefdoms from which it evolved. Up to this point in the monograph, three hypotheses based on irrigation, environmental diversity, and resource competition have been examined and rejected as adequate explanations for the observed social development. These are all ecological explanations in which specific environmental factors operating at the community level are seen as requiring social differentiation and management. Such reflexive explanations of cultural evolution have consistently failed anthropologists in their search for the ecological conditions of development in human societies. General explanations of *structural forms* are bound to fail because they ignore the limitations of an evolutionary process. Evolution is descent with modification; it involves selection between alternative forms. Evolution is not a creative process, and, therefore, any explanation for the present structure must consider carefully the unique history of the society.

This chapter begins by evaluating the structural principles and dynamic processes of Polynesian society. As I will argue, certain aspects of this organization result in an inherently developmental economic and political system. Specifically, a distinctive maximizing strategy resulted in a series of positive feedback loops responsible for rapid evolutionary elaboration. The specific nature of positive feedback will be examined in detail for Hawaii. The main point to be made is that the evolution (elaboration) of chiefdoms is inherent in the social organization and becomes manifest under specific ecological/economic conditions. It is through such an analysis of the interplay between social organization and the environment that an understanding of cultural evolution is made possible.

POLYNESIA: STRUCTURE AND PROCESS

To understand the evolutionary development represented by aboriginal Hawaii, it is first necessary to understand the social organization of Polynesia chiefdoms. This section will attempt to show that (1) Polynesia society is structured according to basic principles of social inequality and centralized leadership. Although these principles are fundamental to centralized political organization, in fact most Polynesian chiefdoms are only weakly centralized and tend to segment into politically autonomous village units. (2) The realization of political centrality depends less on jural rules (which are generally shared) than on specific dynamic processes inherent in the competition for political office (Goldman 1970). It is my position that such intense competition creates a dual economy — a subsistence economy and a political economy. A subsistence economy has a minimizing strategy for which the goal is to meet the needs of the household unit (cf. Sahlins 1972). In contrast, a political economy has a maximizing strategy for which the goal is to produce the greatest income possible to finance political aspirations. While a subsistence system is self-dampening and thus inherently stable, the political economy is self-amplifying, as income is used in part to expand productive capacity. Such a positive feedback system is inherently developmental and will expand until external factors inhibit its growth. This section will examine both the property of growth in Polynesia chiefdoms and the factors limiting this growth.

The Evolutionary Transformation

Polynesia chiefdoms are structured as conical clans, based on the principle of rank (cf. Chapter 2). The conical clan, theoretically, has the capacity to expand indefinitely; after initial colonization, the conical clan expands by the successive imbedding of lineages until the island is fully colonized. This process of expansion and imbedding creates a regionally integrated social structure for the whole island. Because this regional organization is based on rank, the organization is both hierarchical and centralized. The highest ranking individual (focal member) of a group acts as leader for the group and its representative to higher levels in the hierarchy. This potential structure for a regionally integrated society is, however, only partially realized.

In most instances, Polynesian chiefdoms are only weakly centralized, and the regional organization operates in only limited, often ceremonial contexts. For all intents and purposes, the territorial community is the most important social, political, and economic unit. The community is centered on a dominant lineage and community leadership is provided by the highest ranking individual of that dominant lineage. This lineage/village chief is the generalized leader providing direction in all community affairs from cooperative economic ventures to religious ceremonies. The role of village chief is, in other words, very broad and largely unspecified. As the senior member of the dominant lineage, he shares kinship ties with his community, which looks to him as a paternalistic leader. He is the elite member of the local community, not a representative of an elite class. In sum, although a structural principle of regional integration exists, the simple Polynesian chiefdom approximates a segmental organization with considerable autonomy at the village level.

As illustrated by the Hawaiian, Tahitian, and Tongan societies, the complex Polynesian chiefdoms counteract local segmentation and form regionally centralized societies. For Hawaii, the ahupua'a was the functional equivalent of the localized lineage, because it functioned as the generalized subsistence group. In contrast to the lineage, however, the ahupua'a was not organized as a corporate kin group but was organized as unfocused, overlapping kindred networks. The leadership roles which, in a simple chiefdom, are handled by the lineage/community chief, were in Hawaii handled by the konohiki. These konohiki were not high ranking members of the local group but were members of a non-local elite stratum (Earle 1973:158-60; Sahlins 1971). In other words, the local community had become structurally truncated as its leadership roles were removed from local control and were filled by representatives of the regional elite.

In Hawaii, an elite stratum had superseded the many, autonomous lineage chiefs to form an integrated regional group positioned hierarchically above the local community. The Hawaiian chiefs were organized by typical Polynesian conical clan principles but this organization was structurally isolated from the commoner population. The elite lineages were no longer linked to community populations as kinsmen, but were superimposed on these local subsistence units as their leaders and landlords. The Hawaiian chiefs were both an aristocracy composed of hereditary elites and an incipient government, controlling inter- and intracommunity affairs.

In an article on cultural evolution, Flannery defines the evolutionary process of promotion whereby "an institution may rise from its place in the control hierarchy to assume a position in a higher level" (1972:413). This is apparently what happened in the Hawaiian Islands. For an island chiefdom, a single subsystem (an elite lineage) assumed the decision making roles held normally in Polynesia by the autonomous lineages. Promotion, therefore, resulted in regional centralization as the integration between localized subsistence units (the ahupua'a) was strengthened by the creation of a higher order control in the form of the elite lineage.

In order to explain the conditions resulting in this evolutionary change, it is necessary to reexamine briefly the generalized model of Polynesian society which, it has been argued, presents the prototype for all Polynesian societies. Four salient points concerning this model are the following: (1) the Polynesian society is adapted to an island ecosystem typically rich in agricultural and fishing resources, but severely limited by total area; (2) the population of an island or small group of islands is organized as a single conical clan composed of related lineages; (3) the conical clan structure forms the basis for a redistributive hierarchy which can mobilize goods for clan activities, especially ceremonies; and (4) this hierarchy functions as a decision making system for activities associated with any given level. In sum, the prototypical Polynesian society is based on centralized economic and decision making principles integrating the limited populations (perhaps 3000) living on small volcanic islands.

As populations organized by these principles colonize other island types, it should be obvious that specific aspects of this social organization will come under extreme stress. For example, if a large island group, like the Hawaii Islands or the Society Islands were colonized by a small founder population representing a single conical clan, the clan would expand during population growth and continue, by repeated imbedding of lineages, to be the single all-inclusive social structure for the total area. With each successive segmentation and imbedding of a lineage, a new level would be created in the social hierarchy. Specifically, an increase in scale and complexity in the social hierarchy would result in a very indirect system for information processing and a dizzying array of overlapping levels of decision makers who would be in potential conflict with each other.

Two alternative ways in which these organizational weaknesses might be corrected are: (1) increased centralization by promotion of a single lower order subsystem to a differentiated control position; and (2) segmentation of the system into autonomous systems. In many instances in Polynesia, such as for the Maori or the Marquesans, groups simply segment into separate communities after exceeding a certain size. Intercommunity relationships exist but are operationalized only in times of stress like warfare and famine. Conversely, in the Hawaiian

Islands, chiefdoms remained integrated at the level of a whole island by the development of a nonlocalized elite. Selection between the alternatives of promotion and segmentation is governed by the interaction of various systemic characteristics. Specifically, the importance of a maximizing political strategy and limitations to its operation will be examined.

Competition among Polynesian Chiefs

The three evolutionary explanations, investigated so far in this volume, offer functional interpretations. Functionalism, both in social anthropology and cultural ecology, relies on an organic analogy; a social institution like centralized government is explained by reference to its presumed function in the social system analogous to an organ's function in a living body. In this way, centralized government may be seen as a response to managerial requirements in the subsistence economy, regional exchange, or warfare.

This view of societies as integrated, goal directed systems belies much of the dynamic interaction observed in societies. It will be the purpose of this and the following sections to examine the competitive character of Polynesian social systems and to show how this structure results in evolutionary change.

In his comparative analysis of Polynesian societies, Goldman argues that sociopolitical organization is characterized by "powerful internal movement" (1970:xx).

> Polynesian status systems are all strongly dynamic. All are based upon complex patterns representing opposing concepts of ascription and of achievement, of sacred and secular, of formal and pragmatic. [Goldman 1970:8]

Goldman's "opposing concepts of ascription and of achievement" represent (1) a social structure determining status on the basis of rank and religious sanctity vs. (2) a competitive process determining status (especially political office) on the basis of operational power. Goldman (1970:20-22) interprets the evolution of Polynesian society as involving shifts in the relative importance of these alternative mechanisms. Initially, the prototypical ("traditional") Polynesian society was based on a ranked structure (the conical clan) in which an individual's social position was dictated by his birth. Because of intensive status rivalry resulting from certain ambiguities in the ranking system (cf. Sahlins 1958:139-47), competition intensified and brought about a dissolution of structural rules. In the resulting "open society," political office was achieved through competition involving the amassing of a personal following and often the forceful elimination of rivals. "Stratified society," as typified by Hawaii, represented a restructuring of society along traditional lines but including a chiefly class in which a certain amount of status rivalry was still common.

To varying degrees, political office was obtained through competition, which required the collection and use of wealth. Political power in Polynesia was firmly grounded in economic viability and there was a strong inducement for individuals committed to political achievement to maximize their personal incomes. A chief's efficacy was measured "by his ability to promote economic growth, and by his capacity as a donor" (Goldman 1970:18). In order to gain and maintain political position, an individual had to uphold a posture of generosity to supporting chiefs and to his dependent population.

Competition can be seen as having two significant implications: (1) competition is divisive; and (2) competition is financed by economic intensification. These two implications affect alternatively the opposing processes of segmentation and promotion (centralization). Competition factionalizes a group into rivals vying for support. On the other hand, the positive feedback relationship of a maximizing strategy results in the intensification of production and, as Sahlins (1958) shows clearly, the production of a surplus, which is necessary for the elaboration of social stratification. This surplus mobilized from the subsistence economy is used to finance the governmental superstructure and the distinctive elite life style of the chiefs. The specific operation of this maximizing, expansive economic system in Hawaiian is described in a later section.

Aboriginal Polynesian society represents a full range of social complexity from the small scale village chiefdoms of Tikopia or Pukapuka to the regional, "stratified" chiefdoms of the Hawaii Islands and Tahiti (cf. Goldman 1970:21; Sahlins 1958:11-12). Sahlins (1958) argues convincingly that the level of social stratification is closely related to the level of surplus production or more specifically the size of the redistributive hierarchy. The two factors which appear most important in this evolutionary development are size of island group and environmental potential for intensification.

First, and perhaps most elemental, is the size of the island group, which determines the potential scale of the social system. The largest island groups correspond approximately with the largest aboriginal population (cf. Goldman 1970:580). For example, with the exception of New Zealand (the temperate environment of which is marginal for the tropical agriculture practiced by Polynesians), the Hawaiian Islands have the largest land surface (16,700 km^2) and the largest aboriginal population (approximately 300,000). Evidently, the size of an island and its corresponding population determine the potential size of a social system. Assuming no segmentation, an increase in population size is related to an expanded size of the redistributive hierarchy and thus the total surplus available to finance the sociopolitical superstructure.

Size of island and population are together insufficient cause for social development, because a society may simply segment during expansion into small politically autonomous units. It is, therefore, essential to investigate the factors affecting segmentation and centralization. For example, the relatively large total population of the Marquesas (100,000) did not result in regional centralization because extremely rugged topography inhibited intercommunity, intervalley communication. Alternatively, environmental conditions favorable to agricultural intensification would permit economic development and a surplus production available to finance the political superstructure. The significance of Hawaiian irrigation becomes evident in this context. In Polynesia, the extensive alluvial plains were unique to Hawaii and nowhere else could the pondfield and fishpond complexes have been built with such ease. Irrigation, with its potential for intensification (cf. Geertz 1963), was the ideal economic base for an evolved chiefdom, because capital investment in irrigation technology permitted an expansion of surplus production.

In summary, political rivalry (competition) in Polynesian chiefdoms resulted in a positive feedback, maximizing economic system. The expansion of this system was limited either by the size of an island or the environmental potential for intensification. In Hawaii, the relatively large land mass and extensive alluvium permitted the expansion of the social system and the financing of an elaborate sociopolitical superstructure through intensive agricultural production, especially irrigation. The specific conditions of the Hawaiian political economy and social organization are described in the following section.

THE HAWAIIAN CHIEFDOM: THE EVOLUTION OF REGIONAL CENTRALIZATION

The aboriginal Hawaiian chiefdom was a good example of Goldman's "stratified society." The chiefly class had solidified power by holding a monopoly on status positions and on ownership of strategic resources. The redistributive hierarchy usually encompassed an entire major island and often extended to include additional smaller islands. Although political power was monopolized within the elite stratum, there was intensive and pervasive rivalry among chiefs for political power. This competitive process resulted in a cyclical pattern of chiefly expansion and segmentation. The Hawaiian chiefdoms were highly dynamic, constantly expanding by conquest warfare and fragmenting by internal rebellion.

This section begins with a description of competition and warfare in aboriginal Hawaii and especially for Kaua'i. The implications of this competition for a maximizing public economy will then be described and the multiple strategies of capital investment will be outlined. An important ramification of the regional political and economic system is the means by which the local community is articulated with this regional organization. Several specific characteristics of this articulation resulted in a virtual dependency of the local community on the regional organization.

Competition among the Hawaiian Chiefs

Competition among the Hawaiian chiefs for political power was an explicit aspect of social existence. The traditional histories (cf. Kamakau 1961), which served as a mythic charter for political action, concentrate on examples of rebellion and warfare. As will be discussed, competition was implicit in the complex and ambiguous social organization of the Hawaiian chiefs. In addition, because of the system of land tenure, competition among individuals ramified into major confrontations between elite factions whose rights to land and office rested on the outcome of the dispute.

Hawaiian elites were organized on the basis of conical clan principles for which rank, as measured by genealogical distance to senior line, was central. These formal rules were, however, greatly complicated by a number of particular modifications. For the Hawaiian Islands as a whole, there was not one, but several, senior lines loosely associated with specific islands, yet closely related to each other through marriage and subsequent descent. Because status was heritable through both males and females, persons often held status claims to positions in more than one line. A man or woman of high status often married and had children with multiple individuals of greatly varying status.

A person, usually but not exclusively a male, wishing to maximize his political position by laying claim to high status positions, had several options. He could press any of multiple possible claims traceable through a near endless number of male/female, biological/sociological genealogical relationships. Alternatively, or in addition, he could select high status spouses and lay claim to their status rights directly as husband or indirectly as father/guardian of their children.

Because of bilateral inheritance and multiple marriages, in most instances several individuals could lay claim to a single political office. As Goldman (1970) has argued for Polynesia generally, this ambiguity creates intense status rivalry. While many individuals might lay claim to a position, the ability to assume the office depended on an individual's capacity to marshal material support and often to take the office by force, eliminating any competitor.

The importance of competition over the major political office of paramount chief is documented for the early historic period on Kaua'i. Because of the right of each paramount to redistribute the major land holdings among his followers, this competition also involved major confrontations between chiefs aligned with the principal combatants. As will be shown, the succession of paramount chiefs on Kaua'i was a complicated line resulting from descent and alliance, and from inheritance and rebellion. A base line of succession in the Kaua'i senior line can be traced for three generations; however, the actual person in power was determined not by inheritance alone, but by the pattern of rebellion/competition between established political factions.

In the discussion which follows, frequent reference will be made to individuals whose relationships are shown in Figure 9.1. This chart is a partial genealogy for the ruling lines of Kaua'i, Oahu, and Maui but, for ease of handling, only those individuals mentioned in the text are included. Individuals are numbered consecutively and paramount chiefs are shown in capital letters.

Ideally, the paramount chief was recruited by patrilineal primogeniture — the eldest son of the *highest ranking wife* of a ruling paramount should ascend to his father's office. As seen in the case history of Kaua'i, the reality of succession was considerably complicated by factionalism both between and within chiefly descent groups. Six paramounts representing three major chiefly descent groups have been identified for the eighteenth and early nineteenth centuries on Kaua'i (Table 9.1). Almost nothing is known about the actual Kaua'i line. Kaumeha'iwa (5) is described by Barrère (1972: personal communication) as a Kaua'i paramount, but I have been unable to trace his ancestry. Because he had no sons with his highest ranking wife, the social rank descended to his eldest daughter, Kamakahelei (10), whose husbands ruled as

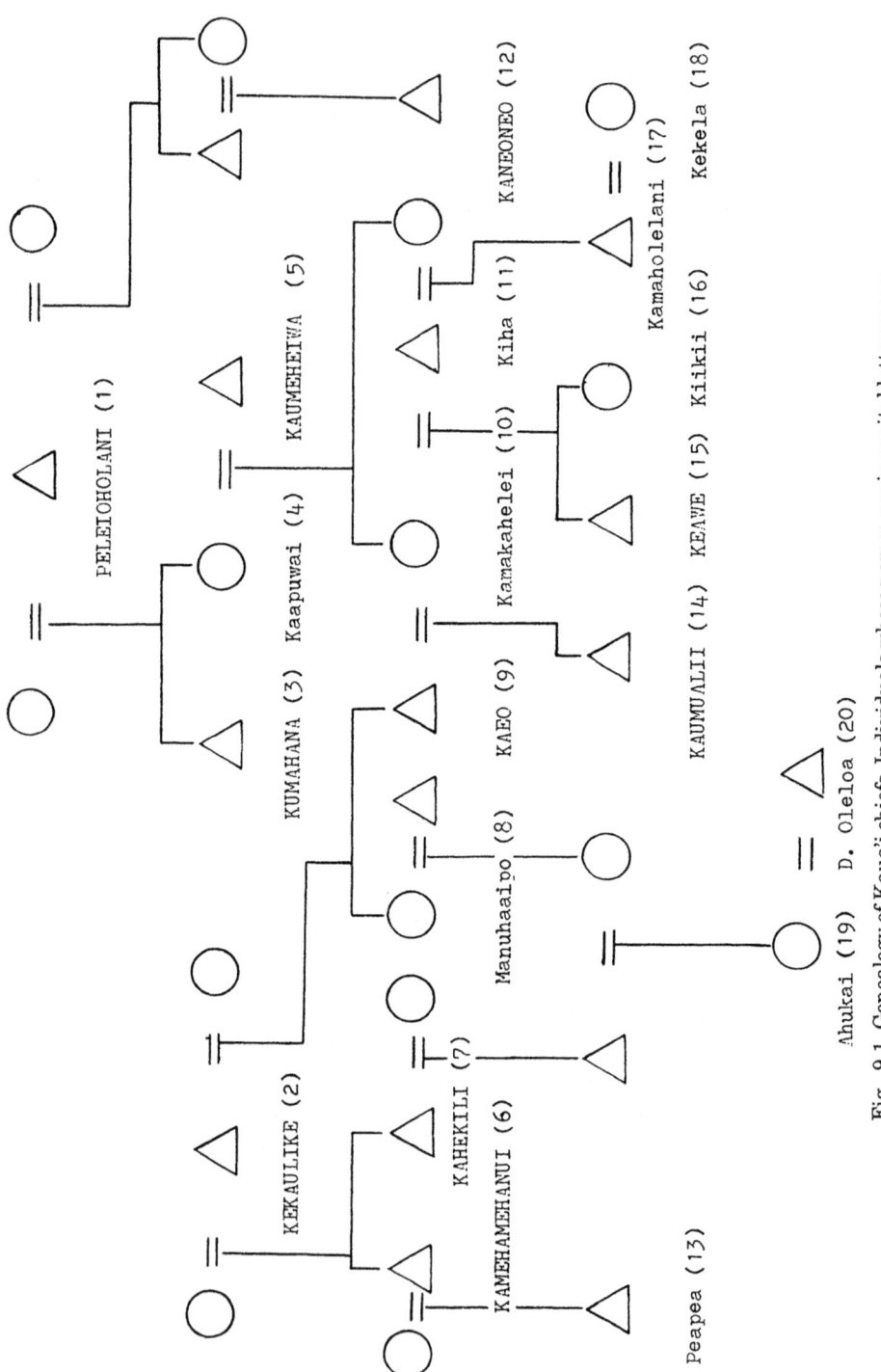

Fig. 9.1 Genealogy of Kaua'i chiefs. Individuals whose names are in capital letters were paramount chiefs of Kaua'i, Oahu, or Maui. Only the individuals mentioned in text are included. Numbers are simply for ease in referencing.

TABLE 9.1

APPROXIMATE CHRONOLOGY FOR AHUPUA'A CHIEFS OF HALELEA
AND FOR PARAMOUNT CHIEFS OF KAUA'I

Approximate Date	Paramount Chiefs Kaua'i	Ahupua'a Chiefs Lumahai	Ahupua'a Chiefs Wainiha
1825	—	Paki	Kalaimoku
1800	Kaumuali'i (14)	Kaumuali'i (14)	Kamaholelani (17)
	Keawe (15)	Ki'ikiki (16)	
	Kaumuali'i (14)	Keawe (15)	
	Ka'eo (9)		
	Keawe (15)	Manuha'aipo (8)	Peapea (13)
1775	Kaneoneo (12)		
	Kiha? (11)		
1750	Kaumehaiwa (5)		
1725	Peleioholani (1)?		

paramount. In a fairly complex pattern which will be described later, rule then descended alternately to her sons, Keawe (15) and Kaumuali'i (14).

Added to this dominant line of inheritance was a conflicting claim from the Oahu chiefly line. Peleioholani (1) was a famous paramount chief of Oahu, but in addition he was described as the ruling chief of Kaua'i during the eighteenth century (Kamakau 1961:71). His son, Kumahana (3), by his first marriage succeeded his father as paramount of Oahu. His son and daughter by his second marriage formed a sibling union and their son was Kaneoneo (12). It was Kaneoneo whom the members of Cook's exploring expedition described as the paramount chief of Kaua'i in 1778 (Beaglehole 1967). When one of Cook's ships returned the following year, various journals described Kamakahelei (10) as now the "Queen of the Islands" (Kaua'i and Ni'ihau), her new husband Ka'eo (9) as "her generalissimo," and her son Keawe (15) by an earlier husband as "King" (Beaglehole 1967). Kaneoneo, described now as a "usurper," was on the other side of the island "gathering forces" but soon arrived for a visit with the foreigners.

The exact nature of the counter-claim by the Oahu line is difficult to reconstruct. The genealogical ties between Oahu and Kaua'i predates Peleioholani (Barrère: personal communication) and were strengthened by the marriage of his high ranking daughter Ka'apuwai (4) to the Kaua'i paramount Kaumeheiwa (5). The absence of a male child from this marriage and the subsequent marriage of their daughter Kamakahelei (10) to a high ranking Maui chief, Ka'eo (9), probably combined to give cause for rebellion. Because of long standing hostilities between Maui and Oahu, the two chiefly descent groups probably viewed each other with distrust. The chiefs on Kaua'i with strong Oahu ties would then have viewed the marriage of Kamakahelei to a Maui chief as a threat to their privileged position and would have supported a rebellion by an Oahu line chief. Kamakahelei's first marriage was to Kiha (11) who may well have been one of the husband of Peleioholani's daughter Ka'apuwai (4) *and* a grandson to Peleioholani (Barrère: personal communication). Kamakahelei's change in husbands would, therefore, be a dramatic shift away from Oahu domination, because, as it should be remembered, Kamakahelei would not occupy the office of paramount herself but would give power over to her husband.

Kamakahelei's new husband, Ka'eo, was the son of Maui's paramount chief Kekaulike (2) and half brother to Maui's two succeeding paramounts Kamehamehanui (6) and Kahekili (7). His close association to the Maui senior line is clear. As already mentioned, after marriage to Kamakahelei it was not Ka'eo who was called paramount chief *(ali'i nui)* but Kamakahelei's young son Keawe from her earlier marriage with Kiha. By 1786, however, Ka'eo is described as "King of Ni'ihau and Kaua'i" and has assumed the office of paramount (Portlock 1789:86). The birth of his son Kaumuali'i (14) may have been the significant factor in his change of status. At this point, Keawe appears to have lost all immediate claim to the office of paramount. When Vancouver visited Kaua'i in 1792, it was reported that Ka'eo had gone to Maui "with all the warriors and double canoes" in support of his half brother Kahekili who was at war with Kamehameha I of Hawaii (Menzies 1920:27). At this point, Kaumuali'i "was left invested with regal dignities under the care of Inamoo, an elderly chief, during the king's absence" (Menzies 1920:27). At the death of Kahekili in 1793, Ka'eo succeeded his half brother as paramount of Maui, Molokai, and Lanai but was killed in a battle on Oahu (Kamakau 1961:168).

On the death of Ka'eo, Kaumuali'i (14), Ka'eo's son by Kamakahelei, would have succeeded to the office of paramount. When Broughton (1804) visited Kaua'i in 1796, however, Kaumuali'i's half brother Keawe (15) was leading a rebellion. Keawe held the southwest district of Waimea and Kaumuali'i probably held the northeast. It is significant that Broughton (1804:44) described Keawe as an Oahu chief. Both Keawe and Kaumuali'i shared the same mother Kamakahelei, but the Oahu-Maui opposition already noted for their different fathers was transferred to the sons. In July 1796, Broughton (1804:73) returned to find Keawe in full power and Kaumuali'i (divested of power) living with his half brother. The rebellion of Keawe as representative of the Oahu faction had been successful. By December 1802, Kaumuali'i was again paramount and no mention was made of Keawe (Turnbull 1813:213). An old Kaua'i resident told the story of Keawe's death (Lahainaluna student composition 1885). While making a tour of the island, Keawe was killed by two members of his train, Kaneeku and Ki'ikiki. Ki'ikiki (*not* 16) had been a counselor of war to Ka'eo and was most probably a Maui chief. A Maui chief, therefore, killed the Kaua'i paramount representing the Oahu line and allowed for the resuccession of the Maui line representative, Kaumuali'i.

Kaumuali'i was the last paramount chief of Kaua'i and he relinquished his authority to Kamehameha I of Hawaii. At Kaumuali'i's death in 1824, a rebellion of Kaua'i chiefs against rule by the heirs to Kamehameha I was decisively put down and Kaua'i became fully integrated into the newly formed Hawaiian Kingdom (Kamakau 1961:268).

In summary, the succession of paramount chiefs can be treated in part as an inheritance of status by established relationships to the Kaua'i ruling lineage. However, the dynamics of succession can only be understood as the resolution of competing claims between social and political factions. The historical descriptions of the fighting between Kaneoneo and Ka'eo and between Keawe and Kaumuali'i illustrate the political significance of Hawaiian warfare. The combatants in both cases were allied with very high ranking chiefs who were distinguished not by the relative legitimacy of their claims but by their representation of the opposed interests of chiefly groups.

The reasons for the strong opposition in interests lay in the nature of the land tenure system. As discussed in Chapter 2, after his ascendance to power, a new paramount apportioned stewardship in the ahupua'a to the chiefs closely associated with him. Competition between individual chiefs for the paramountship involved, therefore, the competition between whole groups of associated chiefs for rights in the chiefdom's ahupua'a. Perhaps the most important document located during the archival research for this project described the succession of ahupua'a chiefs for Wainiha and Lumahai (Table 9.1; Barrère ms.). The two earliest known ahupua'a chiefs were Peapea for Wainiha and Manuha'aipo for Lumahai. Manuha'aipo (8) and Peapea (13) were both the children of Maui paramounts and they were respectively sister and nephew to Ka'eo. Before Ka'eo's marriage to Kamakahelei, there was no recent connection between the Kaua'i and Maui ruling lineages. Therefore, the rights of both Manuha'aipo and Peapea to their ahupua'a must have been established through Ka'eo and his marriage to Kamakahelei.

When Ka'eo arrived on Kaua'i, he was obviously not alone; an entourage of related Maui chiefs must have accompanied him. What is perhaps more startling is that Ka'eo, although paramount only by marriage, redistributed the Kaua'i ahupua'a to his Maui following. The "rebellion" by Kaneoneo as a representative of the Oahu line may well have been an attempt on the part of Oahu aligned chiefs to retain their ahupua'a rights which extended back to Peleioholani (1) or earlier.

After the 1824 rebellion against the domination of Kaua'i by the Kamehameha descent group, there was another major redivision of ahupua'a among chiefs. All chiefs receiving ahupua'a were closely linked to the Kamehameha line which was, by then, the newly formed Hawaiian monarchy. Out of the nine Halelean ahupua'a, only Kalihikai was granted to a Kaua'i chief. He was Keli'iahonui, son of Kaumuali'i, but also a resident of Oahu and a close associate of King Kamehameha III (Kamakau 1961:271).

These two cases show that any major shift in political alignment within the office of paramount resulted in a major reshuffling of chiefly rights to ahupua'a. This would act to solidify power of the ruling paramount, but it would also be a main cause for factional warfare during the transition period between established paramounts.

In sum, one of the major causes of warfare was clearly competition among elites for control of strategic political offices. For any given chiefdom, this resulted in a cyclical pattern of internal warfare/rebellion, solidification, and then expansion. The more general significance of warfare will be discussed in the next section as a central aspect in the maximizing strategy of the Hawaiian elites.

The Role of Capital Investment in Status Rivalry

A primary goal of Hawaiian chiefs was to maximize political power and this was accomplished by using accumulated wealth to finance political activities. This section describes the many ways in which this was executed. The redistributive economy of the Hawaiian chiefdom was structured according to strict hierarchical rules which led to the concentration of wealth at each node in the social hierarchy. The social structure dictated the pattern of economic flow, but a chief at any point in the hierarchy held rights to a percentage of goods which he could use as a capital investment in opportunities resulting in increased income flow through his nodal position. In other words, the Hawaiian political economy was structured such that a chief might manipulate various positive feedback loops (i.e., through capital investment) so as to maximize his economic and political position.

The close relationship between the political power and the economic fitness of a chief has been described for Polynesia generally (cf. Goldman 1970:18). In chiefdoms, political power results from a chief's careful use of the goods mobilized in the redistributive hierarchy, because it is these goods which must finance activities aimed at increasing and maintaining a political following. Specifically for Hawaii, goods mobilized through the redistributive hierarchy had three main uses: (1) support of the chiefs; (2) establishment and maintenance of political relationships; and (3) capital investment.

Support of the Chiefs

Hawaiian chiefs were largely removed from subsistence production and so they were dependent on the mobilization of basic food and clothing from the commoner population (Malo 1951 [1898]). However, the chiefs were supplied with goods well beyond basic needs and they lived with an aura of abundance. By conspicuous consumption, chiefs demonstrated their social distinctiveness and economic efficacy. As will be discussed later, in addition to their personal support, chiefs were also responsible for supporting numerous personal retainers including military and craft specialists. Numerous individuals clustered around the paramount's court and it was largely his responsibility to feed these people.

Establishment and Maintenance of Political Relationships

Political relationships in Hawaii were structured as a redistributive hierarchy based on principles of the conical clan but altered to recognize the realities of political power. The degree to which the hierarchy was "redistributive" (distributing goods down through the hierarchy after initial mobilization) was contingent on the need to build or to maintain political support. Elsewhere in Polynesia chiefs received definite rights from their position in the redistributive hierarchy and there was considerably autonomy at each level. In Hawaii this autonomy was greatly reduced, meaning that individuals in the social hierarchy were more closely controlled by their direct superiors. To compensate for the loss of autonomy and its associated self-interest, the political loyalty of a chief was guaranteed by payments from the higher levels. This payment took the form of gifts of food and of status goods.

Kepelino (Beckwith 1932:148-51) provides an exceptionally vivid description of mobilization of *ho'okupu* ("the offering of gifts"). The collection followed a strict hierarchical pattern — household head to konohiki to ahupua'a chief to district chief to paramount. At each level, goods were amassed and passed on to the appropriate individual at the next level. A portion was then always reserved and returned to the lower individuals who had just given up their gifts. An individual in the hierarchy, therefore, received a fraction of the total collection but he received this as a gift from his superior!

The social and political hierarchy was composed of a set of superior-inferior relationships structured as a hierarchy of political offices but also involving an important interpersonal dimension. The structured relationship between offices involved defined rights and obligations entered into with expectations of mutual benefits. Because of the competitive nature of succession, these bonds were a necessary basis for political and economic support. An individual officeholder guaranteed his support by liberal gifts to those under him in the hierarchy. Thus, an individual's ability to hold and augment his political status depended on his economic condition. Since an office holder's status depended upon his economic generosity, it was essential for him to attempt to maximize his income flow. This was accomplished largely by a prudent schedule of capital investment.

Capital Investment

Because of the importance for maximizing income flow to finance political activities, capital investment played a critical role in the political economy of aboriginal Hawaii. Capital investment was used by the chiefs as a means to increase the productive capacity of the economic system under their control. The three main forms of capital investment were in the subsistence economy, in expansionistic warfare, and in craft specialization.

The most direct form of capital investment was in the form of capital improvements to the technological capacity of an area. Because of the essentially feudal nature of the land tenure system, a chief received his income from the land division which he controlled. The income was in two forms: produce from ko'ele segments; and a percentage of the general taxation. A chief could greatly increase the productive capacity of an ahupua'a by improving the facilities associated with the ko'ele. If the chief wished to build a new set of pondfields or a fishpond, the konohiki, as the chief's manager, would recruit the required labor from the community. In exchange for their work, the konohiki fed the workers during the project and hosted a feast for them at its completion (cf. Chapter 7). In other words, a chief would invest part of his income (in the form of food) into labor used for major capital improvements.

It was, however, still necessary to recruit labor for the normal productive activities related to the ko'ele facilities. As discussed in the next section, labor for the ko'ele was a contractual responsibility for a commoner receiving land use rights. As a result, it was equally to the advantage of a local chief to expand the subsistence capacity of an ahupua'a as an incentive to new farmers to settle in the community. To balance any increase in ko'ele would have required a comparable increase in subsistence capacity. A new or expanded irrigation system would, in this light, economically benefit both the elites and their dependent population. In addition, an increasing local population would increase the community tax and further augment the chief's income from this source. To a certain extent, the irrigation systems in Hawaii provided an inducement to a commoner population to settle (or at least not to leave) an ahupua'a. By offering expanded economic opportunities, an ahupua'a chief could augment his local labor supply and thus increase his income flow.

Agricultural intensification, through the expansion of irrigation, was therefore an outcome of political competition and *not* of population pressure. In fact, agricultural intensification was a strategy to increase local population as a means to increase surplus production.

Warfare can also be understood as a capital investment. Warfare is often explained simplistically as an aspect of competition over scarce resources; a more comprehensive, economic explanation of warfare would interpret it as a competition over all factors of production including land, labor, and capital improvements. I would argue that warfare in Hawaii particularly, and in complex chiefdoms generally, was not a result of expanding population and subsistence requirements, but was a feature of political competition over the means of production, especially population.

Chiefdoms are expansionistic; this has been noted often (cf. Service 1962:151) but never fully explained. Following Goldman (1970), a characteristic of chiefly organization is competition for limited and economically advantageous social positions. As an outgrowth of this competition, the political economy of the elites is based on maximization of income and to do this, a paramount chief could either intensify production within his chiefdom or expand his chiefdom militarily to include more local communities. For the first option, the exploitation of local community economies has definite limits because, in a "redistributional" society based on mobilization, the government relies ultimately on the local community's strong allegiance. Alternatively, the chief can increase his income militarily by incorporating additional communities. This option does not require intensification but simply the successful truncation of a neighboring region's political superstructure and its replacement with an extension of one's own political hierarchy. In other words, a chief acts to increase his income flow by expanding his redistributive hierarchy through conquest warfare.

Warfare should consequently be viewed as a form of capital investment. Warfare is never a spontaneous action but requires both planning and finance. In Hawaii, the expenses associated with warfare were heavy and of various kinds. On a long-term basis, military specialists were attached to the paramount chief and they were supported by staples mobilized from the commoners. In addition, the technology of warfare (double canoes, special spears, sling stones, etc.) required the collection of raw materials, which were often rare and localized, and payments to the craft specialists who produced the weapons. On a short-term basis, any specific campaign required the mobilization of a commoner army which had to be fed and supplied. All these expenses were met by expenditures of funds, in the form of staples and craft goods, mobilized through the redistributive hierarchy. In sum, capital investment in warfare was a means to increase the productive capacity of a chiefdom through expansion and was therefore a key aspect of the maximizing strategy of the Hawaiian chiefs.

A third form of capital investment in chiefdoms is in craft specialization (cf. Service 1962:148). In Hawaii (and other complex chiefdoms), craft specialists were closely integrated economically with the redistributive system of mobilization. The specialists themselves were apparently attached to chiefly households and supported by the staple goods mobilized from the commoners. In addition, raw materials for the craft goods were collected as part of community taxation. A good example of this is the collection of feathers used to make the elaborate chiefly cloaks ('ahu'ula):

> The lands that produced feathers were heavily taxed at the Makahiki time, feathers being the most acceptable offering to the Makahiki idol ... So greedy were

the *ali'i* after feathers that there was a standing order *(palala)* directing their collection. [Malo 1951 (1898):77]

For an example from Halelea, a konohiki commented: "Because of the plentifulness of noni, the tax of Wainiha is big" (Native and Foreign Testimony 1854, Vol. 10); noni *(Morinda citrifolia)* was an important dye source. In short, craft specialists were attached to the elite hierarchy both as a means of support and as the source for raw materials.

The goods produced by these specialists were then essential to the social and political organization of Hawaii. Many of these goods, like the feather cloaks or the whale ivory pendants, were symbols of office and of eliteness in general.

> The *'ahu'ula* [feather cloak] was a possession most costly and precious, not obtainable by the common people, only by the *ali'i*. It was much worn by them as an insignia in time of war and when they went into battle. The *'ahu'ula* was also conferred upon warriors... [Malo 1951 (1898):76-77]

Ownership of such status goods was conferred on an individual by his superiors in the hierarchy and was a necessary demonstration of an individual's rights to an office.

To put this discussion in a different light, craft specialists, who were supported by staples collected in the general mobilization, were employed to convert raw materials into items of wealth and symbols of authority. A paramount chief, by controlling the production of such status goods, held a monopoly and could use them in partial payment for a wide range of political, social, and economic services.

To summarize this section, the economic strategy of maximization relied on a schedule of capital investment. This capital investment involved the support of a full range of specialists — managers, warriors, and craftsmen. Each specialist in his own way performed an essential role in the expansion of a chief's productive capacity. The land managers handled the organization of local production and special investments in capital improvements. The warriors formed the spearhead for military action which would either defend the chiefdom against attack or expand the territory (and tax base) of the chiefdom. Craftsmen produced the necessary special weapons of war and also produced the status goods which form the basic means of payment among the elites.

THE AHUPUA'A: THE LOCAL COMMUNITY IN A REGIONAL CONTEXT

The social and economic organization of the ahupua'a community has been described in Chapter 8, and this section now concentrates on the articulation between the local community and the regional sociopolitical superstructure of the Hawaiian chiefdom. The local community was comprised of a commoner population primarily involved in subsistence production. The goal of this subsistence economy would have been to satisfy household needs with a minimum of risk and effort. In contrast to this domestic economy, the chiefs were enmeshed in contention for political power requiring a maximizing strategy to finance political challenges. The articulation between the subsistence economy and political economy was critical, because the source of economic goods was in both cases the same, the commoner producer. The relationship between commoner and chief involved radically different goals and potentially conflicting interests, and the ways in which this relationship was maintained is important for understanding the operation of the Hawaiian chiefdom. The two aspects of the relationship discussed here are (1) the system of land tenure as it relates to corvée labor and taxation and (2) the reasons for political and economic dependency of the local community on the regional organization.

Land Tenure and Mobilization in the Ahupua'a

The local commoner population was not economically independent since they received use rights to land and other resources from the chiefs. The relationship between the chiefs and the commoners was mediated by the konohiki, who was appointed as land manager by the ahupua'a chief. In return for land and access to natural resources granted by the chiefs, the commoners provided the konohiki with corvée labor and staple taxes. This section discusses the role of the konohiki as coordinator between the land tenure system controlled by the chiefs and the subsistence economy handled by the commoners.

The konohiki has already been described as a local manager, offering leadership in ahupua'a activities, from the construction of irrigation ditches and the allocation of water to community ceremonies. There was an equally important aspect to the office of konohiki which has received little attention in the literature. The konohiki was first and foremost the representative of the land owning elites. It was a konohiki's primary duty to manage capital investment and corvée labor in order to guarantee maximal yield to the ahupua'a chief and to the paramount chief. The konohiki regulated the production of goods for the chiefs by (1) mobilizing corvée labor for use on the chief's lands and (2) mobilizing goods during periodic ceremonial collections.

Mobilization of Corvée Labor

Corvée labor in Hawaii was part of the more inclusive system of land tenure. A commoner held no rights to land except as granted to him by the konohiki. In the majority of cases (119 of 175) recorded in the nineteenth century land awards, the original basis for a land claim was explicitly traced to the konohiki who granted the land directly to the claimant or a near relative. It is often stated that these use rights were given by the konohiki to a commoner "as lands are given by landlord to tenant" (Foreign Testimony for LCA 7967).

The use right of a piece of land could be revoked by the konohiki at any time, and twenty-five cases of land confiscation were mentioned in the land records. In most cases (eighteen), a cause for the confiscation was described but it would appear that the decision of the konohiki could be arbitrary. In sixteen cases the general reason was the inability of an individual to perform corvée for the konohiki. Specific causes were as follows: eight cases of emigration; five cases of death without a male heir; one case of ill health; one case of old age; one case of "freed" from konohiki work. Two particularly explicit examples follow:

> Lands were given by the *konohiki* in the days of Kaikeoewa [governor of Kaua'i, 1825-1839] and have been held 'til 1849 when claimant was elected superintendent of schools and became freed from the *konohiki* work. The result was that the *konohiki* took away his lands and gave them to another tenant. Kowelo was left destitute of food. [Foreign Testimony for LCA 11063]
>
> *Konohiki* took away [*apana*] numbers 3 and 4 on the grounds that claimant was getting old and his labor on the *konohiki* days of little worth. [Foreign Testimony for LCA 10313]

It is clear that the right to hold land relied on an individual's ability to work for the konohiki.

In testimony before the Land Commissioner, konohiki often described their role as managing this corvée labor:

> Kamoolehua swears: When [my father] died, the konohikiship descended to me, and I put the men of Lumahai to work. [Barrère ms.:4]

The fact that land tenure was directly tied to the labor is strongly suggested by the cases of confiscation and it is stated explicitly in the following testimony:

> Edward Bailey swears: The Konohikis under the old system previous to the award of lands were absolute masters of the main ditch and distributed the water according to what appeared to them to be the necessities of the people. The people who got the water had to work for the konohikis. That work was their mode of land tenure. [Willfong et al. vs. William Bailey 1873]

As discussed in Chapter 8, the patrifocal Hawaiian family was in part a response to this contractual responsibility tied to land tenure.

Although corvée labor could take many forms, from the collection of sandalwood to the building of a new fishpond, the most regular responsibility was the agricultural work on the ko'ele. Ko'ele were sections of pondfields farmed by the commoners, but the produce from them went directly to the chiefly steward. These sections were often referred to as "the pondfields of the konohiki" *(lo'i o Konohiki)* but they were clearly attached to the managerial position and not to the individual (cf. Sahlins 1971:Appendix B). The ko'ele were distributed through the ahupua'a in close correlation with the awards. There was a high correlation ($r = .924$) between the number of farmers on an irrigation system and the number of ko'ele. On the average, there were 5.1 farmers for each ko'ele and virtually all systems with more than three farmers were assigned one or more ko'ele. The largest aboriginal system (number 22) had eleven ko'ele in Waioli and Hanalei. As seen in Figure 8.1, these were distributed fairly evenly through the system. The distinct impression is that a group of farmers, let us say five, received land near a ko'ele section which they were then responsible for.

In sum, the konohiki, as manager for the ahupua'a chief, directed corvée labor in the community. Historically (before 1850) the most important use of this labor was for production on land set aside for the support of the chiefs. Commoners contributed their labor explicitly in return for use rights to subsistence plots and other subsistence resources.

Ceremonial Collections

Goods were also procured directly for the chiefs by a periodic tax *(auhau)* or tribute (ho'okupu). Aboriginally, the major collection took place yearly during the Makahiki ceremony when a representation of the god Lono made a collecting circuit around the island chiefdom. The konohiki for each ahupua'a was responsible for collecting an obligatory gift to be offered to Lono. At the boundary of each ahupua'a, the god was set up to receive his gifts (Malo 1951 [1898]:146; Ii 1959:75; Barrère ms.:3-5, 7) and examined for adequacy. An insufficient gift led to additional requests and the possible removal of the ineffectual konohiki (Malo 1951 [1898]:145-46). According to Malo, these offerings included raw materials (feathers), manufactured goods *(tapa)*, domestic animals (pigs) and some agricultural produce (taro) (1951 [1898]:145).

The ahupua'a with its Makahiki shrine was the aboriginal taxing unit. A commoner's community affiliation was determined by the konohiki who taxed him and by the particular place to which he paid his taxes. This information was critical evidence during the Land Commission hearings:

> Pakee swears: Kanekoa was the konohiki of Wainiha, and the persons who lived on this place [disputed parcel] were Kuehina, the man, and Pukoa, the woman. This man was not taxed by Kanekoa in his day. By the *konohiki* of Lumahai he was taxed from the days of Kaumuali'i until the time of Liholiho. [Barrère ms.:3]
>
> Kanoolehua swears: [At] Keakuakahea [a *makahiki* shrine], when a certain man of Lumahai, whose name was Kula, was offering to the Makahiki god at Lumahai, the god called out to him "E Kuli, do not bring your offerings of fish here to Wainiha," and he fetched the fish and took it back to Lumahai. This is what I heard from my grandfather. [Barrère ms.:4]

The important point is that the territorial unit and its attached population were defined according to how they were taxed. By extension, an individual's rights to land through his community affiliation were determined by his tax payments.

The tie between taxation and land tenure is shown clearly by the historical changes in taxation procedures. Three stages may be recognized: (1) aboriginal ceremonial collections associated with the god Lono; (2) secular collections after the abrupt dissolution of traditional religion; and (3) personal and property taxes after changes in the land tenure system. Aboriginally, taxation was a religiously sanctified collection ceremony. The konohiki as ahupua'a manager was responsible for amassing the required offering. After the breaking of the tabus in 1819, the Hawaiian religious system was largely defunct (cf. Kuykendall 1938) and taxation became secularized. At this time, taxes were no longer paid to a god but were paid to a governmental bureaucrat acting as tax collector *(luna)* for an area:

> I was the head *luna (luna nui)* all around Kaua'i after the war of Wahiawa [1824], and made circuits of Kaua'i. On [my tours of] inspection, the people on this side gave their tribute for Wainiha, and those of that side of this ridge gave their tribute for these lands separated [by the ridge]. I knew clearly the men of these two lands. [Barrère ms.:8]

The basic form of taxation remained, however, unchanged. Collection was still directed by the konohiki on a community basis and was still tied to the traditional system of land tenure.

The major change in taxation took place with the granting of land in fee simple to commoners. As discussed earlier, this change in land tenure eliminated the major function of the konohiki as allocator of use rights and manager of corvée labor. After the land reforms, taxes were no longer assessed at the community level but were leveled on individuals as head taxes and property taxes. The change in land tenure from use rights assigned by the konohiki to fee simple ownership resulted in a complete change in taxation principles and an abandonment of the corvée labor responsibilities.

In summary, aboriginally, the konohiki acted in the critical role of mediating the economic relationships between elites and commoners. In this position, he mobilized goods for the elites through his control of the community land tenure system. With the change in land tenure, the office of the konohiki ceased to have a function and was abandoned.

Community Isolation

The shift from acephalous societies to politically centralized societies is often viewed as the primary development of a regional organization. This is not really the case, for there is more precisely a replacement of one form of regional organization with another. All societies retain some form of intercommunity, regional organization. In acephalous societies, communities are interwoven by bonds of kinship, marriage, and alliance. For example, many acephalous societies maintain rules of exogamy; marriage outside the group creates extensive networks of relations. Such regional organizations are uncentralized but they perform necessary support functions in times of economic hardship or military threat (Dalton 1977). In other words, although the community is politically autonomous, it is closely tied with other communities through numerous interpersonal ties.

In contrast, the Hawaiian community aboriginally was socially isolated from other communities. Because of a high rate of local endogamy, interpersonal ties were largely restricted to within the community. As I will try to show, this community isolation was in part an aspect of the developing regional, political organization and the isolation resulted in a dependency of the local community on that new organizational structure.

Although warfare is often thought of as characteristic of chiefdoms, chiefdoms act to control and to restrict the extent of warfare. In acephalous societies, warfare is endemic; a more or less continual state of war exists between communities (Sahlins 1968; Chagnon 1968; Dalton 1977). Chiefdoms, as regionally organized political units, greatly restrict warfare especially between local communities; in other words, chiefdoms act to establish a regional peace.

The probable effects of this imposed peace on the local community are various. First, with a lower frequency of warfare, the regional interpersonal alliances lose their necessary functions as a source of allies and as a refuge from enemies. Second, an imposed peace removes the most obvious restrictions on community size imposed by defensive needs. Therefore, the size of a community may vary greatly according to its actual resource potential. This would tend to increase the possibilities for community self-sufficiency and decrease the need for intercommunity exchange (cf. Chapter 8). Regional, interpersonal networks are costly in terms of goods required from the participating individuals and such a system should atrophy when its basic usefulness is superseded. It can, therefore, be argued that in the case of Hawaii, the development of a regional chiefdom resulted in a loss of function for regional interpersonal networks and in an increase in community isolation.

In addition, community isolation was further bolstered by the regional political economy. As discussed earlier, the konohiki was directly responsible for community productivity, and therefore he attempted to maintain the maximum possible work force. This was done by discouraging migration and encouraging local endogamy.

Without a regional, interpersonal network the local community was in turn increasingly dependent on the regional political organization for support during infrequent but severe disasters. The importance of disasters, from natural and social causes, has been discussed in the context of the irrigation-based Hawaiian economy. It is sufficient to say that such disasters could extensively destroy a community's productive capacity and leave it largely unable to support itself.

A hypothetical line of argument would, therefore, be that the evolution of the Hawaiian chiefdoms restricted local warfare and thus eliminated the most immediate and pressing reason for interpersonal networks. As a result, the local community could be largely independent and isolated, but, in the specific situation of disasters, the community was largely dependent on the regional chiefdom.

SUMMARY

The evolution of regional social organization in Hawaiian chiefdoms is seen as the outcome of various positive feedback, developmental processes. To understand the evolutionary transformation from decentralized village chiefdoms, the organizational characteristics of Polynesian society were examined and two salient points noted: (1) Polynesian society is structured as a conical clan which offers hierarchial principles to integrate regional populations; and (2) political processes are highly competitive and result in a maximizing economic strategy. The interaction between social structure and political process under varying environmental restraints results in the observed variability in Polynesian social organization. In effect, Polynesian society is seen as inherently developmental but the specific level of development is determined by environmental factors. In the Hawaiian Islands, the unique conditions of large land mass and extensive irrigable alluvium permitted the observed elaborations of social stratification and regional centralization.

Rather than being caused by population pressure, Hawaiian irrigation and warfare were important aspects of the political economy for which expanded productive capacity was an essential goal. A positive feedback relationship existed between the competitive political organizations, environmental potential, and population. The commoner population was essential to the chiefs because the surplus production generated from the total economies was used to finance the political system. The articulation between subsistence production and political finance was critical; through the system of land tenure dominated by the chiefs, labor and obligatory offerings from the commoners were exchanged for land use rights. A significant effect of the expanding regional organization was an increased isolation of the local community socially and economically, and an increased dependency of the total population on the regional sociopolitical superstructure.

CHAPTER X
SUMMARY AND CONCLUSIONS

The sociopolitical organization of traditional Hawaii represented a marked evolutionary change from prototypical Polynesian chiefdoms. Characteristically, Polynesian chiefdoms were decentralized; the village approximated an autonomous economic and political unit, and generalized leadership was provided by a localized lineage chief. In contrast, Hawaiian chiefdoms were regionally integrated and socially stratified; the chiefs formed distinct, nonlocalized lineages that were removed from subsistence activities but were owners of land and other resources. Hawaiian chiefdoms were both centralized in decision making and differentiated in socioeconomic roles. In addition to the differentiated regional aristocracy (the ali'i), there were multiple specialists for land management, warfare, and craft production.

This monograph has investigated three ecological theories of cultural evolution based on the causal factors in irrigation, community specialization/trade, and warfare. These theories are all logically similar — an initial increase in population density selects for a specific cultural adaptation which results in the centralization of decision making. The particular economic and ecological conditions of these theories, however, prove not to be sufficient cause for the evolutionary development observed in Hawaii.

First, various hydraulic theories of civilization have been postulated based on the premise that scale and complexity of irrigation determine the degree of political centralization. In Halelea, the irrigation systems were small scale, typical of village level irrigation elsewhere. In a brief cross-cultural comparison, such village level irrigation systems were not associated with any characteristic sociopolitical organization but were found in societies representing a full range of political types from acephalous tribes to chiefdoms to peasant communities incorporated in states. There was virtually no evidence that Hawaiian irrigation would have required centralized management for construction, maintenance, or water distribution. Irrigation technology was simple, indicating no specialized knowledge or overall design. The scale of systems was generally small and most were apparently built gradually by extension and intensification. Allocation of water presented only limited difficulties because of the general sufficiency of supply, the restriction of systems within community boundaries, and specific features of design, i.e. direct access to ditches by farmers and a restricted number of major water diversions.

There is some evidence that a regional organization was essential for the reconstruction of irrigation systems following destruction and for the protection of irrigation systems from external threat. Irrigation systems were compact, highly productive agricultural facilities located on the low lying alluvial soils of the river bottoms and coastal plain. In these positions, they were particularly vulnerable to natural disasters such as winter flooding and tidal waves. In fact, the productive capacity of a single community was often severely damaged by a single accident. Because of their vulnerability, irrigation systems were often the target of enemy raiding aimed at destroying the agricultural base of an adversary. In both these circumstances, the local community was dependent in part on a regional organization for support and protection. Such functions are, however, insufficient cause for the evolution of a *centralized* regional organization, because other mechanisms, especially the regional reciprocal networks found in acephalous societies, are viable alternatives.

Second, a parallel theory postulates that the evolution of a regionally centralized organization and its associated redistributive hierarchy is a response to environmentally determined specialization of local communities. In Hawaii, the territorial boundaries of the ahupua'a community were laid out to provide each community with access to resource zones for farming, fishing, and hunting-gathering. The economies of the local community were thus generalized and repetitious of each other; by minimizing economic interdependence, this economic justification for a regional sociopolitical organization was largely eliminated.

Third, warfare is also offered as a possible cause of regional centralization. Specifically, population growth in a circumscribed area is seen as resulting in competition over scarce resources. Such warfare, in turn, results in the domination of one group by another and the selection for a centralized social system with its obvious advantages in warfare. In Hawaii, warfare was not a result of competition over subsistence resources; population was apparently well below any potential carrying

SUMMARY AND CONCLUSIONS   195

capacity. Thus, the goal of warfare could not have been the increase of a community's resource base as necessitated by increasing population. Rather, warfare was an aspect of political rivalry in which chiefs attempted to gain power by expanding their redistributive base.

The three reflexive theories have thus been shown to be ineffective explanations for the evolution of regional chiefdoms in Hawaii, but this does not dismiss irrigation, redistribution, and warfare as essential factors in cultural evolution. All three were characteristic of aboriginal Hawaii and their importance in the observed development seems highly probable. A reevaluation of their significance has emphasized the position of these factors in a set of positive feedback relationships responsible for the development of sociopolitical centralization.

Polynesian chiefdoms were highly competitive and were associated with political economies based on a maximizing strategy. In Hawaii, the redistributive hierarchy functioned to amass the staples used to finance political activities, and it was not a means to integrate economically specialized subunits. Specialists fulfilled a vital function in the redistributive hierarchy because it was they who acted to maintain and expand the organization. Local land managers (konohiki) administered the allocation of use rights to commoners in exchange for their "gifts" of labor and goods. The staples mobilized in this manner from the community production then became the basic commodities to finance the sociopolitical superstructure. In addition to providing support of the chiefs and their dependents, the staples formed the capital used to expand productive capacities.

Productive capacity could be expanded either by intensifying local production of a chiefdom's communities or by expanding the chiefdom to include more community units. Intensification was directed by the land manager who organized local labor to construct irrigation systems and fishponds. Expansion, through warfare, was directed by the military specialists attached to the chiefly hierarchy. The significance of irrigation and warfare was not in their organizational requirements but instead was in their central role in the maximizing (positive feedback) political economy characteristic of chiefdoms. Irrigation, through intensification, and warfare, through expansion, increased the flow of staples collected by the centralized redistributive hierarchy. The size and complexity (internal differentiation) of this hierarchy was largely determined by the amount of staples (energy) which was tapped off from the community subsistence economies.

Evolutionary theories discussed in this monograph rely heavily on the ecological and economic conditions of the local community. This emphasis on the local community has obscured the importance of the regional superstructure. All societies require some form of regional organization to buffer their populations against natural disasters and defeat in warfare. In acephalous societies, a measure of security is provided by decentralized reciprocal networks binding politically autonomous communities. In a regional chiefdom or state, the regional superstructure provides comparable functions and tends to replace the extensive reciprocal networks. In Hawaii, the organization of the local community and the regional polity were closely intertwined. Staples mobilized from the local community permitted the elaboration of the regional superstructure; by replacing possible decentralized reciprocal networks (based on marriage, trade, and alliance), the regional organization of the chiefdom actually resulted in a social and economic isolation of the community organization. Such isolation then greatly increased the local community's dependence on the regional organization.

In sum, the evolution of Polynesian chiefdoms was largely determined by a series of positive feedback relationships resulting in cultural elaboration under specific environmental conditions. In order to understand this process, it is necessary to understand the internal organization of a culture in addition to its adaptation. For Polynesia, positive feedback relationships were characteristic of the sociopolitical organization associated with the chiefs, and negative feedback relationships were characteristic of environmental limits to expansion, intensification, and communication. Therefore, the factors responsible for evolutionary development were inherent in Polynesian social organization; the degree to which the various Polynesian societies actually developed was determined by the particular attributes of their island environments.

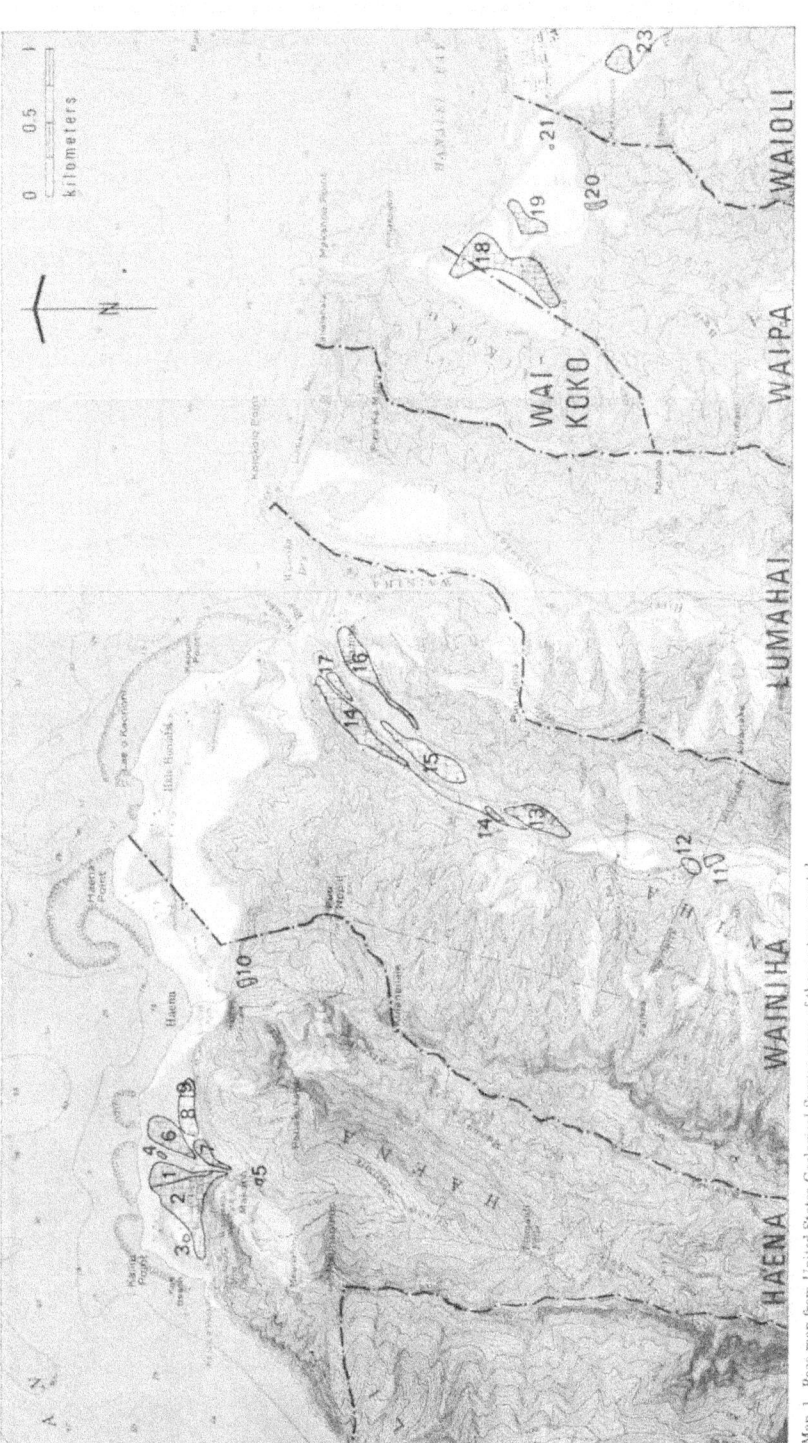

Map 1. Base map from United States Geological Survey maps of the western, coastal portion of the Halelea district. The locations for the modern, historical, and archaeological irrigation systems are indicated.

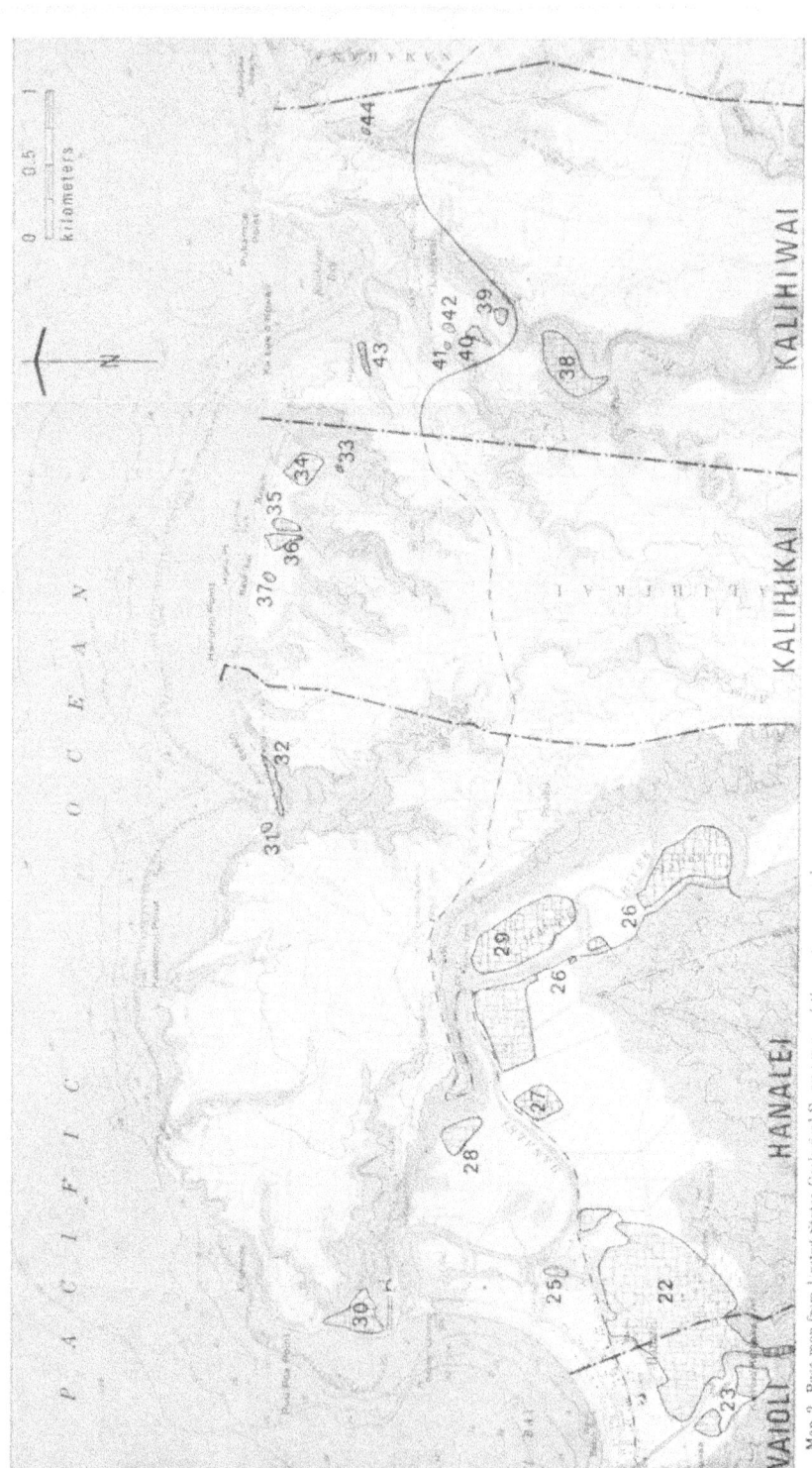

Map 2. Base map from United States Geological Survey maps of the eastern coastal portion of the Halelea district. The locations for the modern, historical, and archaeological irrigation systems are indicated.

BIBLIOGRAPHY

Adams, R. McC.
    1966   The evolution of urban society. Chicago: Aldine.

Alexander, W. P.
    1835   Kauai, Waioli station report, June 1835. Typed manuscript. Hawaiian Mission Children's Society, Honolulu.

Anderson, R. N., J. Barron, and W. G. Marders
    1972   Hanalei development plan: a socioeconomic prelude. College of Tropical Agriculture, Hawaii Agricultural Experiment Station, University of Hawaii Departmental Paper 2.

Arago, J.
    1823   Narrative of a voyage round the world, Vol. 1. London: Treuttel, Jun and Richter.

Barrau, J.
    1961   Subsistence agriculture in Polynesia and Micronesia. Bernice P. Bishop Museum Bulletin 223.

Barrère, D. B.
    ms.   Foreign and native testimony, Vol. 10, pp. 393-99, translated by D. Barrère. Typed manuscript.

Barton, R. F.
    1919   Ifugao law. University of California Berkeley Publication in American Archaeology and Ethnography 15:1-186.
    1922   Ifugao economics. University of California Berkeley Publication in American Archaeology and Ethnography 15:385-446.
    1949   The Kalingas. Chicago: University of Chicago Press.

Beaglehole, J. C. (ed.)
    1967   The Journals of Captain Cook on his voyage of discovery, Vol. 3. Cambridge: Cambridge University Press.

Beardsley, R., J. Hall, and R. Ward
    1959   Village Japan. Chicago: University of Chicago Press.

Beckwith, M. W.
    1932   Kepelino's traditions of Hawaii. Bernice P. Bishop Museum Bulletin 95.

Bennett, J.
    1968   Reciprocal economic exchanges among North American agricultural operators. Southwestern Journal of Anthropology 24:276-309.

Bennett, W. C.
  1931   Archaeology of Kauai. Bernice P. Bishop Museum Bulletin 80.
Bingham, H.
  1969   A residence of twenty-one years in the Sandwich islands. New York:
  (1849)   Praeger.
Boserup, E.
  1965   The conditions of agricultural growth. Chicago: Aldine.
Broughton, W. R.
  1804   A voyage of discovery in the North Pacific ocean. London: Cadell and Davies.
Brown, J. A. (ed.)
  1971   Approaches to the social dimensions of mortuary practices. Memoirs of the Society for American Archaeology 25.
Brown, R. H.
  1920   Irrigation. (3rd ed.) London: Constable.
Campbell, A.
  1967   A voyage round the world from 1806-1812. Honolulu: University of Hawaii
  (1822)   Press.
Carlquist, S.
  1970   Hawaii: a natural history. Garden City, N.J.: Natural History Press.
Carneiro, R. L.
  1970   A theory of the origin of the state. Science 169:733-38.
Chagnon, N.
  1968   Yanomamo: the fierce people. New York: Holt, Rinehart, and Winston.
Conklin, H.
  1967   Some aspects of ethnographic research in Ifugao. Transactions of the New York Academy of Science (Series II) 30:99-121.
  1972   Land use in north central Ifugao: a set of eight maps. New York: American Geographic Society.
  1974   Ethnographic research in Ifugao. In: Aerial photography in anthropological field research, edited by E. Vogt, pp. 140-59. Cambridge: Harvard University Press.
Cordy, R.
  1972   The effects of European contact on Hawaiian agricultural systems — 1778-1819. Ethnohistory 19:393-418.
Corney, P.
  1896   Voyages in the northern Pacific . . . from 1813 to 1818. Honolulu: Thrum.
Dalton, G.
  1977   Aboriginal economies in stateless societies. In: Exchange systems in prehistory, edited by T. Earle and J. Ericson, pp. 191-212. New York: Academic Press.
Dixon, G.
  1789   A voyage around the world . . . in 1785-1788 . . . London: Goulding.

Downing, T., and M. Gibson (eds.)
  1974   Irrigation's impact on society. Anthropological Papers of the University of Arizona 25.

Durkheim, E.
  1933   Division of labor in society. New York: Macmillan.

Earle, E. H.
  1971   A study of taro cultivation with specific reference to Polynesia. Unpublished senior honor thesis, Department of Anthropology, University of Michigan, Ann Arbor.

Earle, T. K.
  1972   Unpublished field notes, Kaua'i. Personal copy.
  1973   Control hierarchies in the traditional irrigation economy of Halelea district, Kauai, Hawaii. Ann Arbor: University Microfilms.
  1976   A nearest neighbor analysis of two Formative settlement systems. In:The early Mesoamerican village, edited by K. Flannery, pp.196-223. New York: Academic Press.
  1977   A reappraisal of redistribution: complex Hawaiian chiefdoms. In: Exchange systems in prehistory, edited by T. Earle and J. Ericson, pp.213-29. New York: Academic Press.

Earle, T., and T. D'Altroy
  n.d.   Social stratification and wealth in mortuary goods: Moche, Peru. Paper delivered at the 1975 Annual Meeting of the American Anthropological Association, San Francisco.

Eggan, F.
  1950   Social organization of the western pueblos. Chicago: University of Chicago Press.

Ellis, W.
  1963   Journal of William Ellis. Honolulu: Advertiser Publishing.
  (1827)

Evans-Pritchard, E. E.
  1940   The Nuer. Oxford and New York: Oxford University Press.

Eyre, J. D.
  1955   Water control in a Japanese irrigation system. Geographic Review 45:197-216.

Firth, R.
  1939   Primitive Polynesian economy. London: Routledge.

Flannery, K.
  1972   The cultural evolution of civilizations. Annual Review of Ecology and Systematics 3:399-426.

Flannery, K., A. Kirkby, M. Kirkby, and A. Williams
  1967   Farming systems and political growth in ancient Oaxaca. Science 158:445-54.

Fried, M.
  1967   The evolution of political society. New York: Random House.

Gall, P., and A. Saxe
    1977   Ecological evolution of culture: the state organization as predator in succession theory. In: Exchange systems in prehistory, edited by T. Earle and J. Ericson, pp. 255-68. New York: Academic Press.

Geertz, C.
    1959   Form and variation in Balinese village structure. American Anthropologist 61:991-1012.
    1963   Agricultural involution. Chicago: University of Chicago Press.
    1972   The wet and the dry: traditional irrigation in Bali and Morocco. Human Ecology 1:23-39.

Goldman, I.
    1970   Ancient Polynesian society. Chicago: University of Chicago Press.

Gray, R.
    1963   Sonjo of Tanganyika. Oxford and New York: Oxford University Press.

Hackenberg, R.
    1962   Economic alternatives in arid lands: a case study of the Pima and Papago Indians. Ethnology 1:186-95.

Handy, E. S. C.
    1940   The Hawaiian planter, Vol. 1. Bernice P. Bishop Museum Bulletin 161.

Handy, E. S. C., and E. G. Handy
    1972   Native planters in old Hawaii: their life, lore, and environment. Bernice P. Bishop Museum Bulletin 233.

Handy, E. S. C., and M. K. Pukui
    1972   The Polynesian family system in Ka'u, Hawaii. Rutland: Tuttle.
    (1958)

Hommon, R. J.
    1972   Hawaiian cultural systems and archaeological site patterns. Unpublished M.A. thesis, University of Arizona, Tucson.

Hunt, E., and R. Hunt
    1974   Irrigation, conflict, and politics: a Mexican case. In: Irrigation's impact on society, edited by T. Downing and M. Gibson, pp. 129-57. Tucson: University of Arizona Press.

Ii, J. P.
    1959   Fragments of Hawaiian history. Honolulu: Bishop Museum Press.

Indices of Awards
    1929   Made by the Board of Commissioners to quiet land titles. Honolulu: Star-Bulletin Press.

Jarves, J.
    1838   Sketches of Kauai. Hawaiian Spectator 1:66-86.
    1844   Scenes and scenery in the Sandwich islands. Boston: James Munroe.

Johnson, E.
    1844   Letter to the Rev. W. P. Alexander, Waioli, April 15, 1844. Mission Children's Society, Honolulu.
    1848   Letter to W. Lee of the Land Commission. Interior Department Papers, January 24, 1848. State of Hawaii Archives, Honolulu.

Kamakau, S. M.
  1961 Ruling chiefs of Hawaii. Honolulu: Kamehameha School Press.
  1964 The people of old. Honolulu: Bishop Museum Press.
  1976 The works of the people of old. Bernice P. Bishop Museum Special Publication 61.
  ms.   Na mo'olelo a ka po'e kahiko. Translated manuscript. Bernice P. Bishop Museum, Honolulu.

Kirch, P.V., and M. Kelly (eds.)
  1975 Prehistory and ecology in a windward Hawaiian valley: Halawa Valley, Molokai. Pacific Anthropological Records 24.

Kirchhoff, P.
  1955 The principles of clanship in human society. Davidson Anthropological Society Journal 1:1-11.

Kotzebue, O. von
  1821 A voyage of discovery into the South Seas and the Bering's straits. London: Longman, Hurst, Rees, Orme, and Brown.

Kuykendall, R. S.
  1938 The Hawaiian kingdom, Vol. 1: 1778-1854. Honolulu: University of Hawaii Press.

Lahainaluna Student Composition, No. 15
  1885 Translated typed copy. Bernice P. Bishop Museum, Honolulu.

Lanning, E. P.
  1967 Peru before the Incas. Englewood Cliffs, N.J.: Prentice-Hall.

Leach, E.
  1959 Hydraulic society in Ceylon. Past and Present 15:2-25.
  1961 Pul Eliya: a village in Ceylon. Cambridge: Cambridge University Press.

Leeds, A.
  1962 Ecological determinants of chieftainship among the Yaruro indians of Venezuela. Akten des 34 Internationalen Amerikanistenkongresses, pp. 597-608. Vienna: F. Berger, Horn.

Lees, S. H.
  1973 Sociopolitical aspects of canal irrigation in the Valley of Oaxaca. Prehistory and Human Ecology of the Valley of Oaxaca 1. University of Michigan Museum of Anthropology Memoir 6.
  1974 The state's use of irrigation in changing peasant society. In: Irrigation's impact on society, edited by T. Downing and M. Gibson, pp. 123-28. Tucson: University of Arizona Press.

Linnekin, Jocelyn
  1974 Land relations and the status of women in post-contact Hawaii. Unpublished qualifying paper, on file at Department of Anthropology, University of Michigan, Ann Arbor.

Macrae, J.
  1922 With Lord Byron at the Sandwich Islands in 1825. Honolulu: Hawaiian Historical Society.

Malinowski, B.
  1922 Argonauts of the western Pacific. London: Routledge.

Malo, D.
   1951   Hawaiian antiquities. Bernice P. Bishop Museum Special Publication 2 (2nd
  (1898) ed.).

Massal, E., and J. Barrau
   1956   Food plants of the south sea islands. South Pacific Commission Technical Paper 94.

Menzies, A.
   1920   Hawaii nei 128 years ago: journal of Archibald Menzies. Honolulu.

Meyen, F. J. F.
   1913   Reise um die Erde . . . 1830-1832. English translation of Vol. 2, Chap. 12, by
  (1834) W. D. Alexander. Bernice P. Bishop Museum, Honolulu.

Millon, R.
   1962   Variation in social response to the practice of irrigation agriculture. In: Civilizations in desert lands, edited by R. Woodbury, pp. 56-88. Salt Lake City: University of Utah Press.

Millon, R., C. Hall, and M. Diaz.
   1961   Conflict in the modern Teotihuacan irrigation system. Comparative Studies in Society and History 4:494-521.

Mitchell, W.
   1973   The hydraulic hypothesis: a reappraisal. Current Anthropology 14:532-34.

Murabayashi, E., T. Sahara, A. Ching, I. Kuwahara, F. Fujimura, E. Awai, and H. Baker.
   1967   Detailed land classification — island of Kauai. Land Study Bureau Bulletin 9.

Nakuina, E. M. B.
   1894   Ancient Hawaiian water rights. Hawaiian Annual 20:79-84.

Newman, T. S.
   1970   Hawaiian fishing and farming on the island of Hawaii in A.D. 1778. Honolulu: Division of State Parks, Department of Land and Natural Resources.

Netting, R.
   1974   The system nobody knows: village irrigation in the Swiss Alps. In: Irrigation's impact on society, edited by T. Downing and M. Gibson, pp. 67-75. Tucson: University of Arizona Press.

Pararas-Carayannis, G.
   1969   Catalog of tsunamis in the Hawaiian islands. Washington, D.C.: World Data Center A, Tsunami, Coast and Geodetic Survey.

Pasternak, B.
   1972   Kinship and community in two Chinese villages. Stanford: Stanford University Press.

Paulding, H.
   1831   Journal of a cruise of the USS Dolphin. New York: Ludwig, Tolefree.

Peebles, C.
  1971   Moundville and surrounding sites: some structural considerations of mortuary practices. In: Approaches to the social dimensions of mortuary practices, edited by J. Brown, pp. 68-91. Society for merican Archaeology Memoir 25.
  1974   Moundville: the organization of a prehistoric community and culture. Unpublished Ph.D. dissertation, Department of Anthropology, University of California, Santa Barbara.

Peterson, G. T.
  1972   Taro farming in Waipio valley on the island of Hawaii. In: Preliminary research in human ecology, 1970: North Kohala studies, edited by R. Armstrong and H. Lewis, pp. 23-45. Department of Anthropology, Department of Geography, and School of Public Health, University of Hawaii, Honolulu.

Polanyi, K.
  1968   Semantics of money-uses. In: Primitive, archaic and modern economies: essays by Karl Polanyi, edited by G. Dalton, pp. 175-203. Garden City, N.Y.: Doubleday.

Portlock, N.
  1789   A voyage round the world ... in 1785-1788. London: Stockdale.

Price B.
  1971   Prehispanic irrigation agriculture in nuclear America. Latin American Research Review 6:3-60.

Queen Emma
  ms.   Observations on varieties and culture of taro; written by Queen Emma, translation by M. Pukui. Typed manuscript. Bernice P. Bishop Museum, Honolulu.

Rappaport, R.
  1967   Pigs for the ancestors. New Haven: Yale University Press.

Rathje, W.
  1970   Sociopolitical implications of lowland Maya burials: methodology and tentative hypotheses. World Archaeology 1:359-74.
  1971   The origin and development of lowland Maya civilization. American Antiquity 36:275-85.

Renfrew, A. C.
  1973   Monuments, mobilization and social organization in neolithic Wessex. In: The explanation of culture change, edited by A. C. Renfrew, pp. 539-58. London: G. Duckworth.
  1974   Beyond a subsistence economy: the evolution of social organization in prehistoric Europe. In: Reconstructing complex society, edited by C. Moore, pp. 69-96. Chicago: American School of Oriental Research.

Ripperton, J. C., and E. Hosaka
  1942   Vegetation zones of Hawaii. Hawaiian Agricultural Experiment Station Bulletin 89.

Sahlins, M.
- 1958 Social stratification in Polynesia. Seattle: University of Washington Press for the American Ethnological Society.
- 1962 Moala. Ann Arbor: University of Michigan Press.
- 1968 Tribesmen. Englewood Cliffs, N.J.: Prentice-Hall.
- 1971 An interdisciplinary investigation of Hawaiian social morphology and economy in the late prehistoric and early historic periods. Grant proposal submitted to the National Science Foundation.
- 1972 Stone Age Economics. Chicago: Aldine.
- 1973 Historical anthropology of the Hawaiian kingdom. Grant proposal submitted to the National Science Foundation.

Sanders, W. T.
- 1956 The central Mexican symbiotic region: a study in prehistoric settlement patterns. In: Prehistoric settlement patterns in the New World, edited by G. Willey, pp. 115-27. New York: Wenner-Gren Foundation.

Sanders, W. T., and B. Price
- 1968 Mesoamerica: the evolution of a civilization. New York: Random House.

Schmitt, R. C.
- 1966 The population of northern Kauai in 1847. Hawaiian Historical Review 2:300-304.
- 1968 Demographic statistics of Hawaii: 1778-1965. Honolulu: University of Hawaii Press.
- 1973 The missionary censuses of Hawaii. Pacific Anthropological Records 20.

Service, E.
- 1962 Primitive social organization. New York: Random House.
- 1975 Origins of the state and civilization: the process of cultural evolution. New York: Norton.

Spooner, B.
- 1974 Irrigation and society: the Iranian plateau. In: Irrigation's impact on society, edited by T. Downing and M. Gibson, pp. 43-57. Tucson: University of Arizona Press.

Steward, J.
- 1955a Theory of culture change. Urbana: University of Illinois Press.
- 1955b Irrigation civilizations: a comparative study. Pan American Union Social Science Monograph 1.

Stewart, C. S.
- 1830 Journal of a residence in the Sandwich Islands. London.

Stolz, L. H.
- 1912 Wainiha to Waimea. Friend, June 1912: 144-45.

Summers, C. C.
- 1971 Molokai: a site survey. Pacific Anthropological Records 14.

Thomas, W. L.
    1965   The variety of physical environments among Pacific islands. In: Man's place in the island ecosystem, edited by F. Fosberg pp. 7-38. Honolulu: Bishop Museum Press.

Tilley, H. A.
    1861   Japan, the Amoor, and the Pacific 1858-1860. London: Smith, Elder, and Co.

Turnbull, J.
    1813   A voyage round the world in the years 1800 . . . 1804 . . . . London: A. Maxwell.

Vancouver, G.
    1798   A voyage of discovery to the north Pacific ocean and round the world, Vol. 1. London: G. G. and J. Robinson, Paternoster-Row, and J. Edwards, Pall-Mall.

Whitman, J. B.
    ms.   Journal 1813-1815. Manuscript. Salem, Mass.: Peabody Museum.

Wilkes, C.
    1845   Narrative of the United States exploring expedition 1838-1842. Philadelphia: Lea and Blanchard.

Wittfogel, K.
    1957   Oriental despotism. New Haven: Yale University Press.

Wolf, E., and A. Palerm
    1955   Irrigation in the old Acolhua domain, Mexico. Southwestern Journal of Anthropology 11:265-81.

Woodbury, R.
    1961   A reappraisal of Hohokam irrigation. American Anthropologist 63:550-60.

Wright, H. T.
    1977   Toward an explanation of the origin of the state. In: Explanation of prehistoric change, edited by J. Hill, pp. 215-30. Albuquerque: University of New Mexico Press.

Yen, D. H.
    1973   The origins of oceanic agriculture. Archaeology and Physical Anthropology in Oceania 8:68-85.

Yen, D. H., P. Kirch, P. Rosendahl, and T. Riley
    1972   Prehistoric agriculture in the upper valley of Makaha, Oahu. Pacific Anthropological Records 18:59-94.

Zimmerman, J.
    1966   Irrigation. New York: Wiley and Son.

Plate 1. Planting taro cuttings in Hanalei, Kaua'i. A string is used to align rows and to maintain proper spacing.

Plate 2. Harvesting in Hanelei, Kaua'i. The root system of the taro clone is broken up with a metal pole prior to pulling.

Plate 3. System 29, Hanelei, Kaua'i. Picture taken from main road, looking south. Taro pondfields in various stages of growth are shown.

Plate 4. Site Ka-D5-8, Ha'ena, Kaua'i. Looking up the stairlike series of pondfield terraces down the center of the site. Photograph by T. Dye.

Plate 5. Site Ka-D5-8, Ha'ena, Kaua'i. Detail of construction of retaining wall for pondfield terrace. Photograph by T. Dye.

Plate 6. Site Ka-D5-8, Ha'ena, Kaua'i. Terrace walls of ceremonial complex, showing main terraces with smaller secondary terraces in front. Photograph by T. Dye.

www.ingramcontent.com/pod-product-compliance
Lightning Source LLC
Jackson TN
JSHW070313120426
100741JS00007B/41